AF497253

Half Moon Series

🌹 🌹 Papers on Historic New York 🌹 🌹 🌹 🌹

Edited by Maud Wilder Goodwin
Alice Carrington Royce, Ruth
Putnam, Eva Palmer Brownell

Second Series

G. P. PUTNAM'S SONS, New York
and London   The Knickerbocker Press
MDCCCXCVIII

Copyright, 1898
BY
G. P. PUTNAM'S SONS

The Knickerbocker Press, New York

CONTENTS.

Contents.

SLAVERY IN NEW YORK

Half Moon Series

Published in the Interest of the New York
City History Club.

VOLUME II.   NUMBER I.

SLAVERY IN NEW YORK,

WITH SPECIAL REFERENCE TO NEW YORK CITY.

BY EDWIN VERNON MORGAN, A.M.

Establishment of Slavery.—In 1625 or
1626, the first negro slaves were brought to
New Amsterdam, the settlement which later
became the City of New York.   Among them
were Paul d'Angola, Simon Congo, Anthony
Portuguese, John Francisco, and seven other
Africans, who were probably captured at sea.[1]
Two years later three negro women arrived,
closely followed by others who are spoken of
as "Angola slaves, thievish, lazy, and useless
trash."   These slaves, apparently, were the
only ones introduced prior to the erection of
patroonships and colonies in 1629, when the
West India Company publicly promised to
"use their endeavors to supply the colonists
with as many Blacks as they conveniently
can," a promise which, from several causes,
was not fulfilled until the arrival in June, 1646,

of the *Amandare*, the first slave ship to New Netherland whose name is recorded. At Barbadoes, where the vessel touched, "three negro wenches were spirited away," but the remainder of the cargo was sold in New Amsterdam for pork and peas. "Something wonderful was to be performed with them, but they just dropped through the fingers." What slaves were brought and whence they came is not stated.

On May 27, 1647, a committee of the States-General of Holland made a full report on the affairs of the West India Company, in the course of which it mentioned the fact that, in consequence of the unsettled condition of Brazil, "The Slave Trade hath long laid dormant to the great damage of the Company." In regard to New Netherland, it said : "That country is considered to be the most fruitful of all within your High Mightinesses' Jurisdiction. . . . The granting of Freedoms and Privileges hath indeed induced some Patroons and Colonists to undertake agriculture there ; but as the produce cannot be sold anywhere except in the adjacent places belonging to the English, who are themselves sufficiently supplied, those planters have not received a return for their labor and outlay. With a view, then, to give greater encouragement to agriculture, and consequently to population, we should consider it highly advantageous that a way be opened to allow them to export their produce even to Brazil, in their own vessels, under certain duties . . . ; and to trade it off there, and to carry slaves back in return. . . . By this means, not only would Brazil be supplied with provisions at a cheaper rate, but New Netherland would, by slave labor, be more extensively cultivated than it has hitherto been, because the agricultural laborers, who are conveyed thither at great expense to the Colonists, sooner or later apply themselves to trade and neglect agriculture altogether. Slaves, on the other hand, being brought and maintained there at a cheap rate, various other descriptions of produce would be raised."[2] In accordance with this report the States-General resolved upon February 10, 1648, that the people of New Netherland "be allowed to export their fish, flour, and produce, . . . to Brazil, in private or the Company's ships, . . . and in return to export, at certain duty from Brazil, to New Netherland and not elsewhere, as much merchandise, such as Slaves." Four years later the slave trade to Africa direct was also opened, but with results so meagre that Fiscal Van Dyck wrote on September 18, 1652, "No requests for Negroes has been presented from Patroons or Colonists here to my knowledge." The burghers of New Amsterdam petitioned Governor Stuyvesant in May, 1660, for " permission to trade free and unobstructed in Ship or Ships, along the whole of the west coast of Africa," since those who would execute "with Skipper or Merchant going to that country a Draft of Partnership, which is beset and pinched by such precise conditions" (as those which at present exist) "would risk their lives and goods, and at best gain nothing." Upon January 6, 1664, the Directors sent word to Stuyvesant that they had entered into a contract with Symen Gilde, of the ship *Gideon*, to take in a good cargo of slaves at Loango, on the coast of Africa, and to fetch them, by way of Curaçoa, to New Netherland, and that Amsterdam was a partner for a fourth of the cargo. Though the ship was due the coming June or July, "with about 300 slaves aboard," she did not arrive until a few days before the Dutch surrendered to the English.[2]

During the war between Spain and the United Netherlands, the privateers which swarmed among the Caribbean Islands and along the Spanish Main occasionally brought prizes into New Amsterdam. After the peace, hostilities were carried on between Spain and France. To privateers under the French flag, New Amsterdam was a neutral port where captive negroes and other prize goods were sold. In 1642 the *La Garce* brought in a few slaves, and in 1652 a lot of forty-five negroes came in on another privateer, which had captured them from a Spaniard. A great part of the slaves who reached New Amsterdam, however, were imported either by private merchants in Holland, under a special permit from the Company, or by the West India Company itself. "We are resolved," wrote the Directors at Amsterdam in 1661, "not only that slaves shall be kept in New Netherland, as we have heretofore ordered, but that they shall moreover be exported to the English and other neighbours." In 1644, the Secretary of the Colony received from Governor Kieft, for four years, a young girl belonging to the Company, "daughter of great Peter, a black man," who, after the expiration of the specified time, "if yet alive," was to be returned. The Directors and Council resolved, in May, 1664, to pay a certain Captain Willet "in Negroes at such price as may be agreed on for a quantity of pork and beef equal to 600 lbs." Two months later they desired "to negotiate a loan of five or six thousand guilders in Wampum for the Honorable Company," to be paid "either in good negroes or other goods," although in November, 1661, they had been sufficiently prosperous to present New Amsterdam with three negro slaves.[4]

Civil Status of Negro and Indian Slaves. —The change of government which occurred in 1664 did not materially affect the status of negro slaves. The "Duke's Laws," published in March, 1664, declared: "No Christian shall be kept in Bond-Slavery, except such who shall be judged thereto by Authority, or such as willingly have sold or shall sell themselves." Fearful that this provision might be misunderstood, the framers added hastily: "Nothing in this law shall be to the prejudice of Master or Dame who have or shall by indenture take Servants for a term of years or for life." [1] In the amended laws, published about 1674, this provision appeared: "This law shall not set at liberty any Negro or Indian Slave, who shall have turned Christian after they had been bought by any person," a declaration which implied, but did not state, that inhabitants of New York might be born slaves. An act to encourage the baptism of negro, Indian, and mulatto slaves, passed October 24, 1706, established, however, the latter point. It provided that every negro, Indian, mulatto, and mustee should follow the state and condition of the mother and be adjudged a slave to all intents and purposes whatsoever. Slavery, therefore, might exist by reason of birth, voluntary sale, or by way of punishment for crime. [2]

The civil position of a slave before the law was determined by a number of acts, one of which, relating to minor offences and dated November 27, 1702, allowed masters to "punish their slaves for their crimes at discretion, not extending to life or member." An order of the corporation of New York, dated March, 1736, suggests the manner in which the right was used. It declared that citizens had free licence to send to the house of correction all servants and slaves, there to be kept at hard labor, and punished according to the direction of any one justice, with the consent of the master or mistress. Serious offences, such as murder, rape, or arson, were tried by a court peculiarly composed.'

By an act of December 10, 1712, three justices and five of the principal freeholders of the county constituted judge and jury, seven making a quorum. For this usual jury the jury of twelve might be substituted, provided the master so desired and paid the jury charges of nine shillings. The prosecution furnished the accusation, to which the offender was obliged to plead, apparently without the aid of counsel. How effectively an ignorant slave would conduct his defence one can imagine. In case of conviction the sentence was immediate death, "in such manner and with such circumstances as the aggravation or enormity of the crime," in the judgment of the judges, required. On March 11, 1684, a barn belonging to Jan Nagel, in Harlem, was burned with twelve head of cattle. It was fired by his negro slave, who ran away, and was found next day "hanging to a tree at the Little Hill by the common." The Mayor was asked what should be done with the body, and he ordered that it should be hanged on a gibbet. But the magistrates, fearing the effect of such a sight upon "their children, who were in the habit of going daily to the fields and woods, and who might be terrified thereby," cut it down and burned it.[8]

By the act of 1702, in a special class of criminal cases, the usual practice of English law was also strangely set aside. "Where slaves are the property of Christians and cannot, without great loss to their masters or mistresses, be subjected in all cases criminal to the strict rules of the laws of England," a slave guilty of larceny of not more than £5 suffered corporal punishment at the discretion of any one justice of the peace; his master, meantime, making good the stolen property. Another section of the same act declared that the evidence of a slave was not receivable in any case, civil or criminal, against a freeman. In cases of "plotting or confederacy among themselves, either to run away, or to kill or destroy their masters or mistresses," of arson, or the killing of their owner's cattle, the testimony of one against another was nevertheless admitted.

Turning from the civil disabilities to the civil privileges, we find that although even freedmen were forbidden to "hold any houses, lands, tenements, or hereditaments," and all persons were forbidden "to trade with any slave either in buying or selling, without leave of the Master or Mistress, on pain of forfeiting treble the value of the article traded for," the like restriction was not laid on the possession by a slave of other kinds of property. By the Game Law of November 10, 1702, a slave received £3 for killing a wolf and 30 s. for killing a whelp, in Suffolk, Queens, or Kings Counties, the bounty going apparently into his own pocket. On September 5, 1717, Sam, late a negro slave of George Norton, deceased, complained to the Governor that Ebenezer Wilson detained money and a negro willed him by Norton. The following is a copy of the petition:

"George Norton in his life time by his last Will and Testament in Writing gave to your poor Petitioner his Freedom from Slavery and thirty pounds in Money, as also one Negro Man named Robin; But Mr. Ebenezer Willson, the Executor of George Norton Deceased, will neither pay your poor Petitioner the Thirty Pound nor let him have said Negro Robin, although he has not (as your Excellency's Petitioner is inform'd) Inventary'd said Negro Robin as a part of said George Norton's Estate. And yet in the Winter when said Negro wants Cloaths he is forced to come to your poor Petitioner for a Supply. And so also when he is sick or lame he has come to your said Petitioner several Times and lain upon him for a month at a time. But so soon as he is well and able to work Mr. Willson takes him away and Imploys him in his own Service.

"Wherefore your Poor Petitioner humbly pray that your Excellency wou'd be favourably pleased to take his suffering Case into your Consideration and find out some way (as in your great Wisdom you shall see meet) to induce said Executor to do Right and Justice to your Poor Petitioner in the case set forth." [9]

One case is recorded, if not more, where a slave brought suit against his master. June 25, 1710, Joris Elsworth, of New York City, complained to Governor Hunter, that his negro slave Will, claiming to be a freeman, had brought suit against him for wages. The case was tried before a jury at a session of the Supreme Court of the province, and a verdict was given for the defendant, against whom it is doubtful whether a slave could have brought suit on any other plea than the one offered. [10]

Regulations Governing Slave Life.—The main interest of the slave code turns on the regulations to prevent conspiracy and sedition. The fear of servile risings was constantly in the minds of our ancestors. Their savage legislation governing slave life is only intelligible in the light of this fact. The corporation of New York passed an ordinance, as early as March 15, 1684, that "No Negro or Indian Slaves, above the number of four, shall meet together on the Lord's day, or at any other time, at any place, from their master's service." They were not to go armed, moreover, "with guns, swords, clubs, staves, or any other kind of weapon," on penalty of receiving ten lashes at the whipping-post. "An Act for the Regulation of Slaves," passed November 27, 1702, which extended these regulations through the colony, reduced the number allowed to meet from four to three. The desired end was not even then attained. Four years later Governor Cornbury was obliged to order the justices of the peace of Kings County to take the proper methods for seizing and apprehending all such negroes as had assembled themselves in a riotous manner or had absconded from their masters; and six years later, when William Hallet, Jr., of Newtown, in Queens County, his wife and five children, were murdered by a negro and an Indian slave, the Governor was obliged to assent to another act for preventing the conspiracy of slaves."

The negro plot of 1712, the predecessor of the famous plot of 1741, necessitated yet another,—"An Act for Preventing, Suppressing and Punishing the Conspiracy and Insurrection of Negroes and other Slaves," passed December 10, 1712,—which reiterated former provisions and emphasized special points. By the act of 1702, no person could employ, harbor, conceal, or entertain at his house, outhouse, or plantation, slaves other than his own without their master's consent. By the latter act, any one who knew of their entertainment and did not report it must pay £2 or be imprisoned. The master who did not prosecute the employer or host paid double the sum that the employer or host should have forfeited. On October 27, 1730, the Assembly passed "An Act for the more effectual preventing and punishing the Conspiracy and Insurrection of Negroes and other Slaves; for the better Regulating them, and for Repealing the Acts therein mentioned, relating thereto." This, the last and most comprehensive act relating to slaves passed in New York before the Revolution, announced, however, no new principles, but contented itself with re-enacting former statutes.[12]

The corporation of New York was not behind the Assembly in taking measures to prevent conspiracies and passed several ordinances to reinforce the four acts last mentioned. As Sunday was the slaves' holiday, and a favorite time for the hatching of plots, the Sunday laws were intended to prevent conspiracies quite as much as to enforce the fourth commandment. "Servile labouring and working," riding a horse through any street or on the common, "rude and unlawful sports," and "fetching any water other than from the next well or pump to the place of his abode," and crossing from New York to Brooklyn without a permission were forbidden. On other days of the week no slave above fourteen years could appear an hour after sunset in the streets "within the fortifications, or in any other place on the south side of the fresh water," without a lantern and lighted candle, "so as the light thereof may be plainly seen." Slaves more advanced in years, since they were in the habit, when riding their masters' horses to water, to go prancing through the streets to the danger of passers-by, were forbidden "to ride in a disorderly fashion." They were also forbidden to clip household plate, to gamble with any sort of money, to assault or strike "any freeman or woman professing Christianity," to curse, swear, or "speak impudently to any Christian," to drive any sort of cart without a permit from the Mayor, except a brewer's drag, or to sell oysters, boiled Indian corn, or any kind of fruit."[3]

Restraining measures, such as those embodied in the acts and ordinances just mentioned, were made necessary by the two servile conspiracies, to which reference has already been made as the Negro Plots. The earlier, that of 1712, broke out on a Sunday night in April, "about the going down of the moon," when a large body of slaves, who thought themselves ill-treated by their masters, armed with guns or rude weapons, met in an orchard, set fire to an outhouse, and assaulted those who came running up to quench the flames. In this way they killed nine men and wounded six others before the alarm was given by the firing of a great gun from the fort, and the soldiers dispatched by the Governor appeared and put them to flight. The militia, by beating the forests at the northern end of Manhattan, aided by sentries posted at the fords, succeeded next day in capturing all the conspirators but six, who, in their despair, killed themselves. Of the remainder, twenty-one were executed either by hanging, burning, or by being broken on the wheel. Many arrested for supposed complicity in the plot were afterwards released for want of evidence to prove their guilt.[14]

The second, or "Great Negro Plot," of March, 1741, though much more serious both in its nature and results, producing deeds "which almost parallel those done in the evil days of the Salem witchcraft," was yet, technically, scarcely a plot at all. Undoubtedly a considerable body of discontented blacks—especially those lately arrived from Africa—vaguely hoped and planned for the murder of their masters. But there is little reason to suppose that the negroes who acted as domestic servants, and who constituted the mass of the slave population, ever contemplated, much less deliberately planned, a general servile insurrection. In New York, as in Salem, fear exaggerated the danger.

The first signs of the plot appeared during the weeks between the twenty-eighth of February and the eleventh of April, when nine fires followed in such quick succession that they seemed certain to be of incendiary origin. Meantime the keeper of a low tavern, his wife, two negroes, and Mary Barton, an indentured servant of doubtful reputation, were arrested on a charge of receiving stolen goods. A proclamation, offering a reward of £100 and a full pardon to whoever would give information concerning the supposed plot, was read to Mary, who, seeing a loophole through which to effect her own escape, suddenly remembered that the negroes who were in the habit of meeting at her master's house had planned to destroy the city and the fort, after which they would make her master king, and one of themselves governor. On the strength of her unsupported testimony a veritable reign of terror began. Citizens removed their valuables from beyond the city limits, and every black man not vouched for by a master in good repute was lodged in jail. The catalogue of victims included not only

one hundred and fifty-four negroes imprisoned, of whom fourteen were burned, eighteen hanged, two gibbeted, and seventy-one
transported, but twenty-four whites, four of
whom were executed. Among the latter was
a schoolmaster named Ury, suspected of being
either a non-juring Episcopalian or a Roman
Catholic priest. The magistrates, taking advantage of an old unrepealed law which forbade a priest to come into the province,
condemned Ury on the double count of being
implicated in the plot and of administering the
rites of his religion. When Mary became bold-
er and accused persons of quality and condition, men saw that the panic must be stopped.
But this was not done until a day for general
thanksgiving had been set apart.[16]

The Religious Status of Slaves.—In contrast to the cruel punishments of the negro
plots it is pleasant to find that, since negroes
and Indians were looked upon by our forefathers as children of the devil, efforts were
early made to Christianize them. But the
Dutch were not zealous in this work. Not
until December, 1660, does there appear
among the instructions given by the home
government to the Council for Foreign Plantations: "You are most especially to take an
especial care of the propogacôn of the Gospel
in the several Forraine Plantations. . . .
And you are to consider how each of the Na-

tives, or such as are purchased by you from other parts to be servants or Slaves, may be best invited to the Christian Faith, and be made capable of being baptized thereunto." [16]

Upon the occupation of New Netherland by the English the work went on with greater spirit. The "Duke's Laws" required all constables and overseers to urge the inhabitants to inform their children and servants in matters of religion. The instructions of James II., William III., and Queen Anne to the Royal Governors of New York, bade them, with the assistance of the Council, "to find out the best means to facilitate and encourage the conversion of Negroes and Indians to the Christian religion." Governor Dongan reported that the task was difficult. "It is the endeavor of all persons here to bring up their children and servants in that opinion which themselves profess; but this I observe, that they take no care of the conversion of their Slaves." Twelve years later, in 1699, it was still found impracticable. Governor Bellomont wrote to the Lords of Trade: "A Bill for facilitating the conversion of Indians and Negroes (which the King's instructions require should be endeavored to be passed), would not go down with the Assembly; they having a notion that the Negroes being converted to Christianity would emancipate them from their slavery, and loose them from their service."[17] On October 24, 1706, "An Act to encourage the Baptizing of Negro, Indian and Mulatto Slaves" finally passed the Assembly, and later received the Royal assent. It distinctly stated that the baptism of a slave should not set him free. The preamble and the first section read: "Whereas divers of Her Majesty's good Subjects, Inhabitants of this Colony, now are, and have been willing that such Negro, Indian and Mulatto Slaves, who belong to them, and desire the same, should be baptized, but are deterred and hindered thereof, by reason of a groundless opinion that hath spread itself in this Colony, that by the baptizing of such Negro, Indian or Mulatto Slaves, they would be free, and ought to be set at liberty. In order, therefore, to put an end to all such doubts and scruples as have, or hereafter at any time may arise, about the same; Be it enacted by the Governor, Council and Assembly, etc., that the Baptizing of any Negro, Indian or Mulatto Slave, shall not be any cause or Reason for the setting them or any of them, at Liberty."[18] This Act soothed the fears of masters, and, as the church registers attest, baptisms became frequent. The Rev. Elias Neau, under the patronage of the Society for the Propagation of the Gospel in Foreign Parts, had established a school for the religious instruction of slaves, three years before, in New York City. The slaves met on the evenings of " Wednesday and Friday and Sundays after Church," on the upper floor of Mr. Neau's house. None of the churches could be used for a schoolroom, " because of keeping them clean for the congregation," and there was " no other public building convenient or capacious enuff." The Rev. John Sharp, seeing that the existing arrangements were inconvenient, proposed, therefore, in 1713, that a catechizing chapel be erected, "which would give a favorable turn to the whole affair." His plan seems to have been adopted.

From Mr. Sharp, also, we learn something in regard both to the marriage and to the burial of slaves. The marriages were arranged, he tells us, by mutual consent, without the blessing of Church. Husband and wife often belonged to different families, and after marriage were sold many miles apart. Polygamy, therefore, was frequent. After baptism a few consented to break their " Negro marriages" and " marry a Christian spouse." However highly colored these statements may be, it is certainly true that the marriage of a slave was not made legal before April 9, 1813. The law enacted on that day reads: " All marriages contracted or to be contracted hereafter, wherein one or more of the parties were or may be Slaves, shall be considered valid as though the parties thereto were free ; The children of such a marriage to be deemed legitimate." [10]

The burial of slaves was first made a subject of legislation on October 23, 1684. The text of the act is not accessible, and we are not able, therefore, to state its provisions. They probably forbade the private burial of slaves, for we find that Mees Hoogeboon, of Albany, was fined twelve shillings "for interring his negro in a private and suspicious manner." In October, 1722, the Corporation of New York ordered that all negro and Indian slaves dying within the city should be buried by daylight. In 1731, in 1748, and in 1763 this order was reissued, with the additional provision that not more than twelve slaves should attend any funeral under penalty of public whipping. On these occasions no pall, gloves, or favors were to be used. A slave who held a pall or wore gloves or favors was to be publicly whipped, at the discretion of the Mayor or of that one of the Corporation before whom he had been convicted. These regulations were probably made to prevent the conspiracy of slaves as much as for any other purpose. The fear of servile risings, as we have remarked elsewhere, is the key-note to the slave code of New York, as well as of the other colonies. Mr. Sharp suggests a second reason, when he remarks: "Slaves are buried in the Common by those of their country and complexion

without the office.   On the contrary, heathen-
ish rites are performed over them."[20]

Indian Slavery.—Both the beginning and
the end of Indian slavery are lost in obscurity,
although nearly all the laws enacted between
1664 and 1788 recognized its existence and
treated it as an integral portion of the slave
system.   The first authoritative reference to
its existence appears in the statement of eight
citizens of New Amsterdam to the West India
Company, dated October 28, 1644, which declared that "The captured Indians, who might
have been of considerable use to us as guides,
have been given to the soldiers as presents,
and allowed to go to Holland; the others have
been sent off to the Bermudas as a present to
the English governor."   The second, which
refers to the emancipation of Indian slaves,
points to the conclusion that however desirable Indian slavery appeared to the people of
New York, it was not acceptable to the authorities.   In April, 1680, the Governor and
Council resolved " that all Indyans here, have
always been and are free, and not slaves—except such as have been formerly brought from
the Bay or Foreign Parts.   If any shall be
brought hereafter into the government within
the space of six months, they are to be disposed of as soon as may be out of the government.   After the expiration of the said six
months, all that shall be brought here from

Indian
Children
1750

those parts and landed, to be as other free Indians." This resolve, if put in force at all,
appears ere long to have become a dead letter. In July, 1703, Jacobus Kirstead, of New
York, mariner, petitioned the Governor in regard to an Indian brought by him from Jamaica
and sold as a slave. In the same month,
twelve years later, Colonel Heathcote wrote
home to Secretary Townsend: "The Indians
complain that their children, who were many
of them bound out for a limited time to be
taught and instructed by the Christians, were,
contrary to the intent of their agreement,
transferred to other plantations and sold for
slaves, and I don't know but there may be
some truth in what they allege." As late as
January 22, 1750, Colonel Johnson wrote to
Governor Clinton: "I am very glad that your
excellency has given orders to have the Indian
children returned, who are kept by the traders
as pawns or pledges as they call it, but rather
stolen from them (as the parents came at the
appointed time to redeem them, but they sent
them away before-hand), and as they were
children of our Friends and Allies, and if
they are not returned next spring it will con-
firm what the French told the Six Nations
(viz.): that we looked upon them as our
slaves or negroes, which affair gave me a
great deal of trouble at that time to reconcile.
I cannot find that Mr. Abeel, who has a Seneca

child, or Vandrieson, who has got a Missisa-gey, are to deliver theirs, which I am apprehensive will cause great disturbance."[21]

From the meagre data which these extracts afford, the writer concludes first, that, compared to the body of negro and mulatto slaves, Indian slaves were few in number ; and second, that the majority of them were either captives or the descendants of captives taken in war, or else West Indians who were confounded with mulattos, and imported as such. That a considerable body of kidnapped red Indians existed as slaves in New York at any period he cannot believe.

Price of Slaves.—*I. Price of Slaves Newly Imported.* In 1659, negroes purchased at Curaçoa for $60 could not be sold at New Amsterdam for the same price. In 1661, a few sold there for $176 each, less the freight. Three years later negroes brought $200 at a certain sale, the highest price being $270.60, and the lowest $134.20. On the same occasion negresses brought about $129 each, although in 1694, "good negresses" sold for $240, and in 1723, anywhere from $225 to $300. Negroes had risen in value, meantime, to $250, and there remained, as long as the importation of slaves continued.

II. Price of Slaves whose Character and Abilities were Known to their Masters.

In 1705, a Bermuda merchant sold, in New

York City, a young negro woman, about eighteen, for $200, who had lived in his family some time. A negro wench, nineteen years old, "whom he brought up from infancy," was sold by Dr. Duprey, of New York City, in 1723, for $275. In the same year a negro wench and child, belonging to a former sheriff of Amboy, brought $375. In the inventory of an estate, in 1719, another negro wench and child stood for only $300. Able-bodied men were then selling for about $250.

During and just after the Revolution, the price of slaves appears to have varied exceedingly. The assessors in Ulster County in 1775, valued male slaves between fifteen and forty at $150, those between forty and fifty, ten and fifteen, and seven and ten, at $75, $90, and $50 respectively. Female slaves between the same ages brought $100, $50, $60, and $40. In 1783, the Council of Sequestration sold a negro boy for $56.25. Ten years later another (in Albany County) was bought for $100. Still a third was sold (in Richmond County) in 1798 ; $410 was his price, though by agreement he was to be manumitted in nine years. In the Oswego *Herald*, 1799, appears this advertisement : "A Young Wench—For Sale. She is a good cook and ready at all kinds of house-work. None can exceed her if she is kept from liquor.

She is 24 years of age—no husband nor children. Price $200 ; inquire of the printer." [22]

From the beginning of this century the price of slaves appears to have decreased. In 1801, Wm. Potter and Mary his wife purchased their freedom for $400. A negro nineteen years old brought in Rockland County, March, 1809, $250, and finally a negro woman, aged thirty-seven, with all the rights her present mistress had to the service of her children, was sold for $100.

From these facts we may draw the following conclusions : first, that while agricultural laborers were scarce, male slaves were more valuable than female, but when domestic servants, rather than farm hands, were in demand, the previous condition of things was reversed ; second, that in the years preceding the Revolution, slaves brought their highest price ; and third, that from 1790, when it became apparent that the legislature contemplated measures to bring about emancipation, the price of slaves gradually declined. A fourth and last conclusion is that, during the colonial period, the average price of both male and female slaves varied from $150 to $250.

CENSUS.

Until 1790 the censuses of New York were inaccurate, and it is well-nigh impossible to compute the number of slaves in the State before that date.   The following figures are the best available * :

	WHITES.	SLAVES.	TOTAL POPULATION.
1664	7,000	" Very few."	
1678	2,000 " able to beare arms."	" Very few."	
1698		Kings Co., 293	18,067
1703	Five Counties about N. Y. City, 7,767	Five Counties about N. Y. City, 1,301	
1712	Five Counties about N. Y. City, 10,511	Five Counties about N. Y. City, 1,775	
1723		6,171	40,564
1731		7,231	50,291
1746		9,717	Without Albany Co., 61,584
1774		21,149	182,247
1790	314,142	21,324	340,121
1800	557,731	20,903	589,051
1810	918,699	15,017	959,049
1820	1,332,744	10,088	1,372,111
1830	1,873,663	75	1,918,608
1840	2,387,890	4	2,428,921

* Colonial Documents, F. B. Dexter's pamphlet, Censuses of the U. S. (since 1790).

IN NEW YORK CITY.

	WHITES.	SLAVES.	TOTAL.
1703	3,634	801	4,435
1712	4,880	960	5,840
1731	7,045	1,571	8,616
1737	8,945	1,719	10,664
1746	9,279	2,444	11,723

REFERENCES.

1. O'CALLAGHAN, *Voyages of the Slavers " St. John " and " Arms of Amsterdam,"* p. 13.
2. *New York Colonial Documents*, i., p. 246.
3. *Ibid.*, ii., pp. 222, 430.
4. *Ibid.*, ii., pp. 371, 474.
5. *Collections of New York Historical Society*, 1809, pp. 322, 323.
6. *Laws of New York*, 1752, p. 69.
7. DUNLAP, *History of the New Netherland*, ii., p. 165.
8. RIKER, *Harlem*, p. 438.
9. *New York Colonial MSS.*, lvi., p. 172.
10. *Ibid.*, lix., p. 21.
11. *New York Colonial Documents*, v., p. 39.
12. *Laws of New York*, 1752, p. 193.
13. DUNLAP, ii., pp. 129, 132, 159 ; VALENTINE, *Manual of the Common Council of New York*, i., pp. 571, 580.
14. *New York Colonial Documents*, v., pp. 341, 346, 356, 367, 371, 525 ; COFFIN, *Slave Insurrections.*
15. *New York Colonial Documents*, vi., pp, 186, 196, 199, 201-203 ; HORSMANDER, *Journal of Proceedings ;* HORSMANDER, *The New York Conspiracy.*
16. *New York Colonial Documents*, iv., p. 36.
17. *Ibid.*, iv., p. 510.
18. *Laws of New York*, 1752, p. 69.
19. *Ibid.*, 1813, ii., pp. 201–202.
20. VALENTINE, i., pp. 566, 571.
21. *New York Colonial Documents*, v., p. 433 ; vi., p. 546.
22. LIVERMORE, *Cooperstown*, p. 171.

TAMMANY HALL

Half Moon Series

Published in the Interest of the New York
City History Club.

VOLUME II. NUMBER II.

TAMMANY HALL.

BY TALCOTT WILLIAMS, LL.D., L.H.D.

TAMMANY, for nearly a century, has constituted the political agency by which
the major mass of the voters of New York City
has made effective its preferences in regard to
the rule of the city for good or for ill to the worst
harvest yet reaped in the wide field of universal
suffrage. This ruling organization of adult male
voters has sometimes been for years together
only a plurality of the voters of the city profiting
by the divisions of its opponents, and it has
sometimes itself divided by fission, a part preferring to use one of the many agencies organized in imitation of Tammany ; but for seventy
years there has never been a time at any election when it was not perfectly clear to every
unprejudiced observer that a clear plurality of
the voters resident on Manhattan Island, preferred, other things being equal, to re-elect
rulers whose primary selection had been determined by this political agency.

It has been associated with the most gigantic spoliation of a civilized city known under manhood suffrage, though the aggregate of its levies has been small by the side of the gigantic fine inflicted on Paris and France by the military despotism, which ruled both with the applause and approval of liberal England and despotic Europe, from the *coup d'état* to Sedan.   Until the close of the last century, it was expected in Europe, as it is still expected in all Oriental countries, that those who governed a nation or conducted the higher and more important duties of its religion would enrich themselves in the process. The princely palaces of Rome record the splendid, sumptuous and successful application of this principle to the fruits of the faith of Christendom. So the "great families" of Europe, their homes, their fortunes, and their rent-rolls, save when the reward of military sack or service, nearly always represent the lucrative use for private emolument of the control of public revenue on a larger or smaller scale, through the exercise or inheritance of feudal agencies of rule, or a share in the more modern agencies of administration.   The faith and the patriotism of men, their fears for the next world and their civil necessities in this, have in all ages up to our own been regarded as the legitimate sources of private fortune, by those who allayed the one or supplied the other.

It is only under democratic conditions that men are expected to gain power without losing their poverty, and even the rapid acquirement of wealth by legitimate means during public service, is deemed a cause for scandal and suspicion. To the usual rule of popular institutions that public servants should leave the public service without money and without debts, their stipends permitting not even the honorable acquirement of a competence after years in positions of power and responsibility, Tammany Hall has been not the only exception, but the one most conspicuous, significant, and scandalous. Yet the prodigious and colossal thefts of certain of its leaders have never permanently destroyed the confidence of a plurality of the voters of New York City in its value as a political agency, which, by and large, gave them the kind of city government which they preferred. They have returned to its banners, its ballots, and its candidates whenever an exposure too scandalous to be endured drove them from it, and they never more unhesitatingly adhered to their faith in it under untoward circumstances than in the election, which in November, 1897, surrendered to Tammany the entire government of Greater New York, in whose history and management that of Tammany will, in future, be merged.

Tammany, during its periods of success, is

the strongest and most convincing argument
which exists to-day against the extension of
the principle of manhood suffrage to the administration of urban affairs. The principle
itself is only a form of government, or to speak
more accurately, a form of the consent, on
which all rule rests. The most arbitrary despotism, in its ultimate analysis, springs from
general consent, and the "freest" institutions
have no other basis. The issue between the
two is, whether this consent shall be exercised
by submission, or through the periodical
choice of rulers by all the voters of a community. If the admitted evils of Tammany for a
century are the normal fruits of the direct rule
of a great city by its voters, free institutions
are doomed. The ultimate verdict of civilization and of honesty will be against the form
of government on which, for over two centuries, as has been confidently believed, rested the
hopes of man and the progress of the race.
If, however, these evils are not physiological
but pathological, if they are not the normal results of conditions either natural or inevitable,
but pathological instead, the normal results of
abnormal conditions, then the final fruit and
result of this great object lesson on the political consciousness and convictions of mankind
depends upon whether these abnormal conditions are reparable or irreparable ; due to
circumstance or to human nature, the out-

come of a special environment, or of the general working of the democratic principle.

So momentous are the consequences involved in a solution of the cause and working of Tammany Hall that neither its assailants nor its supporters, and much less those who discuss it from the general standpoint of past politics or present history, have been able with an even temper to contemplate its disastrous operations, for three generations a constant encouragement to those who honestly believe that privilege and the government of the few are necessary to the happiness and security of the many, and a discouragement as perpetual to those whose confidence in the righteousness and worth of the visible recurrent and articulate control of the many, is unshaken even by Tammany Hall. Yet the facts of the case, neither few nor complex, are both accessible and apparent, enacted on a scene more than any other in the world's history, the object of constant unsparing and contemporary record.

The largest city of the Western World is situated on an island whose shape, size, and surroundings deprived it of an homogeneous civic population, while its own growth was a part, and the most conspicuous part, of that great stream of emigration which has transferred 15,000,000 persons, or half the present population of the United Kingdom, during the last seventy years, from one side of the Atlantic to the other. Our daily and practical morality is, in large measure, the result of our consciousness of the social conscience of the community of which we are part. Every man who travels is aware, always by observation, and but too often by experience, of the sudden shattering of moral observance which befalls those of training, character, and years, when they suddenly find themselves strangers in a strange city, free from the observation of those who do or may know them. A not dissimilar moral deliquescence is the inevitable result of immigration. If it has furnished more than its proportionate and numerical share of crime, corruption, and imprisonment, the wonder must be that it has not done more.

While in London but a small percentage of the population is of foreign birth, while the rapid growth of foreign cities, whose swift increase during the present century is often cited by the unfriendly critics of our municipal affairs as proof that our urban problems offer no peculiar difficulties, has, with negligible exceptions, drawn its accretion from a surrounding population of the same race, language, and institutions; New York City has been a vast sand-dune, without integral relations, swept across the Atlantic and deposited in the most convenient coign of vantage on the coast of North America. Deprived of all the myriad stay and support to sound political action which comes from coherent and uninterrupted mutual personal acquaintance and tradition, these unrelated units represented, for the most part, that precise stratum of society where generations of relentless toil had ingrained the impression that all social institutions worked together for the advantage of the few. It is, inevitably, those who most bitterly feel this disadvantage in the Old World, who seek the New. This great mass, in its diverse language and with very varied traditions, but alike in a past training of profound distrust for both the honesty and good faith of those who enjoy privileges of education, wealth, and refinement, of direction in business, of supremacy in affairs, or of influence through ability, was certain to find its natural and necessary leaders in the members of that class of the community which, by supplying his first wants, comes into direct personal, and more or less selfish or unselfish contact with the stranger laboring with his hands to seek new fortunes in a new home.

The class to which he turned for direction could not be the employer, for he represented the restraint and the *bourgeois* opportunity from which the immigrant fled, and which he hated in his old home and new. It could not be in religion he would find leaders, for through all its early stage, the great mass of immigrants were of a faith deemed alien by the organized churches of the community to which he came. The small grocer and the liquor-seller, the mechanic foreman or superintendent, and the contractor risen from the ranks of laborers, and for whom he was able to furnish the employment the raw newcomer first seeks, constituted the directing force of society brought most directly in contact with the immigrant and his offspring, new landed or long resident. Coming as strangers and unorganized, the immigrant population fell under the immediate direction of that stratum of society which lay nearest, and which had none of the objectionable features of other strata whose rule was resented, and whose privileges elsewhere were remembered with bitterness. The precise classes which have been described constituted, and still constitute, the backbone of Tammany Hall.

It is a grave error to confound the natural, praiseworthy, and often sound desire of the men of this class of lesser retail dealers, liquor-sellers, and contractors, to be of political influence, and to bear a share in the business of government, with the organized and continuous plunder of some of their higher leaders. To many in the rank and file of Tammany Hall, no pecuniary advantage, but the reverse, has come from their membership. They are in it because, being what they are, and the city what it is, it offers the readiest channel to gratify the laudable wish to be of weight and moment in the community in which one lives. Flagrant and flagitious corruption of voters has existed, but corruption only lubricated the machine. It was not its prime motor. The wish and will of a well-organized plurality was this. Tammany has been the agent of this wish. The not infrequent result has been a corruption unexampled under democratic and liberal institutions, though easily matched among despotisms to whose types, methods, and institutions, Tammany of late constantly tends to revert.

These influences would not have become paramount and predominant on Manhattan Island, if it had contained a city normally constituted as to its population, or normally housed as to its dwellings. For the first half-century, New York was such a city, and Tammany Hall, while powerful, was not despotic. But between 1840 and 1870, a large portion of the middle class of New York was siphoned off by insular conditions of territory into Brooklyn, which has often had its boss, always its political independence, and never a Tammany Hall. No insignificant share of the same general class was diverted to the suburban settlements of New Jersey and Connecticut. This left New York City without that precise social enclave which might have saved it, and which in all cities and all times is the salva-

tion of the commonwealth, the class which
filled the trainbands of London in the fight
with Charles, and the Continental Army in
the fight with George.   The instant this class
was restored by the charter of Greater New
York to the constituents of the city, Tammany
Hall was seen to be reduced in its relative
vote, though on Manhattan Island it retained
its usual plurality.[1]

This double circumstance, a population immigrant in fact or by descent, which found its
natural leaders in the lower retail ranks of
economic distribution and social direction,
and an urban community, in which a valuable
and necessary constituent had been decanted
off of the island by its shape and by the pressure of trade and population, was undoubtedly
aggravated by the conditions of American society.   Fugitive in all its relations, American
life has reduced to its final contractual nexus
the relations of domestic service.   Where domestic service is personal and continuous, it
and the relations which grow up under these
conditions, furnish an important agency by
which the political opinions of the well-to-do
are filtered through all social strata.   The
American habit of discharging servants in the
spring and re-engaging them in the fall, and a
domestic habit and attitude which, from faults
on both sides, renders this relation still more
precarious, completely sundered and separated

the more fortunate social strata from the less fortunate, in which lie most of the votes of Tammany.

Since those in need were, for the most part, strangers in a strange land, without personal relations, a vicarious charity system developed, under which most New Yorkers commuted the personal service each man and woman owes to those about him in want, into a money payment. While this disbursed the vast sums which render New York City one of the most liberal in its charities the world over, it divorced and deprived these charities of the personal influence which is the just fruit of an honest personal charity which seeks, first, not to relieve the needs of another, but to discharge one's own personal debt and duty to society, and the relief of human want. In the end, also, these charities themselves, in more than one instance, became the scandalous beneficiaries of Tammany Hall, and were harnessed to the car of its organization, so that their work presented itself to a great mass of the poor and struggling as part of a system which, whether it plundered the rich or not, at least relieved the poverty-stricken.

Lastly, there existed the pressure of American life, quite as much a matter of nervous imagination as of actual exertion, and the more serious social fact that a torrid summer drove from the city for a long absence the class which

was most needed for daily personal influence,
women of character, cultivation, and well-to-
do surroundings.   This summer absence deprived them of the network of myriad contact
which insensibly diffuses social ideas.   The
tenement-house system, due to the limited
area of the city, aggravated and exasperated
all these conditions by preventing among the
great mass of its population those neighborhood relations, and that personal acquaintance
which are only possible where each family has
its separate home.   New York for half a century has been berthed, not housed.

Tammany Hall began in a secret organization, the Tammany Society or Columbian
Order, whose membership was drawn from
the precise stratum already described.   Organized a little over a century ago, the political
drift of this Society, and the political organization which grew out of it, was for forty years
towards universal suffrage ; for forty years its
tumultuous gatherings directed a growing immigrant population, and for nearly thirty, the
heads of this body have led a well-organized
body of all classes, partly foreign and partly
native, for the exclusive object of ruling the
city.   The earliest of these periods ended with
the first elected mayor in 1834.

It saw the destruction of the more or less
aristocratic society of the colonial period, and
the opening of the Erie Canal, both incidents in

the commercial expansion, which in England led to the Reform Bill, and in this country to universal white male suffrage. The next period ran to the end of the war, and saw New York established as the gate of the West, while here, 1865 to 1870, the centralization of Federal power, with the destruction of slavery, was accomplished, and household suffrage established in England. The third, covering the last thirty years, has been marked by the transformation in all fields of individual into corporate activity and the multiplication of a myriad complex and specialized agencies, through which a population of 73,000,000 nominally carries on its varied business—social, economic, and political—through institutions originally devised for a population of 3,000,000, and still bearing their old names.

The Tammany Society, which on its celebration of the ter-centennial of Columbus's discovery in 1792, became also the Columbian Order, was organized by William Mooney,' an upholsterer by trade, and its first celebration, May 12, 1789, on the banks of the Hudson, is usually treated as the beginning of the society, though its original organization took place at the City Hall, and it was itself an imitation of an earlier Philadelphia society. In New York, as elsewhere, the close of the war saw return to power the colonial better class, recruited by those who had led the Revolution.

Tammany stood for popular resistance to this. New York City had a restricted suffrage based on a property qualification, and the ancient forty-shilling homeholder of the English borough. The population of the city in 1790, was 33,131, and its voters numbered 5,184,[3] of whom half, or 2,661, were of the forty-shilling class, not owning freeholds to the value of £20. Even at this early date, a majority of voters were without a property stake, and less than one-fourth, or 1,209, held over £100 of realty. Of these voters less than one-half came to the polls, though it is a persistent political fiction that in earlier and better days all good citizens, when all citizens were good, both voted and attended the primary.

In 1789, when George Clinton defeated Robert Yates, only 2,760[4] votes were cast, or less than half the vote lists. To-day a vote of 90 per cent. of the registry is the normal proportion, and the registry is nearly this proportion of the vote. Where in 1790, 54 per cent. of the registered voters seek the polls, the proportion now is for the most part over 90 per cent. In addition, on the usual basis, New York in 1790, would have had with its population a vote of about 6,600, so that about 1,500 persons must have been disfranchised. An important work which Tammany has discharged, and one essential to the final success of our institutions, is of breeding the habit of voting. Abroad, in France, for instance, not over half the voters vote. However, it has failed at other points, Tammany has always been faithful to the work of extending the basis of suffrage, so far as white males were concerned, and in drilling them to the habit of voting. There is to-day no voting body of equal size, or approaching its size, which so fully exercises its political right to vote as that on Manhattan Island. The work of ensuring that this vote shall be cast to the best interests of the city remains to be done.

In 1789, government was still in the hands of the few. The inauguration of Washington was a turning-point in more than Federal affairs, and the Tammany Society represented more than one of its events. As the Indian was driven back from the coast, and his character and habits became legendary, there sprang up an innocent admiration for qualities which Cooper was soon to make a part of fiction, and which were never a part of fact. The Middle States, in particular, had been brought into close contact with Indians of a tribe and type less savage and more peaceful than any along the coast. Among the Lenni Lenape Indians, Tamanend, whose grave is still cherished,[*] and whose memory was long revered, was a chief who signed one of Penn's treaties, purchasing part of Philadelphia. He became, during the Revolution, the pseudo pa–

tron saint of the younger officers and men of the line. His day, May 12th, replaced that of St. George. There was also in this aboriginal worship and admiration, relic and reflection of Rousseau's apotheosis of primitive man and the dawn of a protest against English supremacy, always strongest in an American community in the stratum from which Tammany's membership was drawn. In organizing the new society in New York, but one of many, the ritual and organization of an Iroquois lodge was imitated, and the "long room" at Martling's had its name, not from its length, but because this was the term, still familiar, applied by the Indian to his tribal assembly-room. The Tammany Society was, therefore, divided into thirteen tribes,[6] each with its totem, and while the Society itself remained active in its membership and meetings, each initiate was assigned to one of these tribes. Time and tendencies are, however, stronger in determining totems than paper constitutions and rituals. The symbol upon which Tammany and the public have finally settled, with the agreeable unanimity of the captor and his prey, has been the Tammany Tiger, first emblazoned on the engine of "Big Six,"[7] and conspicuous under Tweed in the heavy gold badge of the Americus Club. The year[8] in the ritual of the Society was divided into the four seasons, and their elaborate and artificial return to the savage still appears after a century in the advertised notices of the meetings of the Society, jostling more modern forms and phrases. These mild fooleries were all only part of a like spirit perpetually out-cropping in our cities in "Sir Knights," in regalia, and in rituals of whose complexion, extent, and important influence on the character of individuals many of those who deem themselves familiar with American society are profoundly ignorant.

Tammany's original political action was along lines suggested by the "Committee of Correspondence," whose revolutionary plots, success has turned into patriotic projects. It formed the usual medium of inter-state political action in the first forty years after the close of the Revolution, and slowly developed into its present system of party government. Similar Tammany societies had been organized in other States. That in Philadelphia, parent of all the rest, was first organized May 1, 1772,[9] when the sons of King Tammany met at the house of James Byrns to celebrate the memory of a chieftain already associated with American opposition to the European spirit. Reorganized in imitation of the New York exemplar, the Tammany Society, or Columbian Order of Philadelphia, at the Columbia Wigwam, on the Schuylkill, showed its opposition May 12,

Creek
Indians

1798, to Federalism and its sympathy with the French. It paraded in costume in honor of Jefferson's election, its Wiskinski to the front, carrying a key ; it celebrated, in 1802, the acquisition of Louisiana, always supported the ruling demagogues of a day of demagogues, and its celebrations were still in progress in 1814. In Rhode Island [10] it was not until 1819 that a Tammany Society was organized and continued for five years with various branches and much success to lead the Democratic party to short-lived victory. These societies, wherever organized, displayed everywhere the same revolt of the class newly arrived to the suffrage, or desiring it, and made in all places the same appeal in parade, buck-tail, and ritual.

The original Tammany Society was at first welcomed as an aid to the effort Washington was making at the opening of his Administration to conciliate all classes at home, and receive peace on our Indian frontier. A year after its first organization, when Col. Marinus Willett brought to New York a deputation of Creek Indians, they were the guests of Tammany Society during their visit. The occasion was serious. Our Western march was barred at the north by the British forts and at the south by the Creeks and Cherokees, the most powerful confederacy on our frontier. Their reception and entertainment at the new Federal capital by the Tammany Society, in full costume and regalia, was a public service whose importance it is not easy now to appreciate.

Before three years had passed, the Tammany Society was in full, though unavowed, opposition to Washington's Administration, its first conspicuous sign of changing views being its elaborate celebration [11] of the landing of Columbus, October 12, 1792, whose odes, inscriptions, and ceremonies were devoted to the pledge that:

> Secure for ever and entire
> The Rights of Man shall here remain.—

language which in that day and date was the dialect of the supporter of France and the opponent of the policy of Washington. Two months later the Society met, December 27, 1792, to celebrate the victory of Dumouriez [12]—a meeting whose last midnight and perhaps maudlin toast expressed the fervent hope that the American fair would ever keep their favors for the Republican brave. Nor from that day to this has the elaborate political machinery of Tammany Hall failed to appreciate the necessity of keeping in close union the social pleasures and the political action of great masses of voters. The winter ball and the summer excursion, whose heavy expense is no small part of the annual budget of a district leader to-day, echo the determination of the toast in Brom Martling's Hall a century ago.

The Revolution had been precipitated, as far as physical force was concerned, by "Liberty Boys," led by a few men who represented the secondary colonial aristocracy of wealth, for which Adams stood in Massachusetts, Clinton in New York, and Morris in Pennsylvania. Ten years after the struggle found the officer better rewarded than the private both by Legislatures and the public. Mooney had been a violent "Liberty Boy." He and his found little to admire in the waiting policy of Washington. The turmoil of Europe added immigration to domestic ferment, and the Revolution of '98 sent to New York the ablest Irish immigrants of the century, the last immigration of birth, abroad. With it closed colonial conditions of political emigration. Thenceforward European emigration was economic. New York's trade was gaining what Philadelphia lost by yellow fever. The Tammany Society became the nucleus about which centred the unsatisfied turbulence of the Revolution, the rapidly increasing ranks of labor deprived of a vote, and the new wave of immigration stung to bitter revolt against Federalism by the Alien and Sedition laws of 1798. The immediate local leader was Daniel D. Tompkins, a young graduate of Columbia, who began his political career by marrying the daughter of the Alderman of his ward, and, having married her, demonstrated his right to become a district leader by carrying his ward, the Seventh, and reversing, in 1800, the Federal majority of 200 in the year before. He ended his typical Tammany career under charges of pecuniary dishonesty. His integrity was in the end vindicated, but only at the expense of his administrative ability.[18]

For ten years, after George Clinton, in 1789, by a narrow majority of 429, defeated Robert Yates, the candidate of a conservative reaction, the rapid development of politics went on. The population doubled. The voters increased but two thirds; in 1801, 8,088. The men without a vote trebled. Dangers environ a democratic community when population outstrips voters. The halves of the city pulled apart. Realty owners over $500 in value doubled. Men owning $100 to $500 nearly disappeared. The landless 40-shilling householder more than doubled. The landless voteless men trebled. Tammany steadily gravitated from social to political action. It denounced Jay's treaty, and the distinguished author of the Louisiana code began his public career by flinging the missile which cut open the face of Hamilton. It went in a body to help fortify Governor's Island when war with England looked near. It welcomed Priestley, but his New York friends did not, as in Philadelphia, attend his sermons. Its reception to the discoverer of oxygen was the last sign of the scientific interest which, in 1790, led to an American Historical Museum, first opened in the City Hall, and removed later by Gardiner Baker, its founder and curator, to the open triangular space where Broad and Pearl join. Three weeks after its reception to the fugitive from the mob of Birmingham, the society surrendered to the curator its museum on condition that it should bear its name, and that its members should enjoy a family free ticket, an early application of the principle of free passes which has distinguished the Society for a century.

Meeting, as most of the societies of the day did, in a tavern, Tammany began at Borden's in lower Broadway, and its annual procession on May 12th, "St. Tammany," and July 4th, for the "long talks" and "short talks" of its celebration, marched up Broadway with feathers and leggins to the old Presbyterian Church on Wall Street, or to the Brick Church which faced City Hall Square, on the triangle at whose apex is the New York *Times* building. In 1798, it moved to Martling's, on the southeast corner of Nassau and Spruce Streets.

This long, low building, opening on Nassau, was kept by "Brom" Martling (Abraham B.

Martling), and for twenty years, even after a new hall was built, the members of the Society, and the political party which clustered about it, were known as "Martling men." The use of Tammany as a political term did not begin in 1818, but until that date was infrequent. It became common, not because the Tammany Society itself grew more immediate in its political action, but because it had built the first of its permanent homes. Incorporated in 1805, during the next ten years Tammany Hall men held the most lucrative posts in a Federal administration far more extravagant in the emoluments of its offices than in the present day, when salaries have replaced fees. The city itself was passing through a period of rapid commercial expansion, whose first check was the embargo, which Tammany supported, with the result, as a fruit of the policy of which the embargo was a part, that the relative growth of the city was less than one half as rapid in the second decade of the century as in the first. In 1811, at the end of the first decade, Colonel Rutgers was able to raise $28,000, a large sum, but no more than a single Tammany Federal officer had drawn in a year as fees, and "Martling's Long Room" was replaced, not far from its site, by the first Tammany Hall, at the corner of Frankfort Street and Park Row. The walls of the building then erected still stand, the office of the New York *Sun*. It held originally a hall and hotel, where board was $7 a week, the second leading hotel of the city. It had behind it the shipyards and tanneries on the East River. It had before it the City Hall. The better residence quarter was passing up the island, along another channel in whose currents Tammany Hall has never found the stream to grind its mill.

"Martling's Long Room" had been the resort of "Sons of Liberty" and of the "Sons of 1776." The close connection was one of the causes which made it natural for Tammany Society to give funeral honors to the bones of the Revolutionary prisoners of war, of whom 11,500 had sickened and died in British prison-hulks, treated with no more and no less inhumanity than was the brutal custom of the day. Congress had neglected, in 1803, the memorial of the Society. In 1807, Tammany appointed a committee, and a year later, May 26, 1808, Tammany Society in its regalia, the buck-tail conspicuous, led a civic procession which buried the bleached bones, and returned to the weather-beaten, unpainted structure which had survived the Revolution. Its bar-room was on Spruce, its kitchen on Nassau. Its "long room" ran parallel with the latter. Built when a mere road ran before it up the island, the street had risen in grade. The floor of the hall was reached by two

or three descending steps. Uncouth, dirty,
stained, the merest shanty, it was known by
Federalist opponents as " the pig-pen." It
deserved the name. Its selection, and Borden's, the churches in which the Society held
its larger and more decorous meetings, Campbell's in Greenwich village, where its May and
summer outings were held, all bespoke the
small merchant, retailer, and mechanic, out of
whose ranks the Tammany machine was to
grow and to control the vast foreign vote of
the future.

The Federal party lost its power and its
head together, and drove the immigrant into
Democratic support by passing the Alien and
Sedition laws. In spite of this it won the
Congressional election of 1798, and the scandal attending Burr's Manhattan Bank charter
gave the Federalists the city by 900 majority
in 1799. Sinking step by step, from Washington to Clinton, and from Clinton to Tammany, he came to New York, organized the
landless vote, which could not elect a Governor but could determine the choice of Federal electors, and the spring election of 1800
saw the first New York contest in which
voters were enrolled, canvassed, and voted
with ordered precision. " Faggot "-voters
were created by uniting a number of men in
the ownership of the same property, poor men
were deeded free-holds, the Society kept open

house in its hall, voters were carried to the poll, the last man was voted, and the first victory of Tammany Hall was won.

Jefferson was elected President and Tammany was placed in the relative position which it has ever since occupied. In New York City it had opposed to it, the well-to-do, the better-educated, and the mass of property-holders. In the State, the State Administration and the vote of the State was in general marshalled in the opposing party. The instant its leader, Aaron Burr, appeared in Washington, where he had been nominated for Vice-President, and began to act for himself in national affairs, Tammany broke with him and united with his enemies, as Tammany has dealt ever since with every political leader in New York State of its own party who with or without its votes, rose to a national position and began a national career. Lastly, without backing in the Northern States, except in the Tammany societies of the larger cities, the new organization found its natural allies in the Southern slave States, and received first from Jefferson and later from Madison and Monroe the aid of Federal patronage, which, as Governor DeWitt Clinton charged twenty years later, was "an organized and disciplined corps in our elections."[14]

The political history of Tammany Hall began with this victory. The Society and its committee of correspondence gave a nucleus for political action, secrecy, and contact with other States. The "general meeting" gathered voters for assemblies which ratified nominations and passed resolutions already decided in the Society. Federal offices gave patronage and the Albany Legislature a long series of corrupt transactions in which nearly all public men shared. When Burr, in 1804, was nominated for Governor, Tammany Hall, following Jefferson's wishes and its own inclination, supported Morgan Lewis. He was nominated at a Legislative caucus, whose chairman, Ebenezer Purdy, was later expelled from the Senate for corrupt practices; and whose clerk, Solomon Southwick, was later charged with bribery in procuring the charter of the Bank of America.[16] DeWitt Clinton, the municipal rival of Burr, resigned his seat in the United States Senate to become Mayor, a post with four times the salary of the Federal position and proportionately greater power, the first instance, frequent through the century, of a Tammany man preferring the better-filled manger of its service to the higher but emptier stall of a national career. As with all its Mayors, Tammany early gave him the alternatives of submission, retirement, or the organization of his own political machine. Men like Clinton, Wood, and Grace have done the last. Men like Hone and Hewitt, the second.

Other more recent Tammany Mayors have selected the first.

The precise difference in Clinton's case had
as its occasion, not its cause, his sentence of
Gulian C. Verplanck for his share in the riot
which marked public disapproval of the Federalist sympathies of the Columbia College
authorities. Separating himself from the system which placed in a caucus of Congressmen
at Washington the nomination of President, De
Witt Clinton began the modern national convention, and organized the alliance between
the interior of New York and the Federal Whig
and Republican vote of the city which opposition to Tammany has marshalled through
the century on all State and National issues.
Tammany had developed from its own ranks,
Tompkins, its leader in this struggle ; he had
the support of Ambrose Spencer and other
Federal office-holders under him. Tammany
Hall vigorously supported the war of 1812, a
most important public service. It aided in opposing Federal aid to the Canals, which were,
under De Witt Clinton, at length built after
political victories, due to his city machine,
which organized a lower level than Tammany,
as Wood and Morrissey did later, and the interior rural vote, first Tompkins's and later his.
Through all, Tammany steadily held its grip on
the city. In 1818, its entire ticket for Congress
and its corporation officers were chosen by

1,200 majority."[16] In 1819, its average majority on Assemblymen was 2,301 and on Senators, elected by a limited suffrage, 850.[17] One year later, the "Tammanies," thanks to various coalitions in the State, had 41 Assemblymen, the Federals 39, and the Clintonian Republicans 46. These dissensions in Democracy, Niles lamented, as Democratic editors did like divisions due to like causes seventy and eighty years later.[18] From year to year, through this period, the Tammany Society and the General Meeting issued addresses to the branches of the one, and the Democratic-Republican fellow-citizens of the other, deploring in 1817 the spread of the "foreign" game of billiards among the upper, and vice among the lower ; and in 1819[19] its address led Adams, who with Jefferson and Madison responded to its utterances, to wish it success "in discountenancing all pernicious customs and usages, and deviation from a wise and virtuous national economy." Through all its first period, Tammany spoke with the accent of a middle-class precisian. In the next period, it sank to the street-rough. In the close of the third, grew up the intimate connection of some, not all, of its leaders, with the semi-criminal classes. But this affected only a part. The great mass of the active membership of Tammany Hall as a political organization has always consisted of the civic stratum made up of daily labor with its immediate direction in the stratum just above.

A Tammany "general meeting" began the movement which ended in the constitution of 1821 and white male suffrage. This somewhat increased the number of voters, but not much. Under a restricted suffrage, the ingenuity of politicians manufactured a registry of 19,925 voters in New York City in 1821, where the census in 1826 could count only 18,283 adult male citizens. The real change was an increase in the habit of voting. In 1826, only 31.12 per cent. of the voters voted ; in 1828, 75.69 ; and by 1840, 91.96 per cent.—the modern average. Nor had naturalization added much to the vote. Even in 1840, the New York Assembly had in it but one person of foreign birth[20] and 75 were native to the State. In 1855, New York City still had 46,173 native and 42,704 naturalized voters ; in 1855, 51,500 native and 77,475 naturalized ; in 1875, 90,-973 native and 141,179 naturalized. This eloquent proportion remains the rule. Yet the earlier American municipality was a filthy, pestilential city, enduring countless nuisances, with a general death-rate comparable to the tenement-house districts of seventy years later.

Tammany shared with the rest our transition period, 1820–1830, Buck-tails casting in their lot with Van Buren's Jackson men, and Clintonians developing into anti-Masons—

spurred by the wide influence of secret societies like Tammany—and Whigs. For a few years, an election of mayor by the aldermen put Tammany at a disadvantage, as the Whigs held the less populous wards, and the successive ballotings were full of shameless scandal. When a constitutional amendment, 1833, made the mayoralty elective, Cornelius A. Lawrence was nominated, 1834, after old forms. Posters announced the "general meeting." A flag was hoisted over Tammany Hall. The hall was open to all comers. He polled 17,575 votes, and his Whig opponent, Gulian C. Verplanck, 17,373. Since then the tides of votes have ebbed and flowed with a periodical regularity.²¹ Tammany held five successive terms and the opposition two; the organization elected five mayors and the opposition one ; Tammany two and the opposition one ; Tammany one and the opposition two ; Tammany three and the opposition four ; Tammany four and the opposition one; Tammany two and the opposition one ; two candidates endorsed by Tammany and the opposition one ; a compromise candidate and Tammany three ; the opposition one, and Tammany the last. This steady alternation has given Tammany about two thirds of the mayors, and its periods of defeat and victory have only been broken (during the war) by Fernando Wood and the Mozart Hall Democracy.

Tammany Hall, in full communion with Jackson, was already in fatal alliance with Southerners, who figured as prominently as its speech-makers then as now.[22] In 1831, the Hall made the serious blunder of trying to support Jackson and to sympathize with South Carolina in the same resolutions. New York was roused, and a great meeting of merchants passed an uncompromising resolution. The blunder severed a reputable vote never regained. The Equal Rights, or, as we should say, labor party, in 1829 cut off another body of voters. Growing, the new labor party in October, 1835, started from its Bowery headquarters[23] and stormed the "general meeting" in a riot which gave birth to the "loco-foco" party, which owes its name to the matches used when the Tammany janitor turned off the gas. In 1837, after two Tammany victories, the split cost the mayoralty,—Aaron Clark, Whig, 17,044; John D. Morgan, Democrat, 13,763 ; and Moses Jaques, bolter, 4,239. Again, in 1838, Tammany was defeated, borne down by the scandal of wholesale defalcations, Samuel Swartwout, Collector, for $1,200,000, and William M. Price, District Attorney, for $75,000. Both fled, and neither was pursued. The public conscience was inconceivably low. "Defalcations are no crime," said a leading New York paper[24] in a cynical vein. For five years, for the pendulum swung back in 1839, Isaac L. Varian winning by a narrow majority, Tammany Hall elected its mayor by a constantly increasing plurality and an enlarging poll, which, in 1844, prompted charges of fraud from Whigs who found, as often since, that Tammany won as well without Federal and State patronage as with. Twice, 1844 and 1845, the American party elected its candidate, James Harper, but disappeared as rapidly as it had arisen, and, in 1846, Tammany elected W. F. Havemeyer by the crushing majority of 6,822.

The victory was decisive. The city was passing out of its provincial stage. A police force was about to be organized. The water works were completed. The internal trade and foreign commerce of the city were about to enter on the amazing expansion which culminated in 1857. The adoption of a new constitution and its re-apportionment gave the Democrats an advantage retained for thirty years. Immigration was transforming the city. When the Mayor first became elective, American workmen and Whig majorities held the first to the fifth wards in the lower end of the Island and went up the ridge with the eighth and fifteenth wards. The new foreign element had settled in the low ground of the sixth, and the seventh and ninth to fourteenth were Tammany. Fifteen years later, the lower end of the Island was Irish and Democratic, and the American Whig mechanic was elbowed north and west, coloring the seventh, ninth, and thirteenth wards, long Whig and later Republican.

If Tammany lost two or three elections, 1847, 1849, in part because its vigorous support of the Mexican War was unpopular, its supremacy was growing, and in 1850, Fernando Wood, the first man who attempted to be boss in Tammany Hall after fifty years of joint leadership, organized the brute vote which radiated from the "bloody Sixth." Beaten for the first two-year term by Ambrose C. Kingsland, Whig, who polled the Free Soil Democratic vote, predecessors of the "State Democracy," two years later, 1852–1856, Wood was laid aside for Jacob A. Westervelt, who was pulled through by the Presidency and Seymour, in 1852, with 10,000 majority. In 1853, the Democratic party split into "Softs" and "Hards." Slavery is the cause usually assigned.[1] The real one was that the "Hards," the reputable office-holders, were vainly trying to hold power against the rising tide of rowdy "plug-ugly" and bruiser led by Wood and organized in "clubs," "gangs," and fire engine companies, and all the manifold machinery by which an ignorant foreign vote and a depraved native vote as ignorant, was manned, managed, manipulated, and made ready to share and dare the plunder of the city ten years later under

Tweed.　Winning the regular Tammany nomination in 1854, Wood was elected over a divided vote, polling but 20,033 out of 56,-972 votes cast.　With his term began the reversion to earlier methods in the attempt to govern New York from Albany through a non-partisan police.　It failed, and only gave a new demonstration that Tammany's power is independent of mere patronage.　Enjoying boss control of party machinery, Wood, in 1856, polled ninety-nine votes against ten for all other candidates in the regular Tammany convention.[26]　A most reputable bolting convention nominated James C. Libby.　He polled scarcely 5,000 votes and Wood 34,566, a plurality of 9,384 over his next antagonist, Isaac O. Baker, the Know-nothing candidate.　In the regular course, Wood would have become and remained the first boss of Tammany Hall. His respectable opponents had control, however, of the Tammany Society.　A hot canvass, in 1857, ended in the selection of a Board of Sachems, who, by a vote of seven to six, closed the doors on Wood and his General Committee.　For the first time, the Tammany Society, which is only the landlord of the political body which leases its hall, exercised its singular power of deciding between rival organizations.　Again in 1872, it closed its doors.　During the last illness of John Kelly, it was deemed possible that it might be called upon again to decide between rival claimants.

Driven from Tammany Hall, Wood found the city alarmed and aroused, and, in 1857, he was defeated by Daniel F. Tiemann, a Democratic candidate who gathered to his support all dissentient elements, the first instance in the history of the city. Organizing Mozart Hall, in 1859, Wood defeated divided opponents and was elected Mayor a third time in a canvass in which the Democratic vote was evenly divided. The war now broke the continuity of local traditions. Tammany Hall organized a regiment, the 42d New York, and sent it to the front, and its monument, with its Indian wigwam and Indian chief, was dedicated at Gettysburg, September 24, 1891.[26] Of the steady service of the regiment, its record in thirty-six battles and engagements is a sufficient proof. The war period saw George Opdyke, the only Mayor New York has ever had elected on a Republican ticket, chosen by 613 votes over two Democratic candidates, Wood and Gunther. Two years later a brief-lived "Hall," led by John McKeon, elected C. Godfrey Gunther over a combined Tammany and Mozart Hall candidate by 6,524 votes.

The close of the war found Tammany Hall, whose local ranks were bitterly disloyal, divided, defeated, and discredited. If it promptly rose to supreme civic power and decided the national Democratic nomination in 1868, it was because it represented certain stable social conditions and a permanent political force. New York was now a city, and no accretion of population or territory has altered its character. Its great population was, and for forty years and more was destined to remain, with a majority of foreign birth. With this majority was associated another great stratum, descendants of the Irish immigration of twenty years before. The two were crowded together in a great tract of dense population, the needs of whose days and the amusements of whose nights were furnished by the grocer, the retailer, and the liquor-seller, while the associations best known and most familiar were those of the volunteer fire company, the beer garden, and the "club" dance-house. Reorganized with district leaders drawn from these sources, Tammany Hall was led by Tweed in the riotous assault of its chiefs on the city treasury, while the rank and file believed themselves on the high road to regain the Democratic supremacy enjoyed before the war. After the fall of Tweed, crushed by the revelation of his wholesale plunder—though if he had gone to England instead of to jail he might have returned to power—Tammany was again reorganized by John Kelly, a man of a different type, sober, patient, industrious,

Reorganization

and of such honesty as was possible for a man bred in his surroundings. Of the three bosses of Tammany Hall, I once reported the sentence of the first for his embezzlements, and the trial of the third for murder; the second once said to me, when, in a moment of youthful enthusiasm, I urged on him the demerits of a local candidate for district judge, "If I go into these local fights, I can't pick good men for the Supreme Court, which is my business." To this business, he devoted himself for ten years of patient and stubborn assiduity, accepting the evils he found and increasing them by consolidating the power of the organization he led—in some sort its Augustus. He found it a horde. He left it a political army. In 1871, by bolting the nomination of Lucius Robinson, he detached this army from all allegiance but that of Tammany Hall. This supreme stroke of statecraft completed the slow development of a century by rendering the boss of Tammany a supreme ruler within his political limits. Twice he elected his mayors, Wickham, 1874, and Ely, 1876; once he was defeated, Schell by Cooper, 1878, and twice he accepted a coalition Democrat, Grace, 1880, and Edson, 1882, but he ended with the election, 1884, of Grant, a straight Tammany candidate. After his death, John Kelly was succeeded by Richard Croker, a man whose reign is still too incomplete to admit of complete analysis. An investigation in 1894 showed, however, that the early and direct plunder of Tweed had been replaced in the city government of New York by indirect pillage through blackmail, whose responsibility Tammany shares with other political organizations, but in which its portion was larger, its methods more systematic, and its evil success more complete.

The political army which has raised these three bosses to despotic rule, and won this extraordinary succession of political victories through a century, has slowly reached its present organization under which a single man exercises unchallenged supremacy. When New York had 5,000 voters, a single hall enabled a majority of the majority of these voters to meet and decide the nominations and the general policy of the party. This "general meeting" is, by two channels of succession, the lineal predecessor of the General Committee which now crowds Tammany Hall, able to accommodate only a third of the body which is supposed to meet there. During the first thirty years of Tammany, the "general meeting" had two functions ; it directly made nominations and issued addresses, which later became platforms. This use of the "general meeting" survives in the direct use of the "general committee" as a county convention to nominate county officers without calling primaries or electing delegates for the purpose. The "general committee" is to-day, however, the symbol rather than the survival of the "general meeting," which was once the ultimate authority in Tammany Hall.

At the "general meetings" committees were appointed to prepare addresses and to carry on the campaign. These also acted as "committees of correspondence," following Revolutionary precedent, an atrophied organ still surviving in the "Committee on Correspondence." [27] Each ward, at an early day, had its ward committee, appointed at a general meeting of the ward. The same machinery existed in Congressional and legislative districts when these were created. There is a curious political myth that at some early period the general body of voters attended their meetings and made them the direct utterance of popular will as apart from that of politicians directly interested in office-holding and the profits of place and influence. For this legend there is absolutely no evidence whatever. When Tammany Hall, at its primaries in September, 1897, polled 35,000 votes, [28] a larger vote was cast than had ever been before recorded, and there is every reason to believe that it was also a larger proportion of the vote cast in New York City for Tammany candidates at the last election. These "general meetings" and primaries began in the grossest disorder. Clinton's meetings, which drew from a social stratum lower than that of Tammany Hall, were regularly mobbed. The ward meetings from 1820 to 1840 were the constant scene of boisterous and violent combat. From 1840 to 1870 they were normally in the hands of the bully, the black-leg, and the prize-fighter. Tamed by a police, efficient, with all its blackmail, in preserving external order, they have been for the past quarter-century incomparably more orderly, no more corrupt, and no less illusive expressions of the popular will than in the past.

Until the passage of the "Cassidy resolution,"[29] in the State Convention of 1871, the ward and its election district were the units of political representation. By 1822, the ephemeral "general committee," most of whose members were also members of the Tammany Society, and sometimes acted through it, were consolidated in a permanent "general council" of three members from each of the eleven wards, into which (1825) the city was divided. New wards increased the membership to forty-five, and in 1836 to seventy-five. There was here for nearly twenty years a ward general committee, a "general meeting" which tumultuously acted for the party, and a network of local ward and district committees. These last often filled ten to twelve columns in the daily papers, and were, like the Tammany General Committee of to-day, a tolerably complete roster of the office-holding class and the working army of Tammany Hall.

Between the disappearance of this organization in fact, though not in name, and the appearance of current conditions, political power between 1845 to 1865 passed to the many voluntary civic organizations of which the fire companies were so easily chief. Some social, some useful, and some purely predatory, these varied bodies first controlled Tammany Hall, and, when they were turned out of it, for ten years made the fortunes of various "Halls," more permanent. The most important were drafted into the service of the city in a paid fire department, and the rest were subdued by the police.

They became in this condition accessions to a political organization which controlled the police. When John Kelly undertook the work of reorganizing Tammany, the Assembly District and Election District were the units of organization, the latter giving a member each for the General Committee and the former supplying the Assembly District leader, who sat on the old "Committee of Organization." This useful and powerful body was employed by John Kelly "to discipline" John Morrissey, and was for nearly ten years the centre of the organization. It began by choosing its ruler. It ended, as is the fashion of despotism, by its ruler choosing it. It remained the ruling body in December, 1885, when Croker controlled seventeen out of twenty-four members and assured his succession in the organization.

The election district, which with its single member furnished a sufficiently large base in the city of about a million with 160,000 voters in 1875, had become an unsuitable unit twenty years later, when both the city and the voters had nearly doubled in number. The Democratic vote was made a basis of representation in the General Committee for each Assembly District on the ratio of a vote—not member—to each fifty votes cast. The delegation thus determined was "elected" in a nominal poll, until 1895 open only two hours, at a single place in each Assembly District. The delegation has, necessarily, one from each election district and as many more as choose to serve and pay a fee. This procedure has swollen the General Committee from 700 or 800 in 1874 ; to 4,562 in 1890 ; to 8,000 in 1892; and to upwards of 12,000 now. Its committees are correspondingly enlarged, the committee on organization having in 1892, 768 members or 32 from each Assembly District.

Real power and control rested with the "leader" in each Assembly District, named by the "boss," but holding his place by the feudal tenure of constant and unbroken victory. In December, 1893, a running mate for the leader in the shape of a business man was devised. Each "leader" knows the citizens, families, homes, and business of an Assembly District, containing from 5,000 to 14,000 voters, and keeps an amazing knowledge of their votes, habits, needs, desires, pursuits, pleasures, and crimes. Each election district with its 300 to 500 voters has its leader. This organization is customarily supposed to be devoted to marshalling, managing, and polling the vote. But this is only the culmination of its arduous duties. It forms a vast net-work through which a host of daily and necessary civic duties are discharged. Through it, foreign voters are naturalized and trained to new duties, employment is procured for the idle, aid distributed to the needy, the unfortunate are befriended in hospital and court-room, the semi-criminal receive immunity, the honest are guided and aided to those extra-legal advantages a policeman conveniently blind can give to the peddler, the vendor, huckster, and small store-keeper ; and there is furnished, besides, the centre of an active social and political life. A part of these duties involve breach of the law and lead to thinly disguised blackmail. Most are part of that mutual civic help, busy men, however public-spirited, utterly neglect. Done for selfish motives doubtless by the district "leader," they are none the less necessary.

Their discharge renders the Tammany organization a daily fountain of benefits to the ignorant and helpless, whose votes, won by these dubious means, are made the bulwark of daily wrongs public and private. This union of crime, oppression, and benevolence, of malfeasance, blackmail, and largess, has held its power for a century, neither by corruption nor by patronage, but by its hideous imitation and wise use of important civil duties, neglected by the well-to-do. Their sedulous and righteous discharge will supplant Tammany by supplying something better. No other method, machinery, or management will, for no form of government, however free, no law, however wise, and no political machinery, however adroit, can ever be a substitute for civic courage, civic virtue, and the daily discharge of mutual civic duties. If these duties are neglected by good men, bad men will use them to evil ends.

Civic Duties

NOTES AND REFERENCES.

1. In 1897, the vote of the Tammany candidate for Mayor was in New York City (Manhattan and Bronx), 16,607 less than the united vote of its opponents, and in Greater New York (whose total vote was only 75 per cent. greater than that of New York) its own total vote fell 51,562 short of the total of its opponents, or nearly fourfold its New York minority.

2. The first officers were William Mooney, White Matlock, Oliver Glenn, Philip Hone, James Tyler, John Campbell, Gabriel Furman, John Burger, Jonathan Pierce.

3. *New York State Census*, 1855, p. ix.

4. HAMMOND's *Political History of New York*, i., 41.

5. Grave of Tamanend. H. C. MERCER, *Magazine of American History*, March, 1893.

6. New York was the Eagle tribe; Delaware, Tiger; Virginia, Wolf; North Carolina, Buffalo; Pennsylvania, Bee; Connecticut, Beaver; New Hampshire, Squirrel; Maryland, Fox; New Jersey, Tortoise; Rhode Island, Eel; South Carolina, Dog.

7. "Big Six" was the term applied to Engine Company No. 6, in the Sixth Ward, the foreman of whose big "double-decker" was William M. Tweed.

8. The year was divided into the seasons of Snows, Blossoms, Fruits, and Hunting.

9. SCHARF-WESTCOTT's *History of Philadelphia*, i., 265.

10. MARCUS W. JERREGAN, *Tammany Societies of Rhode Island.*

11. EDWARD F. DELANCY, *New York Historical Society*, Oct. 4, 1894.

12. *American Daily Advertiser*, Jan. 3, 1793.

13. In 1806, Tompkins was elected Governor of New York, and in 1816, Vice-President of the United States.

14. *Niles Register*, N. S., vii., 208.
15. Hugh J. Hastings's *Ancient American Politics*, p. 28.
16. *Niles Register*, xii., 192.
17. *Niles Register,* N. S., ii., 192.
18. *Niles Register*, N. S., ix., 354.
19. *Niles Register*, N. S., v., 387.
20. Hazard's *United States Register*, ii., 140.
21. Thomas E. V. Smith, " Elections of New York." *New York Historical Society*, 1893.
22. *Niles Register*, 4th S., vii., 295.
23. *Niles Register*, 4th S., xiii., 163.
24. *New York Herald*, Dec. 10, 1838.
25. *The Tammany Hall Democracy*, 1875, p. 38.
26. *Tammany Hall Souvenir*, 1893, p. 71.
27. *By-Laws General Committee of Tammany Hall*, viii., 2, 1893.
28. *New York Sun*, Sept. 25, 1897.
29. This resolution required the New York Democracy to elect delegates by assembly districts.

OLD PRISONS AND PUNISHMENTS

Half Moon Series

Published in the Interest of the New York
City History Club.

VOLUME II. NUMBER III.

OLD PRISONS AND PUNISHMENTS.

By ELIZABETH DIKE LEWIS.

THE Dutch settlers of New Amsterdam,
having founded their colony in a spirit
more commercial than religious, felt earlier
than did their Puritan neighbors, the need of
a place of imprisonment. This does not mean
that the wicked flourished there to an alarming degree. In fact the city was well advanced in years before it felt the presence of
crime, or the want of anything like a penal
system. A means of punishing peccadillos,
of frightening scolds, and of maintaining
military discipline, was all that was at first
necessary. Consequently more than a century passed before there was a prison building on Manhattan Island, space having been
easily provided for offenders in the town's
official headquarters, wherever such government as there was, had chanced to house
itself.

As is perfectly natural, therefore, the first

dungeon was within the ramparts of Fort
Amsterdam. Somewhere in the quadrangle,
along with the Governor's mansion, the military post, and the little church, was a lock-up,
no doubt of the most primitive order, and
probably of a migratory habit. The earliest
prisoners were the Indians captured in skirmishes, who were confined in some part of
the barracks of the soldiers who had taken
them. It is not certain that any civil offenders were ever imprisoned there, but even
after the building of the Stadt Huys, the captive Indians seem to have been kept in the
Fort dungeons.

In 1644, one Lieutenant Baxter marched to
the "castels" of the Westchester Indians,
destroyed their crops and killed many of
them, and returned to the Fort with several
prisoners.[1] At about the same time an expedition to Heemstede, where troubles had
become complicated, resulted in the capture
of two Indians, who were brought to the Fort
and cruelly dealt with. One was dragged
into a circle of soldiers, abused, and cut at
with knives till he whirled in his death-dance,
and finally dropped amid the jeers of his per-
secutors. The other was also mutilated, and
the same horrible scene might have been repeated had not another party of soldiers interfered and mercifully beheaded him on a block
behind the barracks.[2]

While the colonists were few and mutually dependent, there was no mention of any prisoners save those of war. But other than warlike measures soon became imperatively necessary to protect the community from its terrifying foes. A drunken Indian was a menace to a whole neighborhood, and one armed with civilized weapons was a trebly dangerous enemy. It was, therefore, ordained at various times that he who should be found selling liquors to Indians should be "arbitrarily corrected," or imprisoned, or "condemned": or if the selling could not be proved on any one person, then the whole street in which the drunken Indian had been found was fined.[3] From very early times death was the penalty for providing Indians with firearms, or any munitions of war.[4]

Other offences less serious than these, and generally of a personal character, were none the less deemed a menace to the dignity of the colony, and as early as 1638, a record is opened of curious sins, and still more droll punishments. A certain Hendrick Jansen, convicted of having slandered the Governor, is compelled to stand at the Fort gates at the ringing of the bell, and to ask the Governor's pardon.[5]

The Reverend E. Bogardus—who had succeeded Dominie Megapolensis as pastor of the church within the Fort—is "scandalized by a female," who is forthwith summoned to appear, also at the ringing of the bell, and "to declare before the council that she knew he was honest and pious, and that she had lied falsely." The Bogardus family seem to have been the objects of something like animosity on the part of their fellow-citizens, for presently the wife of the reverend gentleman is accused of "having drawn up her petticoat a little way." Several people were involved in this case, among whom was Hendrick Jansen, perhaps the same who had slandered the Governor, seeking an indirect revenge for his own public humiliation.

A Solomon-like judgment is that in another slander case, in which Jan Jansen complains of a party who has "lied falsely" about him, and *each* side is ordered to contribute twenty-five guilders to the poor box! Guyshert Van Regerslard, apparently a sailor on the yacht "Hope," having drawn his knife upon a fellow, was sentenced to receive three stripes from each of the crew, and to throw himself three times from the sail-yard of the yacht.

The famous wooden horse makes his entry into the annals of the city in December, 1638, when two soldiers were condemned to bestride him for two hours. This punishment seems to have been brought from Holland, where it had long been used as a military discipline. The horse had a razor-like back, upon which the prisoner was forced to sit, while weights and chains were hung on his feet.

The only recorded case of any criminal proceedings during the days of the Fort is that of Manuel Gerrit.[6]

More serious attempts at local discipline began in 1642, when the Stadt Huys was erected on Dock, now Pearl Street,[7] at the head of Coenties Slip. This building, which Kieft had ordered for the Company's tavern, soon entered on its generous career as tavern, court, city hall, and prison combined. All the courts and public meetings of the citizens were held here, and although there were two stories—with perhaps a third under the gables—only one small room on the first floor in the rear could be spared for the prisoners. Their quarters were nevertheless far more ample, and their doings more carefully regulated than they had been in the dungeons of the Fort.

The Provost Marshal, as combined sheriff, warden, policeman, and jailer, had entire command of the prison, and frequent ordinances controlled his various duties.[8] He was to live in the town, where a dwelling was provided for him. He was to visit the prison constantly, to feed and lock up the prisoners, and to be responsible for the keys and for the state of the locks, taking especial care that no "file or rope or anything sharp" be left on the premises.

The weight and amount of irons necessary to secure each prisoner, were determined at his condemnation, by the Fiscal, and the Provost was at liberty to alter the fetters only when a prisoner had attempted to break out, or had in other ways proved himself dangerous.

The Provost had power to place in confinement any persons brought to him, on condition that he make a report at once to the Fiscal. Many persons thus committed were mutinous sailors who had been thrown into irons while on the high seas, and on landing were handed over to the authorities by their ship captains. A mariner bringing any strange or foreign passengers to port, was forced to register them on pain of a fine of forty shillings. He was also commanded to report pirates ; and "An Act for Restraining and Punishing Privateers and Pirates" declared that such should be "fellons" and should suffer "pains of death without benefit of clergy."[9]

Any soldiers found with drawn swords either within their barracks or on the street were liable to arrest by the Provost. Any persons drawing knives and inflicting any wounds whatever were fined fifty florins, or, in default, were sent, "without respect of persons," to work three months with the negroes in chains. A few years later, in 1647, the penalties were doubled—one hundred florins or six months' hard labor.[10]

The number of slight offences against which it was thought necessary to issue ordinances, increased each year, but in most cases only "arbitrary correction" or "corporal punishment" was threatened. These, however, are mentioned constantly. It is no wonder that the old prints always represent the whipping-post and pillory, which stood in front of the Stadt Huys, as provided with incumbents." "Corporal punishment" could be administered "in the discretion of the magistrates provided it did not endanger Life or Limb," and the whippings so ordered were applied either by the public whipper or by any other person desirous of undertaking the same!" A fine opportunity for a personal and yet authorized revenge.

For every prisoner committed to jail the Marshal and bell-ringer received one shilling each, while the Judge's fee was five shillings for each indictment." The Marshal was paid twelve stivers a day for the support of each prisoner. The bill of fare was prescribed in advance by the Company, and was to consist, weekly, of the following rations:'

> One and a half lbs. of beef
> Three quarters of a lb. of pork
> One lb. of fish
> One gill of oil
> One gill of vinegar
> Suitable pottage, and
> A Supply of Bread

Persecu=
tion of the
Quakers

Social offenders were not the only ones who suffered under the Marshal's hands, or behind his bars. Religious persecution had already set in, and Governor Stuyvesant, in spite of injunctions issued against him by the mother country, was busying himself with devising humiliations for the Quakers.

In 1657, a number of them were thrust into the Stadt Huys prison for several weeks, and Robert Hodgson, who had imprudently tried to preach, was fined and scourged, thrust into a cell, and chained to a wheelbarrow ; but all in vain. He refused to acknowledge himself guilty of any law-breaking, and finally, after he had suffered the most frightful tortures, he was released on the intercession of the Governor's sister, Mistress Bayard.[3] John Bowne was freed from prison only to be banished; and many others were thrust upon the wooden horse, or into the stocks ; while any one housing a Friend was fined fifty pounds.

It was many years later, in 1694, that the persecuted sect seems to have won its first concession, by an " Act to Ease Peple that are scrupulous in Swearing." This new law allowed a solemn " promise before God " to have the force of an oath, and made false promising the equivalent of perjury.[4]

As the Provost's duties became more and more complicated, he was relieved of those which lay outside the prison, and they were entrusted to a second official called the Schout. This personage was directly subordinate, however, to the Koopman, who acted as secretary and was second in authority to the council.[2] The Schout was sheriff and prosecutor all in one, as may be seen from the following instructions:[15]

" . . . He shall *ex officio* prosecute all contraveners, defrauders and transgressors of any placards, laws, statutes, and ordinances, which are already made and published or shall hereafter be enacted and made public, as far as those are amenable before the Court of Burgomasters and Schepens, and with this understanding that having entered his suit against the aforesaid Contraveners, he shall immediately rise, and await the judgment of Burgomasters and Schepens who being prepared shall also, on his motion, pronounce the same. . . . He shall take care that all judgments are pronounced . . . according to the stile and custom of Fatherland, and especially the city of Amsterdam."

The Schout was empowered not only to complain of culprits to the Burgomasters and Schepens, but also to recommend a suitable penalty for the offence.[16] Fortunately for the cause of mercy, the magistrates were not bound to accept his suggestions, many of which seem more severe than the occasion required. For the crime of impertinence to the Schout, that officer demanded that a sinner be placed on bread and water for a month. The Schepens' verdict in this case was fifty guilders, or confinement for three days; whereupon the defendant remarked that the devil would take him who should first attempt to arrest him.

Another mutinous prisoner who had insulted the Fiscal, De Sille, and his wife,—"so that they had to have the soldiers called,"—being ordered to pay a fine of two hundred guilders, exclaimed that he "would rot in prison first!" And opportunity to do so was promptly afforded him.

For a small theft, the Schout recommended scourging at the post and banishment for four years, but the culprit was let off with a few days in a certain part of the Stadt Huys. Another, however, met with all that the Schout asked; was scourged, gashed on the cheek, and banished for twenty-five years, all for having noisily demanded wine in a private house.

A little maid of ten, Lysbet Anthony, was arrested by the Schout in the act of stealing, and brought before the council with vigorous demands for imprisonment on bread and water. The common-sense verdict, however, was that "Mary her mother be ordered to chastise her with rods in the presence of the Worshipful Magistrates."

The Schout's sense of his duty evidently did not stop at the living sinners under his jurisdiction. He pulled the poor suicide, Hendrick Smith, from the tree where he had hanged himself, and brought the body to court that it might be drawn about town on a hurdle and then shoved under the same tree again. But the Worshipful Magistrates listened to the pleas of the neighbors and the good reports of the suicide's character, and finally accorded the body decent burial.

The charges of the hard-worked Schout were adapted to his broad field of duty, as may be seen by the table published in 1693:[12]

	£	s	d
" Serving a writ, taking into custody, and bail Bond (without any pretence of riding in the county)	0	6	0
Returning a writ	0	1	0
A venire	0	3	0
Returning the same	0	1	0
Serving an execution under 100 pound . . .	0	5	0
Every ten pound more	0	1	0
Serving a writ of possession	0	12	0
Scire facias serving and return	0	3	0
Every person committed into the common prison,	0	3	0

" . . . In criminal matters fees to be correspondingly the same."

The Stadt Huys continued to serve as the civil and judicial centre of the town through its first period of domination by the English ; again during the Dutch restoration, and even after the English power was finally established, until 1699, when the building was condemned as unsound, and sold to John Rodman.[17] The Government removed the bell, the King's arms, iron-work, fetters, and other accessories of the prison, and reserved the right to have the "cage, pillory, and stocks before the same remain one year, and prisoners within said jail within the same City Hall remain one month," after the sale.[9]

The new City Hall was on the site of the present United States Sub-Treasury building in Wall Street, fronting Broad Street, on the corner of Nassau. It was completed in 1700, and was a fine building for the time, though it did not suit the "Congress" until numerous alterations had been made. The whole building projected over the street, and formed an imposing arcade across the sidewalk, under the lower story.[10] The ground floor was an "open walk" except for the jailer's rooms.

As soon as it was ready to open its doors for the courts and public meetings, it received also the prisoners, who were put in the basement. Later, the cellar below was used as a dungeon for dangerous characters, while debtors and other transients were lodged in the garret.[19]

The stocks and pillory were not placed immediately in front of the prison this time, but were on Broad Street, a little below Wall. From here the cart used to start when criminals were whipped around town at its tail, and here, too, were formed the processions which attended the wooden horse and its unlucky rider. The victim at this time was put on the horse, and then both were placed in the cart and trotted up and down, with added suffering and humiliation. In honor of the first person treated to the torture in its improved form, this device was always after called "the horse of Mary Price."

The city at this time was obliged to maintain a long list of officials: a mayor, recorder, town clerk, six aldermen, six assistants, one chamberlain or treasurer, one sheriff, one coroner, one clerk of the market, one high constable, seven sub-constables, and one marshal or sergeant-at-mace. The mayor, recorder, and aldermen might commit any persons for misdemeanors, and the mayor and aldermen alone were to try offenders who could not give bail. The sheriff was appointed yearly, and was obliged to give "a thousand pounds bonds for his faithfulness."[18] There were also a number of justices of the peace, and the prevailing impression seems to have been that they were not only too numerous but too ignorant. Many of them were appointed with no higher qualification than a seven years' apprenticeship in some clerk's office.[19] The Court of Chancery was also very obnoxious to the people, and altogether it was an open question whether New York, with her complicated system imported from the mother country, or New England, with her own cruder experiments and innovations, was the better fitted to cope with new and problematic conditions.

The City Hall was the only prison until about 1760, and it must therefore have been in one of its rooms that Zenger was confined [20] during his notable struggle for the freedom of the press.[21] Here, too, suffered the negroes and the whites concerned with them in the supposed plot of 1741.[22]

After this great panic the blacks were more carefully restricted. They were not allowed to sell anything at any price whatever, on pain of a fine of five pounds or under; and if more than three of them met and talked together anywhere, they were to be arrested and whipped at the post.[11]

At the same time several new penalties were established. Any person working on the Lord's Day was fined ten shillings; and children breaking the Sabbath by playing, one shilling. It was forbidden to build on any street not yet laid out, on pain of forty shillings,—rather a tardy effort to guard against tangled city streets. Six shillings was the fine exacted from a householder who had no fire buckets, or who did not keep them in good condition; and firemen who failed to answer the alarm bell promptly were also fined.

For many years the jail in the basement of the City Hall had been pronounced unsafe, and in 1727, extra precautions were taken by appointing a watch of four men to guard it and prevent escapes. In this same year, too, a new gallows was placed at the upper end of the Fields.[17] About 1756, though the date cannot be ascertained within a decade, a new stone prison, with four stories, grated windows, and a cupola,[18] was erected in its neighborhood.[19] This, the first real jail of the city, still stands as the Hall of Records, at the northeastern corner of the City Hall Park.

It was called at first the New Gaol, but from the wretched purpose it served, soon won the title of the Debtors' Prison. The history of imprisonment for debt is a long record of stupid injustice; and nowhere was its folly more bitterly fruitful than in old New York. It was upon the laborers and mechanics, who relied wholly on their daily efforts for their daily bread, that the prosperity of the growing city depended; and they were, of course, the very people most likely to get into debt. Let a workingman fall ill, and immediately on his recovery he would be clapped into jail, because he had not paid for his provisions and medicine; while the family either starved or piled up more debts, which kept him still longer in idle captivity.[20] An advertisement in a newspaper of the time[21] shows both the painful condition of the men thus confined, and the peculiar attitude of the public toward them.

"The Debtors confined in the Gaol of the City of New York, impressed with a grateful sense of the obligations they are under to a respectable publick for the generous contributions that have been made to them, beg leave to return their hearty thanks, . . . because they have been . . . preserved from perishing in a dreary prison, from hunger and cold."

Among these men was one Major Rogers, who was the innocent cause of a serious riot. The soldiers, to evince their contempt of civil power, forced an entrance into the Gaol, and demanded his person. They opened all the doors, and told the prisoners they had leave to depart freely, which, says the chronicler, they were "too honourabel to do"; and the only real outcome of the disturbance was the death of one of the sergeants."

The Fields—later called the Common, and now the Park—was in 1769, and the years following, so decidedly the centre of the struggle for Independence, that it has been called "the Fanueil Hall of New York." It was the scene of many of the riotous meetings of the Sons of Liberty, and the poles repeatedly erected by them and torn down by the soldiery stood at its northwestern corner. The handbill calling one of these meetings, though signed merely "A Son of Liberty," was traced to the office of James Parker, and he was thrust into the still extant dungeon in the Fort." The printer then betrayed the writer, Alexander McDougall, who many years later was to be the Major-General in charge of West Point. He too was arrested, and thrown into the Debtors' Prison; whence in April, 1770, he was released on bail to await his trial.

While confined there he published a "personal" in the *New York Journal*, inviting his friends to an original kind of afternoon tea.[19] He would be, he notified them, "Glad of the Honour of their Company from Three O'clock in the afternoon till Six," and the date affixed was "New Gaol, February 10, 1770."

As the Debtors' Prison was not large enough to accommodate all classes of prisoners, the city authorities had seen fit to order a new city jail;[30] and in 1775, the Bridewell came to make part of the historic surroundings of the Common. It stood to the west of the Debtors' Prison, between Broadway and the site of the present City Hall, and would have been a handsome building if the original design, calling for a pediment and columns, had ever been carried out. It was of dark gray stone, two stories high, and contained, on the ground floor the jailer's quarters and the famous Long Room for common prisoners,—on the upper story, apartments for the better class of convicts.[20]

It was not finished, however, when the Revolution opened ; and on the twenty-seventh of August, 1776, when the British took possession of the city, they found not only the wooden barracks just abandoned by Washington's troops, but the Debtors' Prison on one side and the new Bridewell on the other, all empty, and ready for their occupation.

The Debtors' Prison was placed in charge of the wicked Provost Marshal Cunningham, and was thereafter called The Provost. It was made the principal prison, though besides the Bridewell and old City Hall, the British pressed into military service the old sugar houses, the churches, Columbia College, the hospital, and the abandoned, half-rotten ships-of-war in the Bay.[31] Space requires the omission of any details regarding these temporary prisons, whose interesting history does not, strictly speaking, form a part of the history of the prisons of the city.

The Provost and its peculiar terrors were reserved for the most important prisoners. Compared to the physical sufferings of the men confined in the hulks of the *Jersey*,[32] and the other "floating hells," as they were termed, the discomforts of the prisoners in the Provost were mild. Though they were too cold, and frightfully crowded, they had less disease and degradation to contend with. But Cunningham was a tyrant who did not stop half way. His was a reign of terror, and a secret scourge, searing-iron, and gallows, awaited the unfortunate man who furnished

him with the slightest excuse for persecution.
There is no evidence that he ever executed
any one without trial; but his trials may have
been conducted in a cursory manner. The
gallows, which was practically a private institution of his own, stood on a little hill in
Chambers Street; and thither he is said to
have accompanied his victims in person, after
giving orders that all householders along the
route from there to the prison should close
their windows on pain of death. He took
care to make this gallows a terror by keeping
it always occupied; and when a real man was
lacking, he would fill it with an effigy of Han-
cock or some other obnoxious rebel.[33]

This infamous marshal deliberately allowed
many men to starve by reducing or withhold-
ing their rations to enrich himself. The extent of his crimes is unknown, and it is useless
to catalogue their reported horrors. Some
writers relate that he was hanged at Tyburn
shortly after his return to England,[3] and even
give in detail his dying confession, in which
he says:[34]

" . . . I shudder to think of the murders I have
been accessory to—both with and without orders from government—especially while in New York, during which time
there were more than two thousand starved in the churches
by stopping their rations, which I sold. There were also
two hundred and seventy-five American prisoners executed
. . . hung without ceremony, and then buried by the
Black Pioneer of the Provost. . . ."

This interesting document is, however, almost a palpable fabrication. No record has ever been found of any such execution, either at Tyburn or elsewhere; and the best authorities insist that Cunningham died peacefully many years later, in a country home.[35]

The most notable of Cunningham's prisoners was Ethan Allen, who, having been released on parole in New York, was seized in January, 1777, and thrust into solitary confinement, in spite of his energetic denial of the charge that he had broken his parole. He had been first taken at Montreal in 1776, transported to England, and after a painful voyage brought back to New York. Here General Howe offered him a commission, with the promise of large tracts of land in Vermont at the close of the war, if he would only "desert his lost cause, and serve his King"; but Allen replied that he did not think the king would have enough land in America at the close of the war to redeem any such promise.[36]

When he had been some eight months in the Provost, he seems to have begun to chafe under the apparent neglect of his countrymen; as Joseph Webb writes to Governor Trumbull, in a letter arranging for an exchange of prisoners:[37]

"Ethan Allen begs me to represent his Situation to You that he has been a most Attached friend to America and he says he 's forgot—he 's spending his Life, his very prime and now is confin'd in the Provost and they say for breaking his parole without he own's it in part—I cou'd wish some of 'em wou'd be more prudent."

Allen was exchanged in May, 1778, not long after this, and joined Washington at Valley Forge.[38]

The Provost had at this time been strengthened by the British. Barricades had been erected between the external and internal lobbies, and grated doors placed at the foot of the stairs, where sentinels were stationed night and day. On the right of the main hall was the Marshal's room, now the Register's office, and opposite was the guard, and the chamber of O'Keefe, Cunningham's deputy and accomplice. Most of the prisoners were confined on the second floor, in the northeast chamber, ironically called "Congress Hall"; and it is here that they were so crowded as they lay down in rows on the floor, that when one wished to turn over, he had to wake all the others, and give the word of command for all to turn at once.

It was to the door of this room that Cunningham ushered his guests, drunk as himself, after a luxurious dinner, while he exhibited his prisoners as one would a cage of animals.

"There is that d——d rebel, Ethan Allen, sir," he would cry; "Allen! get up and walk around!"[39]

It is to be said, on the other hand, that while the seamen on the *Jersey* were being exposed to small-pox and abandoned to filth and starvation,[32] the crowded inmates of "Congress Hall" were carefully guarded against disease and vermin. Their packs and blankets were aired every morning and then hung on the walls during the day; and in illness they received medical attention.[36]

When the British troops evacuated the city, Cunningham and his deputy were among the last to leave. In the Provost there were still a few prisoners, and as O'Keefe prepared to rush off they cried out to know what was to become of them.

"You may go to the Devil!" he exclaimed, throwing the keys on the floor.

"Thank you," they replied; "We have had enough of *your* company in this world."

The chief sufferings of the American patriots in the Bridewell arose from the extreme cold, for the unfinished building had only iron gratings at the windows.[40] There were several old veterans who claimed to have been among eight hundred and sixteen prisoners-of-war confined in these crowded quarters from Saturday to the following Thursday, without food of any kind.[41] No deaths are mentioned, however, and as it is scarcely possible that a large body of exhausted and wounded soldiers can have survived such treatment, the story lacks credibility. It is certain that the rations of the prisoners here were at times withheld from them, but the reports that many men had been poisoned by the physicians have never been verified."

When Washington at one time complained that the men who had been released from New York were in such desperate condition that they were not a fair exchange for the British prisoners, Howe replied: "

" . . . All the prisoners are confined in the most airy buildings and on board the largest transports of the fleet, which are the very healthiest places that could possibly be provided for them. They are supplied with the same provisions as are allowed to the King's troops not on service, . . . the sick are separated and especially cared for by surgeons. . . ."

At the same time Congress was publishing in its *Journal*, regarding the prisoners in New York:

" . . . Many of them were near four days kept without food altogether. When they received a supply, it was both insufficient in point of quantity, and often of the worst kind. They suffered the utmost distress from cold, nakedness, and close confinement."

If we balance the official assertions on each side, we may come to the conclusion that the extreme stories of both should be discredited altogether. The tales, however, were believed by many who heard them and by some who told them, and they played a prominent part in the minds of the people at the time.[41]

After the Revolution the Provost was again used for debtors, and at one time five per cent. of the whole number of citizens were imprisoned for debt.[42] Much of the misery was done away with in 1817, when the laws were so amended as to confine only those who had incurred debts for amounts larger than twenty-five dollars.[43]

About 1787, the Provost was again the scene of a riot.[44] The methods employed by some doctors for obtaining bodies for dissection had aroused the most bitter feeling against the whole profession.[45] A mob gathered, and assailed the houses of the obnoxious physicians, while their friends covered their hasty retreat to the jail. There the mob followed them and did much damage, both to the police, and to the citizens, who made a feeble defence at the prison door. One of the doctors was "wounded by a stone which laid him up some time, in the head," and the riot was quelled only by promises of reform.

A drawing of City Hall Park made by W. G. Wall in 1826, pictures the Hall of Records as of pale gray stone, while the Bridewell is green, with tan blinds. A note in the corner explains that the artist did not "feel justified in representing the foliage of the Park as in a handsome state, because it was n't, being much affected with caterpillars." [10] One might question whether this gentleman had been equally conscientious, when he sprinkled the foreground with ladies in hoops and poke bonnets.

In 1830, the Provost ceased to be used as a prison, and was prepared to serve as the Register's office. The bell was taken down and remounted as a fire-alarm on the roof of the Bridewell. The front and back of the dingy edifice were pretentiously decorated with columns like those of the temple of Diana at Ephesus; [40] and since then, the space thus made has been again walled in so that the columns now appear as mere pilasters. In 1835, the building was ready for the purpose which it has served ever since ; and to-day the title deeds to all the real estate in the city are preserved under its venerable roof. [38]

As for the Old Bridewell, if tradition be true, it followed the injunction regarding coals of fire ; for in the war of 1812, many English captives were confined there, and are said to have been treated by the keeper, old Tom Hazzard, with marked kindness, and even to have been fed in secret at his own expense when he considered their rations insufficient. [42]

After this second experience as a war prison, the Bridewell resumed its uneventful career as the general city jail. At first, trials were held only four times a year, and prisoners committed for slight offences would perhaps have to await examination for nearly three months. Some time before 1828, however, the court began to be held every month. The prisoners were here made to pick oakum or were employed on the city works, and this attempt at prison labor seems to have succeeded better than the earlier experiments at Greenwich prison, of which we shall speak presently.

Although fairly healthy and clean, the Bridewell was far too small to suit the city's growing needs, and the erection of the present City Hall,[47, 48] just before the war with England, had long made its presence in the crowded Park, undesirable. In 1838, it was destroyed, some of its stones being used in the erection of its successor, the Hall of Justice in Centre Street—early rechristened "The Tombs," on account of its gloomy Egyptian exterior.

The old Provost bell, which had served as a fire-alarm on the Bridewell, was sent to the Naiad Hose Company's station in Beaver Street, to continue the same office. It was soon after destroyed by the very fire to which, for the last time, it had summoned the lines of wooden buckets.

The Bridewell and the Provost together had thus served during the latter years of their existence as city jails, though they had been built for special purposes—the one for debtors, the other for a long-term prison. Two reforms had merged their interests. Imprisonment for debt had been practically abolished, and the Debtors' Prison thus left free to receive other inmates. A few years earlier a much-needed State's Prison had been erected, leaving in the Bridewell, too, space for short commitments; while the convicts who were sentenced to three years or more were sent to Greenwich.

The act appropriating about $208,000[49] to relieve the crowded prisons of the city, had at first provided for two buildings, one to be at Albany; but on deliberation it was decided to devote the entire fund to the Greenwich building.[50] It was ready for occupation in 1797, and seventy prisoners were transferred to it from the other prisons. The big pile stood at the head of Tenth Street—then Amos,—on the bank of the Hudson, a mile and a half from the Bridewell and the Provost. Strange to say, the fashionable little village of Greenwich seemed not to resent the intrusion, but rather to hail it as raising the value of property, and giving a stately air to the otherwise rural scenery.[51]

It was the handsomest prison and one of the most imposing buildings the city had yet seen, being decorated with Doric columns, surmounted with a fine cupola, and surrounded by nearly four acres of grounds. The whole was enclosed by a stone wall fourteen feet high in the front, and twenty-three in the back, where the four wings extended from the main building down to the river. Beyond this wall was the wharf where were landed convicts sent from points up the river.[51]

In every earlier prison the criminals had been thrust all together into large rooms.[52] Here an approach to a better system was made, each of the fifty-two cells lodging three persons only; while there were also twenty-eight cells for solitary confinement. In the north wing was a chapel, in the south a dining-room, and the centre was given up to the quarters of the officers. There were also good cellars, an ice-house, and store-rooms of various kinds ; and in the courtyard there was a tank where the prisoners could bathe, so abundant was the supply of water. The women were on the ground floor of the north wing, and had a separate courtyard.[53]

In 1787, the experiment had been tried in Philadelphia, of reserving capital punishment— which had been the penalty of a dozen different crimes—for that of premeditated murder alone.[54] In New York many offences which are now termed misdemeanors had been punishable with long imprisonment, or with the humiliations of the whipping-post and pillory. At the close of the century the example of the Quaker Commonwealth began to be followed, and imprisonment under better conditions, with stated terms and definite regulations, became the rule.

The greatest importance attaches to the persevering attempts here made to introduce prison labor. For the first time it seemed to have entered the minds of the authorities that the work of a prison should be not only to punish, but to reform. A method of accomplishing both ends was suggested to them by a shoemaker who begged for occupation, and proposed to make himself profitable to the institution,—inspiring his fellow-prisoners to do the same." Spacious brick workshops went up in the yards of the Greenwich prison." To a certain extent the men were permitted to follow their own callings. If a man had none, one was assigned him. The principal trades were weaving, spinning, shoe- and brush-making, and carpenter work ; but the locksmith's art was the most popular among the convicts, who hoped to profit by their skill in it on their release. For twelve hours a day they were compelled to work, being marched into the dining-hall at meal-times, and locked into their cells at night. Each convict on his arrival was compelled to strip and wash, and dress himself in the striped prison uniform. This was always made in the prison, and was of different grades. When an offender was convicted for the second time, the right side of his coat and left of his trousers were black. If a third time, he wore a figure 3 on his back, and his food was coarser and less abundant than before.[85]

The keeper's salary was eight hundred dollars. The rations of each prisoner came to about five cents a day, the chief items being oxheads and hearts, indian meal mush and molasses, pork, black bread, and ''lambs' plucks.''

For a few years the system promised wonders ; but the ease of communication soon undid everything. The numerous escapes and extreme corruption may be ascribed to three distinct causes. First, the solitary cells were too few. Second, not even they were secure, as they were not connected by passages, and so could not be easily kept under watch. Third, there was so little hope of pardon, that the men were incited to attempt escapes, rather than to win commutations of their sentences by good behavior.[87]

As the better class of officials became disgusted with the inadequate adaptation of the building to its purpose, and weary of their fruitless attempts to contend against heavy odds, it was natural that inferior keepers should take their places. In a few years a low class of men had control of the prison, and the convicts were corrupted not only by each other's society, but by the example of their officers, who are said to have been profane and drunken tyrants. Laziness ruled everywhere. The men were again herded together, and children thrust in with them, because it was easier to care for a crowded room, than for individual cells. Many prisoners are known to have falsely confessed themselves guilty of special misdemeanors, that they might be confined in the less offensive, solitary cells. Books were withheld on the pretext that the prisoners destroyed them. Inhuman whippings were administered by the keepers for real or fancied personal insults ; and the bodies of dead convicts were either buried without ceremony in the Potter's Field, or disposed of to the dissectors.[68]

The hospital, consisting of four rooms with a straw bed in each, was in the north wing. The resident physician was frequently a youth easily imposed on by the convicts, who were skilled in counterfeiting illness and were generally glad of a few days' rest from the workshop. The most serious of the real diseases treated in the hospital were those unavoidably attendant on the close confinement of the prisoners.[69] Deaths were numerous, being as one in two hundred and fifty each month.

Very few troubles seem to have come from the undoubtedly coarse, but abundant food ; and no complaints are made of uncleanliness. Indeed to such an extent were these humane and saving points insisted upon by the prison authorities, that many citizens regarded the good treatment as equivalent to laxity in discipline! Less easily refuted are the complaints that the system of solitary confinement was never thoroughly tried. The inspectors pointed out that one Smith had been placed in a solitary cell for six months, and had emerged "a revengeful desperado"; while the complainants maintained that, as he had been allowed daily converse with his keeper, extra diet, and reading matter, the experiment had not been a fair one.

In spite of all that was said against the discipline and plan of the Greenwich prison, it marks the beginning of at least an attempt at a system aiming at reform. For the first time punishments were regulated by their duration as well as by mere severity; and the good effects of prison labor were proved, while its weak points began to be understood, and could be guarded against.

It was in 1829, that the prison was sold and destroyed. A small part of its old wall is still in existence, having been built into the brewery on the same site. The prisoners were gradually transferred, in 1828, and 1829, to the enormous new pile at Sing Sing.

In 1826, the penitentiary on Blackwell's Island had been opened; [60] and with the closing of the careers of Greenwich, the Debtors' Prison, and the Bridewell, and the substitution of Sing Sing, Blackwell's, and the Tombs, the old city prisons and the first quarter of the century came to an end together.

REFERENCES.

1. General J. G. WILSON, *Memorial History of the City of New York*, ii., p. 188.
2. BROADHEAD's *History of the State of New York.* MARTHA LAMB's *History of the City of New York*, p. 118.
3. J. F. WATSON, *Historic Tales of Olden Time.*
4. *Laws and Ordinances of New Netherlands*, 1643 and 1645.
5. WATSON, p. 127.
6. *Stadt Huys* of this series.
7. *Century Magazine*, iv., p. 847.   RICHARD GRANT WHITE.
8. Ordinance, August 20, 1664.
9. Acts of Assembly Passed in the Province of New York from 1691 to 1725.   Printed by Wm. Bradford, 1726.   Acts of 1692.
10. Ordinances, 1642, 1647.
11. Grolier Club : Exhibition of Drawings of Old New York.
12. The Charter of the City of New York, and the Act of the General Assembly Confirming the Same.   Printed by Zenger, 1735.
13. Acts of Assembly, 1693.
14. *Ibid.*, 1694.
15. *Dutch Records*, 1652, 1663, Letter V.
16. VALENTINE's *Corporation Manuals*, 1861, p. 533.
17. LAMB, p. 443.
18. WILSON, ii., p. 222.
19. SMITH's *History of the Province of New York*, to which is annexed . . . the Constitution of the Courts of Justice in that Colony.   London, 1757.
20. DUNLAP's *History of the New Netherlands*, i., pp. 297, 302.
21. *Governor's Island* of this series, p. 159.
22. *Slavery in New York* of this series, p. 16.

23. WILSON, ii., p. 165.
24. HASWELL'S *Recollections of an Octogenarian.*
25. *History of the People of the United States*, McMASTER, i., p. 98.
26. *Gazette and Mercury*, July 27, 1772.
27. DAWSON'S *History of the Park.*
28. LEAKE'S *Life of General Lamb.*
29. *New York Journal*, February 17, 1770.
30. WILSON, ii., p. 477.
31. ONDERDONK'S *Incidents of the British Prisons and British Ships at New York.*
32. *The Old Jersey Captive ;* a narrative of the captivity of Thomas Andros, 1781.
33. LOSSING'S *Pictorial Field-Book of the Revolution*, Supplement, iv., pp. 658, 660.
34. WILSON, ii., p. 540.
35. BANCROFT.
36. DUNLAP, ii.
37. S. B. WEBB'S *Reminiscences*, ii., pp. 37, 41, 54, 121, 192.
38. Hour-Glass Series : *A Historic Landmark*, by J. F. McL., pp. 210, 211.
39. *John Pintard's Account of the Time after the Battle of Brooklyn.*
40. *New York and its Institutions*, by Rev. J. F. RICHMOND, 1872, pp. 74, 514.
41. *Journal of Oliver Woodruff.*
42. DAVIS'S *Essay on the Old Bridewell.* Manuals, 1855, pp. 486 *et seq.*
43. *In Old New York*, THOMAS JANVIER, p. 243. Petition to the General Assembly by the Association for the Relief of Distressed Debtors, 1788.
44. The Laws of New York. The Town Records.
45. WATSON, p. 175.
46. WILSON, iii., p. 342.
47. *Century Magazine*, v., p. 865 ; *The New City Hall*, by E. S. WILDE.

References

48. *New York as it was during the Latter Part of the Last Century*, by DUER.
49. *Inside Out; or, An Interior View of the New York State's Prison.* By One Who Knows, 1823. (Probably by JAMES STEWART or W. A. COFFEY), pp. 13, 15.
50. *Harper's Monthly*, 87, p. 339 ; *Greenwich Village*, by T. JANVIER.
51. *Old Greenwich* of this series, p. 292.
52. *Defence of the System of Solitary Confinement*, by G. W. SMITH.
53. *Journal of Prison Discipline*, i., p. 4 ; *Inside Out*, Introduction, p. 8.
54. *An Account of the New York State Prison, by One of the Inspectors*, 1801. Pamphlet of the New York Hist. Soc., No. 64.
55. *Old Greenwich* of this series, p. 290.
56. *Annual Reports of the Inspectors of the State Prison*, 1823 *et seq.*
57. *Old Greenwich* of this series, p. 291 ; *Inside Out*, p. 24.
58. *Inside Out*, p. 10 ; Introduction, pp. 29, 54.
59. *Ibid.*, p. 165 *et seq.*
60. *Grand Jury Reports*, 1849.

THE NEW YORK PRESS AND ITS MAKERS

Half Moon Series

Published in the Interest of the New York City History Club.

VOLUME II. NUMBER IV.

THE NEW YORK PRESS AND ITS MAKERS

IN THE EIGHTEENTH CENTURY.

BY

CHARLOTTE M. MARTIN

AND

BENJAMIN ELLIS MARTIN.

The native Indians of the New Netherland, like the other red men of North America, sometimes sent their news to a distance, scratched on the smooth surface of birch bark : such were the only news-letters that circulated in the colonies in those early days.

As to New Amsterdam, if the records did not tell us that no newspapers existed there, we should know it beyond doubt by the words of Diedrich Knickerbocker, when in one of the serious passages of his brilliant burlesque, he describes the profound repose and tranquility that dwelt in the embryo city : "The very words of learning, education, taste, and talents were unheard of ; a bright genius

Strict
Surveil-
lance over
the Press

was an animal unknown. No man, in fact, seemed to know more than his neighbor, nor any man to know more than an honest man ought to know, who has nobody's business to mind but his own; the parson and the council clerk were the only men who could read in the community, and the sage Van Twiller always signed his name with a cross." These words prove, by implication, and beyond possible doubt, that no newspaper, such as is known to us misguided moderns, existed in the quiet town.

When New Amsterdam became New York, the day of the newspaper was put off longer than in the other provinces; for that broad and enlightened Stuart, James II., sent to his Governor, Dongan, in 1686, the following order: "Forasmuch as great inconvenience may arise by the liberty of printing, within our province of New York, you are to provide, by all necessary orders, that no person keep any press for printing; nor that any book, pamphlet, or other matters, whatsoever, be printed, without your especial leave and licence be first obtained." Even when the press was allowed to be set up in the province, it was kept under strict surveillance and subject to stringent restrictions; the authorities, in the words of Isaiah Thomas, "by keeping the people in ignorance, thought to render them more obedient to the laws, prevent them from libelling the government, and impede the growth of heresy." Not until about 1755 did our press feel any touch of freedom, and gain any small measure of liberty of speech.

It was in January, 1639, that "printing was first performed in that part of North America which extends from the Gulph of Mexico to the frozen ocean"; and it was not till 1690, that a newspaper was issued on this continent. This was a small quarto of short and irregular life, which appeared in Boston. In April, 1704, there came to stay, in that town, the first real newspaper in any of the colonies—*The Boston News-Letter*. Philadelphia came next in 1719, with its *American Weekly Mercury*, and so in succession the other provinces, Maryland, Virginia, North and South Carolina, came out with their papers.

New York saw its first paper on the sixteenth of October, 1725. *The New-York Gazette*, printed and put forth by William Bradford. This worthy man had come to Philadelphia from London by the advice of William Penn, Chief of the State, and armed with a letter from George Fox dated "London, 6th month, 1685," to the Quakers of the colonies, announcing to them that "a sober young man, whose name is William Bradford, is coming to set up the trade of printing Friends' books." So he started his press in Philadelphia, but soon he and his fellow non-combatants fell to fighting over the liberty of that same press, as to which they had opposing views. The weaker one went to prison for a while, then gave up Quakering, and came to New York. It was in 1693, that he set up his press in this little town of four thousand inhabitants, "At the Sign of the Bible," in that wide gate-way between King Street and Old Slip and the river, which has been called Hanover Square since the accession of George I., while King Street has become our present William Street.

To Bradford belongs the glory of introducing the art of printing to this town and this province. In April, 1693, he was appointed by the Council, Printer of the Acts of the Assembly and Public Papers, with a salary of £40 a year, and the privilege and the profit of his own private printing. In 1694, appeared the Laws and Acts of the General Assembly "at New York, printed and sold by William Bradford, Printer to their Majesties, King William and Queen Mary." In 1710—his appointment having been renewed in 1709—appeared a later edition, "Printed by William Bradford, Printer of the Queen's most excellent Majesty for the Colony of New York." He put forth, during these years, and for many after years, almanacs, controversial pamphlets, and public documents; while, as a publisher, he adventured many books now eagerly sought for by collectors and amateurs. In 1723, Benjamin Franklin, coming from Boston to New York in search of work, found Bradford still the only printer here, but with no work for him. The young stranger, and future rival, found kindly entertainment, and was sent on to the younger Bradford—the son—in Philadelphia. Why Franklin called William Bradford "the cunning old fox" in later years, is not apparent.

Bradford was sixty-one years old when the first copy of *The New-York Gazette* was issued from his press in 1725. This weekly, which came out on each Monday, was, until 1733, the only newspaper in the town. At first a single leaf, it was increased to two, three, four, and six pages as its contents warranted. These contents were made up of small doings at home and abroad, in small paragraphs, selections of stale literature, poor poetry, no news of moment, and scanty advertisements. It was a dwarf folio, poorly printed on dirty, grayish paper; on the left of the title, in large Roman type, were the arms of the city—barrels and beavers, and the wings of a wind-mill, supported by an Indian and a soldier—the royal crown over all. On the right of the title was a pine tree, and a post rider on an animal meant for a horse. The foreign news was of such weighty matters as the exploits of an English highwayman at Bath, or the young French king's indisposition, which forced him to put off the ceremony of "touching the diseased," promised for November 23, 1726, until the following day, the twenty-fourth. Of greater import was this from London, March 18, 1727: "Yesterday morning died, aged eighty-five, Sir Isaac Newton, Master of His Majesty's Mint at the Tower, to which place is annexed a salary of £500 per annum, and President of the Royal Society." It is curious, and characteristic, this giving foremost place to the petty office and its salary, his great office being mentioned, quite casually, at the last!

The issue of June 15, 1730, contains matters of more international interest, for it is full of excitement over the election of the Pope, and the probable effect upon European politics; while a later copy gives a detailed account of the coronation of the successful Orsini as Clement XII.

William Bradford was greater as a man than as an editor—a rare, and a strong character, marked by ability, industry, and probity; decent in his own life, kindly to his fellow-men. "No man is born unto himself alone" seems to have been his essential rule of conduct. "So that herein I may but be serviceable to the Truth and to the Friends thereof," he wrote on the first day of the first month of 1687-8. The "old fox" was good to his needy, deserving fellow-creatures, and his quiet influence was felt both in the church and in the little printing world of his day. With few exceptions, the then rising generation of printers was trained under his watchful eye.

He ended his life of uneventful usefulness in 1752: his age being given by differing authorities as ninety and ninety-four. His chipped and stained tombstone, now carefully preserved in the entrance hall of the Historical Society of New York, gives it as ninety-two, and the date of his birth as 1660—an error of the mason, doubtless. This stone was replaced by a new one on the occasion of the memorial service in Trinity Church—of which Bradford was a vestryman—on May 20, 1863, when the Historical Society celebrated the two-hundredth anniversary of the printer's birth. The new stone, standing above his grave in Trinity burial ground, is an exact copy of the original stone, save that it is a trifle larger. The Historical Society has also placed a tablet in the wall of the Cotton Exchange, on the corner of Hanover Square and William Street, marking the site of the building from which Bradford issued his *New-York Gazette*, and commemorating the two-hundredth anniversary of the introduction of printing into New York, on April 10, 1693.

When Bradford retired from business in

1742, his newspaper was taken in charge by Henry De Foreest, an apprentice of Bradford and the first New York printer known to have been born in the town. He had been a partner of Bradford during the last years of the *Gazette*, and it bore the joint imprint of their names. De Foreest succeeded to the entire control of the paper in 1744, and in November of the same year he published it in the afternoon instead of the morning, calling it the *New-York Evening Post*, the first evening issue in the town. It was a weekly like the *Gazette*, but was a great improvement on its predecessor, being well printed, with clean type, not too large for its page, the type page being about five and a half by nine and three quarters inches. It gave special prominence to shipping and foreign news, and there was the customary dose of flimsy literature and feeble verse. Advertisements were still few in number, and their old-time queerness makes some of them worthy of reproduction here. . . . A bookseller publishes *A Short and Easie Method with the Deists*. . . . "To be sold, a Negro Wench, that can do all manner of House Work, fit for Town or Country. She has had the small pox." "John George Cook, Stocking Weaver, can supply all sorts of stockings." . . . "Very good Pot-ash made and sold by Cornelius Brower, living next door to the Widow Killmaster's, near Gold-ing Hill." . . . . " This is to give notice that all persons who are indebted to Rebecca Sipkins are desired to come and pay the same to prevent further trouble, and all who have demands on her to come and receive satisfaction." . . . This *Evening Post* went out of existence in 1752, the causes that brought about its end being unknown.

Among the seven thousand Germans who found their way, from their devastated Palatinate, and from the cruelties of Louis XIV., to England—and there camped out at Blackheath and Camberwell—was a woman named Zenger, with her three children. When Queen Anne's shrewd bounty sent some three thousand of these exiles to help colonize this country in 1708, this family came to New York, and the eldest child, aged thirteen—John Peter —was apprenticed to William Bradford. These indentures are now in the office of the Secretary of State at Albany. Under his master's good guidance the boy's character was formed, and he learned his trade well enough to set up his own printing-press—the second in the town—about 1726. On November 5, 1733, he brought out the first number of his *New-York Weekly Journal*, the second paper in New York, and so the first rival to Bradford's *Gazette*, then over eight years old. However excellent Zenger's training may have been, a proper respect for age and authority seems not to have taken root in him, for when Bradford—who was naturally, by virtue of his official position, and by reason of his social standing in the commonalty, on the side of the " powers that be "—accused him in print of " publishing pieces tending to set the province in a flame, and to raise sedition and tumults," Zenger referred to his former master as " this Scribbler," and " that groaping Fumbler," and continued to publish lampoons against the authorities, and especially against the impotent Governor himself.

The State officials were of the same mind as Bradford in this matter, and in November, 1734, Governor Cosby and the council arrested Zenger for " printing and publishing several seditious libels," and had copies of the offending papers burned. Zenger spoke for the popular party in the politics of the province, and the people were with him, the Crown officials and the conservative classes of the town ranged against him. The Grand Jury would find no true bill against the printer, and the trial was conducted by the Attorney-General, and before biassed judges, carefully selected. Zenger's counsel was the then head of the Philadelphia bar, Andrew Hamilton, whose plea for Zenger and the liberty of the American Press won a verdict of " not guilty " from the sympathetic jury, in defiance of the instruction of the judges. The verdict was

Trial of
Zenger

hailed with shouts by the great crowd within
and without the court ; to Andrew Hamilton
was given the freedom of the city in a gold box,
and Zenger was made a popular hero. Either
he or his verdict—it is difficult to determine
which is meant by the mixed metaphor—has
been acclaimed as "the morning star of that
liberty which subsequently revolutionized
America." It is queer and pitiful, too, that
Bradford, who in his youth suffered imprisonment for the cause of liberty of the press,
should, in his old age, have been on the side
of the prosecutors in this most momentous
trial; and that the victim of this arbitrary persecution should be an apprentice of his own,
the outgrowth of his training in all things,
and doubtless in free speech.

Zenger went back from his prison, after long
months of idleness and growing debts, to his
shop in "Broad Street, near the upper end of
Long Brij.," where he had established himself
and his journal in 1733, and at once issued in
pamphlet form *A Brief Narrative of the Case
and Tryal of John Peter Zenger, printer of the
New-York "Weekly Journal;"* a pamphlet that
had an immense sale at the time and is still
famed. He had published many pamphlets,
almanacs, and sermons in his day, and in 1735
he issued, in a small folio, *The Charter of the
City of New York*, "printed by order of the
Mayor, Recorder, and Commonalty of the City

Zenger's
Publica-
tions

aforesaid." Any one who wishes to be personally acquainted with Zenger's work as a publisher and maker of books may consult, in the Lenox Library, *The Adorable Ways of God*—three sermons printed in 1726. It is a square old volume, roughly bound, with uneven edges. The paper is pale brown, and has that peculiar brittle quality dear to the lovers of old books. The type is clear, but the imprint of each page is slightly confused by the impressions from its other side. The wide margins and curious, decorated initial letters add to the beauty of this valuable specimen of old-time printing.

These books and pamphlets did not interfere with the regular publication of the *Weekly Journal*, which Zenger resumed after his trial. It was a small sheet, with a type page measuring a little over five inches by nine inches and a half, with uncomfortably narrow margins, and not laudable in its printing, its make-up, or its editing. Indeed, its editor was no scholar, and his German boyhood had left him without an exact command of English. But his paper was entirely alive, and his lampoons on the government were novel in their audacity and startling in their strength.

The *Journal* sold at three shillings each quarter, its advertisements paying three shillings a week for the first week, and a shilling each for every succeeding week. It was advertised as "Containing the Freshest Advices, Foreign and Domestick," and although the freshness seems stale indeed in the light of modern enterprise, the news "both foreign and domestick" covered an astonishing amount of ground. Letters from abroad show the constancy with which the people of New York clung to their mother country and her interests. First place was almost always given to these foreign despatches, inter-colonial news being considered of much less importance. Sometimes contributed letters, such as those on "The Liberty of The Press," signed by "Cato," usurped the first page of two or three numbers in succession. On December 24, 1733, one John Gardner, a mariner of Boston, swears to the authenticity of his map of the fortifications of Louisburg, which is published in that issue, and tells the exciting story of his acquaintance with the town, judging that it may be of use to his countrymen in case of a war with France.

When Zenger died, in 1746, the paper was carried on by his widow and his eldest son, in "Stone Street, near Fort George": carried on with great improvement in printing and contents, until 1751, when Mrs. Zenger's death seems to have taken away its controlling force, and it came to an end.

Another apprentice of William Bradford was James Parker, a New Jersey boy, who, tired of work and confinement, tried for his independence by running away from his master. Bradford advertised a small reward for his return ; the boy found his way back, and served out his term faithfully, learning his trade so well that he succeeded to his master's post as Printer of the Province when that good man retired. In that same year, 1742–3, Parker began the issue of the third newspaper in the province—*The New-York Weekly Post-Boy*. In 1746, after Bradford's original *Gazette* had been merged in *The New-York Evening Post*, under De Foreest's management, Parker enlarged his paper, calling it *The New-York Gazette Revived in The Weekly Post-Boy*. At this time, also, he succeeded to a goodly share of William Bradford's subscription list. The paper, in its new shape, a small folio, with a type-page measuring six and a half by ten and a half inches, was pleasant to the eye, well printed and well edited. For these reasons it deserved the good repute and good sales which were its portion, and for more, because it contained real news, having items from St. Petersburg, Vienna, Berlin, Stockholm, Paris, and London ; this newest news being not over two months old ! The interest in the details of foreign affairs remains undiminished, and these details are somewhat better arranged and edited than in Zenger's *Journal*.

The *Post-Boy* of June 10, 1745, contains a careful map and plan of the siege of Louisburg, published in the hope that it will be of value to the subscribers, inasmuch as many of the besieging force had friends and relations in the province. The issue of February 26, 1750, gives notice of the coming of a company of comedians from Philadelphia, who "will give performances in a room of the building belonging to the estate of Rip Van Dam, Esquire, deceased." This building, the first theatre in the town, stood on the site of the present numbers 64 and 66, Nassau Street, that plot of land remaining whole and uncut. This more recent structure, covering its entire site, has yet an air of sedate antiquity to modern eyes, and something in its square stolidity still suggests the "Estate of Rip Van Dam, Esquire." As far as is known, this is the first notice of the first play-acting in the town. The advertisement runs as follows:

" By his Excellency's Permission, At the Theatre in Nassau Street, On Monday the 5th of March, next, Will be presented the Historical Tragedy

of

King Richard 3rd!

Wrote originally by Shakespeare, and altered by Colley Cibber, Esquire. In this play are contained the Death of King Henry 6th; the

The Weekly Post-Boy

artful acquisition of the crown by King Richard, the murder of the Princes in the Tower;
the landing of the Earl of Richmond, and the
Battle of Bosworth Field.

"Tickets will be ready to be delivered by
Thursday next, and to be had of the printer
hereof.

"Pitt, five shillings; Gallery, three shillings.
To begin precisely at half an hour after six
o'clock, and no person to be admitted behind
the scenes."

The Gazette and Post-Boy of September 24,
1750, prints the following:

"On Thursday evening the tragedy of
'Cato' was played at the theatre in this city,
before a very numerous audience, the greater
part of whom were of the opinion that it
was pretty well performed. As it was the
fullest assembly that has ever appeared in that
house, it may serve to prove that the taste of
this place is not so much vitiated or lost to a
sense of liberty, but that they can prefer a
representation of Virtue to one of loose character. 'The Recruiting Officer' will be presented this evening."

From such decorous and unboastful beginnings has the New York School of Dramatic
Criticism "grown so great." The item con-
tinues: "The House being new floored, is
made warm and comfortable, besides which

Gentlemen and Ladies may cause their stoves to be brought." These small foot-stoves— iron cages, with embers in the pan—were in every-day use at this time ; now they are gathered into collections and museums.

In 1770, James Parker "closed all his earthly concerns," and his journal quietly expired three years later.

William Weyman, another apprentice of Bradford, acted as James Parker's assistant for a few years, and then, in 1759, started his own *New-York Gazette*. This was a poor affair, having no vitality. The proof-reading was so wretched that its owner and editor was constantly in trouble; being haled to the bar of the Assembly of New York, and forced to beg for mercy for some of his errors, which had seemed to cast a slight on that honorable body. So early were seen symptoms of sensitiveness on the part of the provincial authorities, signs of the strain that was beginning to be felt. Although poor enough as a newspaper, Weyman's *Gazette* is absorbing reading to the lover of history, for it is full of reports—or rather rumors—from the front, of the way the " French and Indian " War was going. It prints a manifesto from General Wolfe in full, and on August 6, 1759, it joyfully records the taking of Ticonderoga by Amherst, ten days after that almost bloodless victory, which helped to wipe out the cruel repulse of the preceding year. This feeble journal languished until 1767, and then expired of inanition.

A more vigorous personality than Weyman's is that of John Holt, a Virginian, who came to New York in 1759, and soon appears as a partner of James Parker. He was assistant editor of *The New-York Gazette and Weekly Post-Boy,* for a year or two, and had entire control of the paper from 1762 to 1766. Then he quarrelled with Parker, and set up his own paper,—*The New-York Journal,*—"Containing the freshest advices, Foreign and Domestick." It contained, too, the freshest thoughts and deepest convictions of this ardent patriot and devoted Whig, as well as frequent contributions from his fellow-Whigs; and it had a sudden success, and large sales. This was the first paper to be wholly and frankly given over to the cause of the patriots. On June 23, 1774, Holt removed the royal arms from his title, and substituted Franklin's device, the serpent cut in pieces, with the warning motto, "Unite or Die." This simple design held the place of the royal arms until December 15, 1774, when this same serpent appears, united and coiled, with his tail in his mouth, making a double ring, enclosing a pillar crowned by a liberty cap, and held upright by many hands on the firm foundation of "Magna Charta." The following inscription, printed on the body of the snake, follows its double coil.

> "United now, alive and free, firm on this basis, liberty shall
>   stand ;
>   And thus supported, ever bless our land ;
>   Till time becomes eternity."

These two symbols, both strong and suggestive, caught the popular eye, and this object-lesson sank into the popular mind.

In 1776, his fearlessly expressed principles forced Holt to fly from New York. He took with him only his press, leaving behind, and losing, all else he possessed. For seven years, he and his press wandered from one town to another along the Hudson, now at Fishkill, then farther north at Esopus, now farther inland, as he was forced by the advances and retreats of the British lines ; sending out his militant journal, with undaunted courage and admirable regularity, throughout the war. This was the first instance of a printing press being set up outside of any of the large towns, and it was not a financial success, so that, at the close of the war, Holt gladly came back to New York, continuing his paper under the title of *The Independent Gazette or the New-York Journal.*

At his death in the year following the peace, 1784, a notable figure, and a genuine force was lost to the American Press. He was an able editor and an admirable writer as well as a pugnacious patriot. He was a good churchman too, and his slab, in the burial ground hard by the southwest corner of the old Tory chapel of St. Paul's, is in place there, willing as he was to worship in that structure whence every royal sign and symbol had been torn by a revolutionary mob, leaving only—not noticing in the patriotic burst of destruction—the three feathers of Wales, on the sounding board above the pulpit. This princely emblem remains in position to this day, while the words Whig and Tory have been dropped from the vocabulary of American politics.

The Independent Gazette remained in the Widow Holt's hands until 1787, when it was sold, together with Holt's printing-office, to Thomas Greenleaf, who changed the one paper into two, renamed them, and made them the earliest Democratic organs in the country. The later life of these papers cannot be recorded here, for they passed into other hands, and outlived the century.

In marked contrast with Holt's firm character stands, or rather wobbles, the Irishman, Hugh Gaine. His political creed, "it seems"—in the words of a competent witness—"was to join the strongest party," Not certain whether Whig or Tory were to prove the stronger, he actually, after a vain attempt to remain neutral, belonged to both ! He had begun his *New*-

York Mercury in 1752, and had enlarged it, in 1770, under the title, also enlarged, of *The New-York Gazette, and The Weekly Mercury.''* This paper he had kept fairly neutral, when the war first broke out : but he took the precaution to set up another paper of the same name in Newark, New Jersey, where he considered it safe and politic to be a staunch Whig in all his utterances. This Newark edition was begun on September 21, 1776, its first issue being a folio, uniform, so far as externals went, with the New York issue of September ninth, which was its immediate predecessor. The second number came out as a quarto, why no one seems to have taken the trouble to explain, and in this shape the paper was continued until November second, when it ceased abruptly, with no editorial warning. In fact, there is nothing to show that this Newark paper was a new or separate venture in any way, the impression, which was carefully conveyed to the subscriber, being, that Mr. Gaine, like many another ardent patriot, had been forced to seek refuge for his press outside New York. His transplanted patriotism grew smaller as the British successes grew greater. In his New York paper, meanwhile, he published many proclamations of Lord Howe and his brother, and addresses of fulsome loyalty from the citizens who had chosen to stay in the town. In the Newark issue of November

Hugh
Gaine

second he printed a long selection from the
Connecticut Gazette with this explanatory note:
"The following articles are taken from the
New-York Mercury, printed in New York at
the house lately kept by Mr. Gaine—which we
received via Long Island." The article in
question—a detailed account of the various
engagements which gave the British possession of New York, spiced with mockery and
abuse of the American forces,—was taken
from Gaine's own paper, his New York issue
of October 7, 1776; while, in his Newark
paper of October fifth, there is an anxious
letter from a large investor in the English
funds, who is so sure that the Americans will
win within a few months that he bewails the
inevitable fall in British securities and his own
loss of income!

Even Hugh Gaine would be put to the blush
could he see the two records of his great feat
in journalistic hedging, bound in one volume
as they now are at the Lenox Library. *The
Newark Mercury* once abandoned, the New
York paper became so frankly and wholly
loyal, that the evacuation of the city left Mr.
Gaine in a decidedly difficult position, from
which he could extricate himself only by
petitioning the Assembly to allow him to remain in the city and to continue his paper.
The petition was granted, but there was no
room for Gaine's peculiar editorial principles

amid a people so much in earnest, and his paper ceased its existence in November, 1783.

Gaine hung out his sign at the "Bible and Crown" in Hanover Square for full forty years, pouring forth from his press a ceaseless stream of pamphlets, almanacs, and books:—among these last, the first American edition of *Robinson Crusoe*, and another famous volume entitled *Military Collections and Remarks*, by one Major Donkin, published in 1777. It is a well printed octavo, and its frontispiece, representing Lord Percy receiving friendly attentions from Fame, is a fine engraving by J. Smithers. The real and abiding interest of the book is found in the fact that, with the exception of one copy, every existing specimen of the *Military Collections* has been carefully expurgated. The little paragraph which has been "scissored out" does not deserve quotation, for it is only a dastardly suggestion that poisoned arrows should be used against the American forces to inoculate "these stubborn, ignorant, enthusiastic savages" with their dread enemy, the small-pox. Yet the fact remains that Donkin wrote it, Gaine printed it, and some person left just this one paragraph uncut, for the amusement of those who go to-day in search of literary curiosities. Gaine amassed great wealth by his strict devotion to business, and to no principle beyond that of money-getting. As may be supposed, there was much cleverness and even brilliancy in this ingenious time-server, and his paper shows taste and ability; but he lived at the wrong time, either too early or too late for the exercise of his shifty talents.

Among the publishers who were forced to flee from New York in 1776 was Samuel Loudon, an Irishman, who had established, early in that year, his *New-York Packet and American Advertiser*, the last newspaper started in New York before the Declaration of Independence. This paper, which was printed at Fishkill during the years of the war, is interesting to the student of history more for the pleasing variations in its elaborate title, with its fine cut of a full-rigged clipper ship and its old English lettering and delicate scroll-work, than for the dry details in its three-columned page of fine print.

After the declaration of peace, Loudon returned to New York and established himself at 5 Water Street, between Old Slip and the famous Coffee House, on the corner of Wall and Water Streets. Later he turned his paper from a weekly to a daily, and, later still, changed its name to *The Diary, or Loudon's Register*. In its later numbers, his journal, which ran on until 1792, fell below its own early standard, and far below that of its contemporaries, losing even its especial feature of a picturesque title, and becoming content with plain lettering. Loudon's *Magazine*, made up of "elegant extracts," etc., was the first publication of the kind issued in New York.

There was but one newspaper printed in New York during the British occupation that continued to live after the departure of that army. This was the *New-York Morning Post*, established in 1782, by William Morton, with whom was associated Samuel Horner. This paper was changed to a daily in 1786, and had its day until 1788.

James Rivington, a notable figure in these ranks under review, appeared first in New York in September, 1760, when he announced himself, from Hanover Square, as "the only London bookseller in America." He had grown rich as a publisher in Paternoster Row, London, but Newmarket enticed him, and its bookmakers carried off the bookseller's fortune. With his native vigor, and little else, he started out to retrieve his losses in the new world. From New York, he went to Philadelphia for three years, but finally established himself permanently in this town in 1765, and in 1772, added a printing office to his shop. On April 22, 1773, he bought out *The New-York Gazetteer*, adorned with a fine cut of a ship, labelled *The London Packet;* promising, with much flourish, in a long prospectus, that it should be a better weekly than any yet seen in the town.

The promise was kept : only Zenger's paper could compare with the *Gazetteer*. Petty and inadequate as it is to modern eyes, it was an improvement on all preceding papers, in the quality of its writing and the freshness of its news. Sales were large and advertisements—the test of modern success—came in rapidly. Two specimens, among the many, will serve to show the then form of advertisement : "To be lett, and entered upon the first day of May next"—the moving day of modern New York can trace its origin back through more than a century—" the two houses at present occupied by Abraham Lott, Esquire, nearly opposite the Fly-Market. For particulars apply to Mrs. Provoost, on Golden Hill." The "Fly Market"—which took its name from a corruption of the Dutch *Vly* or *Vlaie*, a marsh or salt-meadow—occupies various sites on the old maps of New York, from old Queen Street to the corner now occupied by its lineal descendent Fulton Market. The weight of authority seems to place it at the head of what is now Burling Slip. "Golden Hill" gave its pleasant name to that part of our present John Street which lies between William and Pearl Streets.

The second extract shows that gentlemen were given to letting their mansions, from time to time, even as they do to-day : " To be lett, from the 25th of March next, or sooner if wanted, the pleasant situated, and convenient house and grounds of William Bayard, Esquire, at Greenwich. Any person inclining to hire the same may apply to the owner living on the premises, or to Mr. James Rivington." It is curious to note that the English rental quarter-days had survived the voyage to this country. This house of William Bayard stood on the bank of the North River, just above the present Christopher Street ; thither they carried Alexander Hamilton after his fatal duel on Weehawken Heights, rowing him carefully across the broad river, and there he died after a day of hopeless suffering. A portion of the house was standing until within a few years.

The title of Rivington's paper grew with its growth, reaching its extreme limit in 1775, when it became *Rivington's New-York Ga-etteer, or, The Connecticut, Hudson's River, New-Jersey, and Quebec Weekly Advertiser*, " printed at his open and uninfluenced press fronting Hanover Square." " Open and uninfluenced " for a few months only, for, neutral at the start—or at least impartial and fair— Rivington's press had become a violent Tory in 1774. At about this time, when other printers were removing the royal arms from their titles, Rivington adopted them, giving them the place formerly held by his " London Packet." It is a coincidence, at least, that in

July, 1774, Lord North had sent out a hand-bill, offering £500 to the printer who would steadily advocate and promote all ministerial measures.

The new tone of the *Gazetteer* aroused intense wrath throughout the province ; its libels and fabrications in the interest of the Administration vexed even the Tories; it was more loyal than the king himself ! Perhaps it unconsciously aided "the good cause"—to use the expression of Harvey Birch—by its wholesome stimulation of the " patriots." That stimulus went so far, in 1775, as to move the mob, mainly from Connecticut, to wreck Rivington's shop twice, the second time destroying his presses and melting his type for bullets.   He was forced to cease pub-lication while he went to London to buy new presses.   In 1777, having brought back from England his appointment as printer to the king, as well as the necessary presses and type, he began again the issue of his paper, calling it at first *Rivington's New-York Loyal Gazette*, and later, *The Royal Gazette*, "pub-lished at New York, by James Rivington, Printer to the King's Most Excellent Majesty." Its popular title was short and pithy—"The Lying Gazette."   This came out twice a week. In its columns, August 1, 1781, appeared the first canto of John André's " Cow Chace;" the poem running through three numbers, its last canto being published on the very day of the capture of the jaunty author by the comrades-in-arms of the "Warrio-drover Wayne."

The first attempt at a daily paper in New York was made by Rivington, in connection with the editors of four other Royalist papers, who arranged their weekly issues in such order that, with the assistance of Rivington's bi-weekly *Gazette*, each day had its special paper.

When "the rebels" became the government, Rivington, in his anxiety to retain his subscription list, and to continue his paper, printed the following explanation and apology in its columns :

"To the public :—The publisher of this paper, sensible that his zeal for the success of his Majesty's arms, his sanguine wishes for the good of his country, and his friendship for individuals, have, at times, led him to credit and circulate paragraphs without investigating the facts so closely as his duty to the public demanded—trusting to their feelings, and depending on their generosity—he begs them to look over past errors and depend on future correctness. From henceforth he will neither expect nor solicit their favors longer than his endeavors shall stamp the same degree of authenticity and credit on the *Royal Gazette* (of New York) as all Europe allows to the *Royal Gazette* of London." This did not suffice,

First attempt at a Daily Paper

and his truthful *Gazette* failed to inherit the success of its lying predecessor, and so died a natural death on December 31, 1783.

Rivington died in 1802, in his house in Pearl Street, No 156, on the northeast corner of Wall Street. Rivington Street, which those who remember it as "the prettiest street in all New York" would gladly connect with this picturesque old Tory, took its name from an entirely different family.

Despite the possible indirect influence of Lord North's £500, it may not be said that James Rivington's attitude was not conscientious ; conviction was as common with the Tories as with the Whigs ; there was only one Hugh Gaine, and only here and there, on either side, one who, like a modern Irish "Patriot" was "grateful to God that he had a country—to sell." Indeed, it was the honesty and earnestness on both sides that gave birth to such bitterness, and aroused a more ferocious animosity in the rebel heart against the native "Royalist" than was felt toward the British oppressors. For twenty years before the outbreak of the Revolution there had been agitation, constantly growing stronger ; tumult, and ultimately terror, impassioned men's minds. It was not a period of repose, civic, domestic, or personal ; no man breathed tranquilly, no voice spoke gently, no pen was enlisted for decorous and urbane combat. And many pens—regulars and volunteers—were in motion during these years ; at first only in defence of political rights, urging that they should be preserved within due bounds, with no suggestion of breaking loose from the mother country ; then in defiance, advocating independence, and expressing the conviction of the larger portion of the people that separation was the sole salvation of their constitutional rights.

Throughout this perturbed period, and during the war that followed, there was a plentiful out-put of newspaper-letters from private and official pens, state papers, political essays, addresses and sermons, and especially of pamphlets—then with us the most stirring appeal to the populace, as with France a little later, as with England a little earlier. They spoke on both sides, and were strikingly earnest and authentic documents voicing the sentiments and judgments of the entire country. And these poor, ill-printed, dull-faced little sheets had their share in the work : not by virtue of their editorial pages, which were hardly known as we know them, but through the communications sent to them by the best thinkers and the hardest workers on either side, as has been noticed in the case of Holt's *Journal*, and as was the case with most of the other papers. Each of them had its own corps of contributors, men of ability, character, and standing, who were glad to work, without hire, for the good cause as each one judged it. This form of quasi-editorial writing gave telling impulse to the movement towards revolution, and when war had once begun, contributed immensely to its success.

It is beyond the province of this paper, on a local press only, to do more than refer, with respect and gratitude, to the work done and the help given by the greatest journalist, the most powerful writer of pamphlets during this period, "Tom" Paine. But it is of local interest to note that the latest homes of the man who was a phenomenal force in our early history, who, with his *Common Sense*, wrought an effect "rarely produced by types and paper in any age or country," were in our city, and that one of them is still standing, almost unchanged, at No. 309 Bleecker Street. This street was then named Herring Street, and the little two-story and attic house, which stands so dingily on the street, had its garden once, and was trim and orderly after the fashion of its day, a fashion dimly suggested to us by its delicate dormer windows, and huge chimney.

To this house Paine came in July, 1808—Madame Bonneville, and her two sons, who had followed him from France, living quite near—and here, under the care of his landlady, Mrs. Ryder, he spent quiet and serene months. Here, as we stand in the busy street, we can fancy the worn warrior sitting, reading at his favorite front window, or perhaps in the sunlit little garden. In April, 1809, when his increasing infirmities demanded more constant care, Madame Bonneville moved with him to a house standing well back from Herring Street, approached by a path through the great gardens of that day : there he died on the eighth of June, 1809. Grove Street has been cut through these old gardens, and the site of the room in which Paine died is now occupied by Number 59 in that street. His martial mission to his adopted country had ended with the successful close of the war he had done so much to sustain and speed. "The times that tried men's souls are over," he wrote in the last number of his *Crisis*, after the news of the negotiation of the treaty at Paris had reached him.

But John Jay, three years later, when the first flush of victory had passed and the future was dark with unanswered questions, wrote to Washington; "I am uneasy and apprehensive, more so than during the war." And with reason, for although the question of independence had been answered, other issues almost as vital, were to be discussed, other appeals almost as impassioned, were to be made. And now a new mission began for the New York Press. The writers, who had brought success to the Revolution almost as much as had the men in the field, now turned their pens, with equal energy, to settling the political problems that came with the peace. For this new warfare, with new weapons, men did not stop to put on gloves, any more than did those eager partisans who had thrown the tea into the harbors.

Of the many pre-Revolutionary papers, but one or two survived the seven years of strife, and even this remnant changed hands, and sometimes names. New journals came to fill the vacant places, and the press improved greatly in ability and in influence, dividing its forces between the two great political parties, now first formed on vital national issues : the Federalists, devoted to the new constitution, and to Washington's administration; and the Anti-Federalists—dubbed " Democrats " in derision—reinforced by the Democratic-Republicans, generalled by Jefferson, and guided by the essential principles of the French Revolution. The attempt to create a strong central government and a closer union between the States, met with violent opposition from many men with many motives, some of whom feared to lose their personal advantage and limited glory if their States were merged in a nation.

One New York paper deserves mention here simply for the sake of its issue of October 27, 1787. The first number of the

Federalist appeared, on that day, in the columns of *The Independent Journal*, printed by J. and A. McLean, in Hanover Square. The after numbers of this, "the greatest treatise of government that has ever been written," were published, in the *Packet* and other papers, through the summer of 1788. Each of the numbers was signed "Publius," a pen-name used in common by Hamilton, Jay, and Madison. Three of these brilliant political papers were written by Hamilton and Madison in collaboration : of the remainder, Jay wrote five ; Madison, thirteen ; and Hamilton, sixty-three.

Then, as now, the city of New York was the key to the political situation, and the leaders of the two parties—Hamilton and Jay on the one side, Burr and the Livingstons on the other—turned all their energies toward securing the vote of the town. In this conflict, the newspapers played an important part, carrying the "liberty of the Press" to its farthest limit, in their bitter attacks on their opponents. In addition to the great national points at issue, there were many minor matters that caused what seems to us at this distance ludicrous virulence of feeling and of language : such as the intrigues to remove the seat of government from town to town, with intent to secure a sufficiently central spot, where living should be cheap ; the restoration of the Tories to their former rights of citizenship ; the Alien and Sedition laws of 1798 ; the demand for the suppression of that blameless body, the Society of the Cincinnati, on the ground that it was fated to lead to a "military nobility and an hereditary aristocracy"; the furious electoral struggle between Burr and Jefferson in 1801 ; Burr's trial at Richmond in 1807, for attempted treason "at a certain place called and known by the name of Blennerhassett's Island"; the outcry for the strengthening of the navy, too feeble to protect our fast-growing sea trade ; the rights of search enforced by the British, in all waters, even within sight of our shores ; the pitiable affair of the *Chesapeake* in June, 1807 ; the famous proclamation of President Madison, the embargo, and the embittered negotiations that preceded the war of 1812.

In these discussions, the journals and frequent pamphlets lashed themselves into a fury, hounded on by the powers behind— politicians, place-hunters, patriots — whose patriotism, in too many cases, was covered completely by Dr. Johnson's definition, "the last refuge of a scoundrel."

That the observant foreigner was not lacking to chronicle this unhappy state of affairs is shown by a fat and foolish volume, issued from the press of Cundee, in Ivy Lane, and written by an Englishman, Charles William

Janson, Esquire, under the imposing title of *Observations on the Genius, Manners, and Customs of the United States, Made During a Long Residence in that Country.* "The Stranger in America," as he styled himself, found nothing in this land, during the latter part of the eighteenth and the beginning of the nineteenth century, to please him. His fine feelings were constantly affronted, his dignity rumpled, by all with whom he came in contact, from the "pert virgin" demanding admiration, to the "sullen Yankee" harboring resentment. "Among the lower orders," he querulously complains, "in spite of his endeavors to adapt his behaviour to their satisfaction, he was regarded as proud and haughty ; while a distant kind of envious obsequiousness, tinctured by an affectation of superiority, was but too evident in the majority of his equals." He becomes lachrymose over "their persistent rancour against the mother country ; so pointed also in their press."

With the power and excesses of that press, he is impressed, with real reason, for nothing is more striking than its cruelty and coarseness, its venomous vigor of invective, its contempt of all that should be sacred in political warfare and in private life. Too many of its editors and writers were, in the words of gentle old Isaiah Thomas, "destitute at once of the urbanity of gentlemen, the information of scholars, and the principles of virtue." They raged madly at one another as "vermin and foxes," as "minions of sedition," as "notorious Jacobins." Bache, of Philadelphia, was styled "the greatest fool, and most stubborn *sans-culotte*" in the land. His *Aurora* spoke of Washington as "the man who is the source of all misfortunes to the country," and coarsely quoted, when the first President retired to Mount Vernon after the inauguration of Adams, "Now lettest Thou Thy servant depart in peace, for mine eyes have seen Thy salvation"; exultant that "the name of Washington from this day ceases to give currency to political iniquity and to legalized corruption." Major Benjamin Russell, in his *Sentinel*, is equally hysterical over the election of Jefferson. Callender spoke of President Adams as "a hoary-headed incendiary,—the scourge, the scorn, the outcast of society."

These amenities were not confined to editors, and it is a high government official, Pickering, the Postmaster-General, who expresses his opinion in the following gentle statement : "The critic is a liar, who lies because it is natural to him and because he cannot help it." Among themselves the editors exchanged even more pointed personalities, so that suits for slander,—wherein the defendant had sometimes only to read aloud in court the plaintiff's own words to be acquitted,—street brawls with fists and pistols, duels, and even murders, were not at all infrequent. This astoundingly shabby spectacle ceased to exist only toward the end of the second war with England, when the various American victories, ashore and at sea, were hailed with equal exultation by both factions of the press and the people. Parties were drawn closer together, partisan poison became attenuated in the body politic, and with the election of Monroe, Federalism, as a force, faded away, "the era of good feeling coming in," as Major Russell expressed it.

In the midst of the most rancorous period, a paper was started which took no note of party strife. This was *The Shipping and Commercial List and New-York Price Current*, which was first published on December 19, 1795, by one James Oram, a New York printer, at 33 Liberty Street—the then recently renamed Crown Street. This paper concerned itself with business only, and printed no general news—which, perhaps, accounts for the fact that it was not drawn into the quarrels of the time—and devoted its weekly issue to commercial, financial, and shipping interests, with their allied industries and trades. In 1795, John Jay negotiated his much criticised commercial treaty with England, insuring the American merchant marine from Great Britain's privateers ; so laying the foundation for what was once one of the greatest industries of the United States—its carrying trade to other countries. This new life found no voice in the daily press of that day, and John Oram's paper, a folio of letter-sheet size, which came out every Monday, was of immense value to merchants with its full accounts of all shipping matters, the sailings of every vessel, and the current prices of all staple commodities.

The Shipping and Commercial List and New-York Price Current is still in existence, that old name serving as the sub-title of *The New York Commercial*—a title which it has been allowed to adopt after some legal difficulties with its contemporary of a hundred years standing, *The Commercial Advertiser*—and claims to be the oldest paper of its sort in the country. The little weekly folio is grown to be an important daily of sixteen pages, still devoted entirely to shipping and trade news, finding a large demand for its special information, in spite of the fact that modern journals devote so much space to the same subject.

In 1895, was celebrated the centenary of trade journalism and of American commercial freedom, a fitting commemoration of John Jay's diplomacy and of John Oram's journal, whose file for the last hundred years gives a complete detailed account of one of our greatest interests.

If it were possible to get complete files of the many literary and political papers in our land and in this town that were contemporary with the *Shipping and Commercial List*, one would have at hand all the doings of "History in her workshop." The statistics that cover only so short a period as that between January and July, 1810, are full of interest and surprise, for the proportion of political journals to the population was greater than the world had ever witnessed ; more surprising still when we bear in mind that the great body of the reading and criticising public was employed in daily labor. At no time and in no land had the masses hitherto had access so easily and so cheaply to the news and the knowledge and the discussions of the public press ; and they were bent on improving their opportunities at any cost, even at the cost of the publishers. When unable to pay in current coin, they paid in all sorts of odd merchandise, and distant subscribers were supplied on credit : "which accounts," says a naïve chronicler of the period, "for the large circulation of some journals."

Proportion of Political Journals to Population

REFERENCES.

[Specific references to newspapers are given in the text.]

The History of Printing in America, with a Biography of Printers, and an Account of Newspapers. ISAIAH THOMAS, printer, Worcester, 1810.

Journalism in the United States, from 1690 to 1872. FREDERICK HUDSON, New York, 1873.

Printers and Printing in New York. C. R. HILDEBURN, New York, 1895.

Address delivered at the Celebration by the New York Historical Society, May 20, 1863, of the Two Hundredth Anniversary of the Birthday of Mr. William Bradford, who Introduced the Art of Printing into the Middle Colonies of British America. JOHN WILLIAM WALLACE, of Philadelphia. Albany, 1863.

Military Collections and Remarks. MAJOR DONKIN. Hugh Gaine, New York, 1777.

Old Streets, Roads, Lanes, Piers, and Wharves of New York, Showing Former and Present Names. JOHN G. POST, New York, 1882.

The Life of Thomas Paine, with a History of his Literary, Political, and Religious Career in America, France, and England. MONCURE DANIEL CONWAY, New York, 1892.

BOWLING GREEN

Half Moon Series

Published in the Interest of the New York
City History Club.

VOLUME II.   NUMBER V.

BOWLING GREEN.

BY SPENCER TRASK.

NEW YORK is cosmopolitan, essentially so, beyond all large cities of the world. Absorbed in the whirl and stir of the To-day, occupied with vast schemes and enterprises for the To-morrow, overswept by a constant influx of new life and new elements, it seems to have no individual entity. It does not hold fast its old traditions, its past associations. It is hurried on, in the quickstep of its march of improvement, far away from its starting-point; and as it goes and grows with rapid progress into something new and vast, it ruthlessly obliterates its old landmarks and forgets its early history. It is well, sometimes, to look back and remember the beginning of things, to quicken our civic pride by measuring our growth, to recall the struggles and the conquests which proved the courage, patience, and stamina of the people who made New York what it is.

March of
Improve=
ment

There is no piece of land on Manhattan Island which has retained for a longer period its distinctive name, and at the same time fulfilled more thoroughly the purposes of its creation, than the small park at the extreme southern end of Broadway, known as Bowling Green. It is the one historic spot which has never lost its identity or been diverted from public use since the foundation of the city.

The history of the city from the time when the good ship *Sea Mew* sailed into the bay, May 6, 1626, bearing the doughty Dutch Governor, Peter Minuet,—with no city and no people as yet to govern,—to the present, might almost be written from what has been seen and heard from this small plot of land.

The West India Company was chartered by the States-General of Holland in 1621. In 1625, enough capital had been raised, and colonists obtained, to warrant the Company in beginning to avail itself of the almost unlimited privileges granted, of exclusive trade along the whole Atlantic coast, and of almost sovereign power. The first act of the honest Dutchman on that May morn was to call together the Manhattan tribe of Indians, probably on the very site of the future Green. There he traded for the whole island, named after the tribe, estimated at that time to contain about " 11,000 Dutch morgens," [1] or 22,000 acres, a quantity of beads, trinkets, etc., valued at sixty guilders, or about twenty-four dollars, a sum far less than that now paid for a single square foot of any portion of that land which then came within his vision. From this sharp bargain was to grow the city that was destined to be the commercial metropolis of the new continent, and the second largest city of the world.

In order to insure peaceable possession, a fort was built, seemingly under the direction of one Kryn Frederycke, and in 1635, a larger one was erected at the contract price of $1635. It was 300 feet long, and 250 wide. This enclosed the Governor's house, barracks, and, later, the church. The contract for the building of the church required it to be of "Rock Stone," 72 feet long, 52 feet broad, and 16 feet high. The price was $1000. This fort occupied the space between the present streets called Whitehall, Bridge, State, and Bowling Green. The sally-port was at the north.

The large open space opposite the sally-port was set apart and known at first as "The Plaine," afterwards to become the Bowling Green. It held a place of great importance in the annals of the city in times of peace and times of war. This was the village green, which marked the growing social life of the people. Here the children played, looking far off into the watery distance as they remembered stories of their grandfathers' and fathers' homes beyond the sea ; here the youths and maidens danced on holidays and crowned their loveliest on the first of May, wreathing their May-poles with the early green.   It was also the parade-ground for the soldiers.   On Sundays, we can see it crowded with the country wagons of all descriptions, of those who came to worship at the church "within the Fort," the horses being turned loose to graze on the hillside running down to the water on the site of the present Battery.   Here, also, was the well, built for the use both of the garrison and of the general public.   Tradition has affirmed that the site of this well was originally a spring, the surplus waters of which ran in a little brook down the present line of Beaver Street, and contributed to form the marsh in the present Broad Street, then called "Blommaert's" Valley.

Here Governor Van Twiller proved his valor and his contempt for the English.   An English trading vessel came into the bay to trade with Indians up the river.   One of the sailors deposes that

"The Dutch here inhabitinge send and command all our Companye (excepte one boye) to come to their forte, where they staide about twoe houres and the Governor commande his gunner to make ready three peeces of ordnance and shott them off for the Prince of Orange, and sprede the Prince's Coloures.   Whereupon Jacob Elekins, the merchant's factor of the Shippe, the *William*, commande William Fforde of Lymehouse (the gunner) to go abord the Shippe and sprede her coloures and shoote off three peeces of ordnance for the Kinge of England." [2]

Then Jacob Elekins coolly sailed up the river in defiance of the guns of the fort, leaving the astonished Governor to meditate on his audacity. Thunderstruck at such an act of temerity, Van Twiller summoned all the people to "The Plaine," then ordering a cask of wine and another of beer to be rolled out, he filled a glass and called on all good citizens to drink a health to the Prince of Orange and confusion to the English.

Here, after two years of a bloody and savage war with the surrounding Indians, during which the island was almost depopulated, the farms destroyed, and many adjacent settlements obliterated, the sachems of all the hostile tribes assembled August 30, 1645, smoked the calumet of peace, and buried the tomahawk, pledging eternal friendship with the whites. [3]

In 1641, Governor Kieft established two annual fairs for the encouragement of agriculture, the first for cattle, to begin October 15, and the second for hogs, to begin November 1. These were ordered to be held "att the markett house and plaine afore the forte." This fair was the great annual event of the city, forerunner of the Horse Fair and Dog Show. We can picture the sturdy burghers and their fair vrouws, in all the glory of starched ruffs and variegated quilted petticoats, discussing the respective merits of their Holsteins and hogs. One inducement held out to attract strangers was that no one should be liable for arrest for debt during the continuance of the fair. This must have materially added to the number of visitors.

The peace and quiet of the worthy burghers, as indicated by these fairs and social gatherings, were rudely shaken when, early in 1653, a war having broken out between England and Holland, an invasion from New England was threatened. At a General Session of the Councillors held March 13, 1653,[4] it was resolved,

"1st. That the whole body of citizens shall keep watch by night in such places as shall be designated, the City Tavern to be the temporary headquarters."

"2nd. That the fort be repaired."

"3rd. Because the fort is not large enough to contain all the inhabitants, it is deemed necessary to enclose the city with palisades and breastworks."

"4th. Some way must be devised to raise money."

"5th. Captain Vischer is to be requested to

fix his sails, to have his piece loaded, and to keep his vessel in readiness."

(Whether for fight or flight is not said.)

Evidently not much reliance could have been placed upon the palisades, for on July 28, the Governor sends a missive to the City Magistrates, stating that the palisades are completed, and requesting them "to keep the hogs away from the repaired ramparts of the Fort."[5]   Some years later we find the following entry:

"Whereas, the fortifications of this city have at great and excessive expense, trouble and labor of the Burghery and inhabitants, been mostly completed, and it is therefore necessary for the preservation of the same and better security of this city some orders be made, therefore——

"Ittem.   It is strictly forbidden and prohibited, that any person, be he who he may, presume to land within this City, or quit the same in any other manner, way or means, than thro the ordinary City Gate, on paine of Death.   And finally, as it is found that the hogs which are kept within this city in multitudes along the public streets, have from time to time committed great damage on the eastern fortifications, and that the same are most certainly to be expected in like manner here on the erected works, every one who keeps hogs within this city is there ordered and charged to take care *that their hogs shall not come to, in or on the Bulwarks, Bastions, Gardens or Batteries, under forfeiture of said hogs*, and double the value thereof, to be applied the one half for the informer, the other half for the informer who shall put this in execution. Every one is hereby warned and put on his guard against injury."

"By order of the Heer Govnr. Gen. of N. Netherlands.

N. Bayard, Sec'y."

Fortunately no more serious assaults than these from the hogs and from the horns of the cattle were made against the palisades, for peace was shortly after declared between England and Holland, and their colonies had to restrain their martial ardor.

The following year but one was again full of fears; for in February, 1655, a council of war was held to consider a threatened attack of the Swedes on the South (Delaware) River. It was then "Deemed necessary that the fortifications be repaired "—the cattle probably in the meantime having become obstreperous and displayed their ferocity against the stockade—"by spiking with good spikes, a blind of planks five or six feet in height against the palisades."

Again was all this precaution useless, for, the Swedes not coming, Governor Stuyvesant decided to go to them ; and the council of

war, at a special meeting, having applied for
and obtained "two drummers to improve the
marching of the militia," the valiant army set
forth, and returned triumphant, having destroyed the Swedish fort.   Later in this year
a foray of Indians was made in the surrounding country, and the vigilant magistrates, on
September 20, resolved "to raise up the palisades to the height of at least 10 or 12 feet,
to prevent the *overloopen* [jumping over] of
the savages."

The palisades, or stockade, extended along
the East River, from near the present head of
Coenties Slip, on the line of Pearl Street.
crossing the fields to the North River, on the
present north side of Wall Street (whence its
name), and then along the North River to the
fort, just east of Greenwich Street, which was
then under water.   The map of the city in
1695 shows the line of the palisades.   In
digging the foundation of the new Bowling
Green Offices, 5–11 Broadway, a large number of these old posts were found many feet
under the surface.   Although nearly two hundred and fifty years old, the portions found were
in a wonderful state of preservation. Canes and
other mementos have been made from these.

War's rude alarms for a while having ceased,
the citizens turned their attention to the improving of the city. First, a census was taken,
which showed 120 houses and 1000 inhabit-

City Improvements

ants. The average price of the best city lots was then fifty dollars, while the rent of an average good house was fourteen dollars per annum.

The ditch, which heretofore had run through the centre of Broad Street, was sided up with boards. Several of the streets were ordered paved with stone, whence Stone Street received its name, being one of the first paved streets in the city.

In 1659, an ordinance was passed establishing a public market on the present Bowling Green.[5]

"It is found good and resolved, that for all fat cattle brought to the market (not slaughtered) posts shall be erected by the side of the church where those who bring such cattle to market for sale shall present them.

"It is also resolved, that shambles be built, a cover be made, and a block brought in, and that the key be given to Andries, the baker, who shall keep oversight of the same."

It was at this time made the duty of the Sheriff to go around the city at night. He evidently must have considered this as detracting from his dignity, for he officially complains, "That the dogs attack him; that the people cause frights by halloing 'Indian' in the night, and that the boys cut 'koeckies.'"

For some time the English colonists occupying the country to the north and the south of New Netherland had been restive, and the home government was more than willing to back up their claims that no rival power should separate their possessions, claiming that the Dutch occupation was usurpation of the English rights. Charles the Second, with kingly liberality, granted a patent under date of March 12, 1664, to his brother James, Duke of York, bestowing upon him the whole of New Netherland, and that part of Connecticut lying west of the Connecticut River. That he had no right or title in this property disturbed him little, he believing, with other monarchs of that time, that might made right. The King had previously granted to the Earl of Sterling the whole of Long Island; in order to consolidate his possessions, James bought this of him for three hundred pounds, and then arranged to send an expedition to take formal possession of all his new territory. The utter uselessness of resistance, notwithstanding the amount of work and time that had been spent upon the fort and palisades, was apparent to the Governor's Council and the Burgomasters, even if not to the Governor himself. In vain Peter Stuyvesant stormed around on his wooden leg, endeavoring to infuse his own courage into the others. He finally, however, was compelled to yield to necessity, and on August 26, 1664, the capitulation was formally agreed upon, New Am-

sterdam thenceforth becoming (except for a
short period when, in 1673, the Dutch retook
the city and held it for about a year) known
as New York. The terms of surrender were
most favorable, it being agreed that the West
Indies Company should enjoy all their "fast
property" except forts, etc. ; the then magistrates were continued in office until future
election by the people ; the Dutch inhabitants
were confirmed in their property and liberties.
There seems little question but that the people
generally felt that the change of government
would be for their ultimate good. At any
rate, they accepted the situation gracefully,
for a few months after the capitulation the
magistrates (being the same who had been in
office at the time of the surrender) sent the
following petition : [1]

"To His Royal Highness The Duke of York,
by the Grace of God, our most Gracious Lord,
Greeting."

"It hath pleased God to bring us under
your R. H's obediance, wherein we promise
to conduct ourselves as good subjects are
bound to do, deeming ourselves fortunate
that His Highness hath provided us with so
gentle, wise, and intelligent a gentleman for
Governor as the Hon. Col. Richard Nichols,
confident and assured *that under the wings
of this valiant gentleman we shall bloom and
grow like the Cedar of Lebanon.*"

Assuming that this gracious acceptance of the inevitable, in all the rhetorical splendor of its mixed metaphor, must soften his heart, they at once proceed to request further rights and privileges, and pray to be relieved from certain onerous imposts and burdens for five or six years.

"Doubting not but His Royal Highness will at the close of these years learn with hearty delight the advancement of this Province, even to a place from which your Royal Highness shall come to derive great revenue, being then peopled with thousands of families, and having great trade by sea from New England and other places out of Europe, Africa or America."

Certainly these Burgomasters, with their prophetic souls, could not be accused of any old-fashioned ideas as to loyalty and allegiance to their past, for in the very next year, in the record of the "proceedings of the Burgomasters and Schepens," under date of June 24, 1665, it is recorded: "This day, after the usual ringing of the city-hall bell three times, is published a certain proclamation regarding the confiscation of the West India Co's effects, in consequence of the Company inflicting all sorts of injury on His Royal Majesty's subjects." Thus passed away the last rights of the West India Company.

In 1672, war having been declared by England against Holland, a Dutch fleet appeared in the harbor of New York, and recaptured the city on August 9, 1673. The name was then changed to New Orange. Only for a short period, however, were the Dutch allowed to retain possession, for the next year a treaty of peace was signed between the parent countries, by the terms of which Surinam was given to the Dutch as an equivalent for New York !! The city was restored to the English, November 10, 1674, and the name changed back to New York. Under the sway of the English, increased prosperity came to the city. Among the privileges granted was a monopoly in the bolting of flour and in the exportation of sea-biscuit and flour. The importance of this monopoly, which lasted until 1694, can hardly be over-estimated, since it gave New York a commercial importance which it has never since lost. In 1686, under Governor Dongan, a charter was granted to the city, which still forms the basis of its municipal rights and privileges. At the same time a new seal was given which, with the substitution of an eagle for a crown and a sailor for one of the Indians, is virtually the present seal of the city. This seal retained the beaver from the old seal of 1623, emblematic of the city's commercial beginning, and added to it the flour-barrel and the arms of a wind-mill, as tokens of the prosperity which had come to it from the Bolting Act.

Interesting as it would be to follow the history of the city and its gradual progress towards its present condition, space compels us to confine ourselves more especially to those events and changes which show the evolution of the Bowling Green and its immediate neighborhood. The lower part of Broadway, facing Bowling Green, in common with that upon the east-side, was simply designated as ''The Market-field.'' Afterwards, it received the name of the ''Heere Straat,'' or principal street, and later the name ''Broad Way.'' Grants of lots were first made, and deeds given, in 1642. Until then settlers had been allowed to occupy land as they saw fit, and lines and boundaries were established by chance, or according to each one's own sweet will.

In 1643, the first lot granted on ''De Heere Straat'' was deeded to Martin Cregier. It was thus described (translated from the Dutch) :[8]

''Grant to Marten Cregier, 1643. Lot for a house and garden lying north of the Fort, extending from the house, about west, nine rods two feet ; towards the fort, south, six rods nine feet. Again about east, with a great out-point, fourteen rods six feet ; further, to the place of beginning, four rods five feet. Amounting, in an uneven, four-sided figure, to eighty-six rods three feet.'' This lot is now known as numbers 9 and 11 Broadway, being part of the land upon which the Bowl-ing Green Offices are built.

The city fathers, in their later attempt to lay out the city, and to fix lines and boundaries, in April, 1744, "Ordered: That the owners of the houses between Mr. Chambers and Mr. De-peysters corner house, by the Bowling Green, have liberty to range their fronts in such manner as the Alderman and Assistant of the West Ward may think proper." And again, in May of the next year, they

" Ordered: That a straight line be drawn from the south corner of the house of Mr. Augustus Jay, now in the occupation of Peter Warren, Esquire, to the north Corner of the house of Archibald Kennedy, fronting the Bowling Green in the Broad Way, and that Mr. William Smith, who is now about to build a house (and all other persons who shall build between the two houses) lay their foundations and build conformably to the aforesaid straight line."

The liberty given to the owners of the houses by the ordinance of 1744, " to range their fronts " as might be thought proper, was so thoroughly availed of that even until the present time, one hundred and fifty years af-ter, no attention has been paid to the later order of 1745, for the buildings pulled down in 1895, to make room for the new Bowling Green Offices, were very far from being on a line, and the few buildings still remaining to the north, towards Morris Street, do not even yet front on a straight line. A view taken in 1835, shows the projecting edges of the houses. A map of the city in 1695, shows that the waters of the North River came beyond the present eastern side of Greenwich Street. A later map shows how the city has been gradually extended, the dotted lines marking the water-line at various periods.

In 1723, the city offered for sale the lands between high and low-water mark, "from the house of Mr. Gaasbeck near the fort to the green trees, commonly called the locust trees, near the English Church," [18] or from the present Battery to Rector Street. In 1729, it was ordered: "For the better utility of trade and commerce, and increasing the buildings within the city, and improving the revenue of the corporation," that two streets should be surveyed and laid out along the Hudson River, one street of forty feet in width at high-water mark, and the other of thirty feet in width at low-water mark; the high-water mark to be the centre of one street, and the low-water mark to be the centre of the other." These streets are the present Greenwich and Washington Streets, the former deriving its name from its being an extension of a lane which led to Greenwich Village. Notwithstanding the "order," it was some years before anything was done towards filling in the land and opening these streets, for on a map as late as 1755, these streets are not shown as existing at their southern end.

In March, 1732, the then city fathers "

"Resolved, that this Corporation will lease a piece of land lying at the lower end of Broadway, fronting to the Fort, to some of the inhabitants of the said Broadway, in order to be inclosed to make a Bowling-Green thereof, with walks therein, for the beauty and ornament of said street, as well as for the recreation and delight of the inhabitants of the city, leaving the Street on each side thereof 50 ft. in breadth."

Three public-spirited and sport-loving citizens, John Chambers, Peter Bayard, and Peter Jay,—may their names be placed upon the roll of the worthy,—hired, in accordance with this resolution, this ground, theretofore called "The Plaine," and later, "The Parade," for a term of eleven years, at the enormous rent of one peppercorn per annum, and prepared it for the sport of bowls. Let us hope they did not charge too much per game to recoup themselves. As this lease neared its termination, it was ordered that it be renewed for eleven years, on payment of twenty shillings per annum, the lessees being John Chambers, Colonel Phillipse, and John Roosevelt. We are not told what happened at the expiration of this lease, whether they demanded a reduction of rent, and failing to obtain it abandoned the Green, or whether other sports became the fad of the ultra-fashionables, whose houses then surrounded the Green.

In a map of 1763, we find Greenwich Street has been opened, the Bowling Green being then laid down in the shape of a triangle. The land beside the Fort, on the east and west side, was anciently called "T' Marckvelt," or "The Market-field," from its vicinity to the markets then held on the "Plaine," or Bowling Green. The portion on the east is now Whitehall Street. The name "Market-field," however, remains in connection with the small street originally running from Whitehall to Broad, formerly called "Petticoat Lane," a part of which has since been obliterated to make room for the present Produce Exchange. The name "Whitehall" originated in a large storehouse on the corner of Whitehall and State Streets, built by Peter Stuyvesant, afterwards falling into the hands of Governor Dongan, who named it the "White Hall." This subsequently, for a little while, became the custom-house of the city, which later was moved to number 1 Broadway."

This plot of land, 1 Broadway, had originally been owned by a widow, Annetje Kocks. In 1760, Captain Kennedy, afterwards Earl of Cassilis, built on this corner a mansion, which was destined to be famous for many years. The garden in its rear extended to the Hudson River. Captain Kennedy, returning to England prior to the Revolution, left the property to his son Robert, from whom it passed to the late Nathaniel Prime, a leading banker of the city. In the spring of 1776, General Lee, and afterward General Putnam, occupied this house as their headquarters, and, for a time, Washington." During the occupancy of the city by the English, Sir Guy Carleton and other British officers lived here. Mr. Isaac Sears, one of the prominent "Liberty Boys," lived in it subsequent to the Revolution. He was commonly called "King Sears," and his daughters "The Princesses." Afterward, it was taken by Mrs. Graham for a girls' school, and later was known as the best boarding-house in the city. For many years it was called the Washington Inn. In 1882, it was torn down, and the present structure known as the Washington Building was erected by Cyrus Field, to whose perseverance and skill was due the laying of the first Atlantic cable. After the land at the rear of these houses was extended, a house was built in what had been the garden of the Kennedy house, in which Robert Fulton, the inventor of the steamboat, lived and died. At number 3 Broadway, John Watts, one of the Governor's Council, lived;

his daughter was the wife of Archibald Kennedy.[14]

Next to this was the property of Martin Cregier, already referred to. This same Martin Cregier was a notable citizen. He was by turns an Indian trader, sloop owner, and master. In 1648, he was appointed one of the first four Fire Wardens. He commanded an expedition against the Swedes on the Delaware River, and, in 1663, against the Esopus Indians.[16] He was Captain of the "Burghery," or citizens' company, in all of which occupations he must have been successful, for, in 1659, we find he built upon his lot a tavern, which soon became a place of fashionable resort, the Delmonico or Waldorf-Astoria of the time. Fortune favored him, as before, for, in 1673, during the temporary recapture of the city by the Dutch, at a meeting of the "Valiant Council of War," an order was passed calling for the nomination of six persons as Burgomasters. "To wit : from the *Wealthiest* Inhabitants and those only who are of the Reformed Christian Religion." Cregier, fulfilling all these requirements, was duly elected, further proving that tavern-keeping was equally prosperous then as now, and not inconsistent with religious profession. In 1654, we find that a new seal having been granted to the city, it was publicly delivered December 8, by the Director to Martin Cregier, presiding Burgomaster. (The salary of Burgomaster was three hundred and fifty guilders—when it was paid!) [16] In 1674, we find him superintending the fortifications, in anticipation of the coming of the English force. Whether his Dutch blood resented the final capture of the city by the English, or whether new and more modern taverns eclipsed his own and took his custom, we are not told; but we find that later he abandoned New York, and with his family moved to the banks of the Mohawk, then on the very frontiers, where he died, in 1713, nearly a century old.

As Cregier's Tavern became old and behind the times, a new building was erected, which afterward bore the name of "King's Arms Tavern," and at the time of the Revolution was familiarly called "Burns' Coffee House." It was among the few buildings that escaped the fires of 1776 and 1845. As late as 1860, the same building was still standing, bearing the title of "The Atlantic Garden." This is remarkable as being only the second structure to occupy the site since the foundation of the city. Almost until the present time the garden connected with this property has furnished a place for popular amusement. In Parker's *Post Boy* of May 27, 1762, appears the following notice:

"This is to give Notice, to all Gentlemen and Ladies, Lovers and Encouragers of Musick. That this day will be opened, by Messrs. Leonard & Dienval, Musick Masters, of this city, at Mr. Burnes' Room, near the Battery, a public and weekly Concert of Musick. Tickets, four shillings."

"N. B. The concert is to begin exactly at 8 o'clock, and end at ten, on account of the coolness of the evening. No Body will be admitted without tickets, nor no money will be taken at the door."

In the next year, 1763, a Mrs. Steel, who had kept the King's Arms Tavern in Broad Street (the most noted tavern in the city for thirty years), removed to this house, carrying with her the name of her old place. The announcement is thus made in the *Post Boy:* "Mrs. Steel, Takes this method to acquaint her Friends and Customers, That the King's Arms Tavern, which she formerly kept opposite the Exchange, she hath now removed into Broadway (the lower end opposite the Fort), a more commodious house, where she will not only have it in her power to accommodate gentlemen with conveniences requisite as a tavern, but also, with genteel lodging apartments, which she doubts not will give satisfaction to every one who will be pleased to give her that honour."

Mrs. Steel's move must have been an unfortunate one, for, in 1765, we find Burns again in control (perhaps he married the widow), and from then on the place seems to have been known as "Burns' Coffee House."

On October 31, 1765, a meeting of the merchants of the city was called at Burns' Coffee House, in order to express their opposition to the Stamp Act.　Here they passed and signed the first non-importation agreement of the colonies.　Over two hundred merchants signed the resolutions, thus securing for New York the credit of being the first to sacrifice its commercial interests to the cause of liberty. At this meeting a non-importation association was also organized, and a committee appointed to correspond with the other colonies, with a view to the universal adoption of similar measures.　In the morning of the next day, November 1, when the Stamp Act was to go into effect, handbills mysteriously appeared throughout the city, forbidding any one, at his peril, to use the stamped paper.

In the evening two companies, largely composed of the Sons of Liberty, whose headquarters were at Burns' Coffee House, appeared in the streets.　The first company proceeded to the "fields," or common (City Hall Park), where they erected a gallows and suspended thereon an effigy of Lieutenant-Governor Colden, with the stamped paper in his hand, a drum at his back, and by his side they hung an effigy of the devil with a boot in his hand. The other company, with another effigy of

Colden seated in a chair, broke open his stable, and taking out his chariot placed the effigy in it, and then, joining the other company, both proceeded to the fort, strictest orders having been given that not a word should be spoken or a stone thrown. On arriving at the Bowling Green, they found the soldiers drawn up on the ramparts of the fort, and the muzzles of the cannon pointed toward them. General Gage, who was then the British commander, prudently refrained from firing upon the mob, knowing well that the first volley would be followed by the instant destruction of the Fort. The people having been refused admission to the Fort, tore down the wooden fence about the Bowling Green, kindled a fire there, and burned the carriage, gallows, effigies, and all.

The odious Stamp Act was finally repealed on February 20, 1766. This action of the ministry was received with the wildest enthusiasm. The whole city was illuminated, special bonfires being kindled on the Bowling Green. For a time this action of the home government aroused the enthusiasm of the populace, and on June 23, another meeting was held at Burns' Coffee House, petitioning the Assembly to erect a statue in honor of William Pitt, and also an equestrian statue of George the Third. On August 21, 1770, the statue of George the Third having arrived

Statue of George the Third

from England, it was placed in the centre of Bowling Green amid the general acclamation of the people. In November, it was ordered "That a temporary fence be forthwith made around the Bowling Green, of posts and rails not to exceed five rails high." The following year, 1771, it was ordered: "Whereas the General Assembly of this Province have been at the great expense of sending for an equestrian statue of his present majesty [George III.], and erected the same on the Bowling Green, before his majesty's fort in this city, and this Board, conceiving, that unless the said Green be fenced in, the same will very soon became a receptacle for all the filth and dirt of the neighborhood, in order to prevent which, it is ordered that the same be fenced with iron rails, in a stone foundation, at an expense of £800." This fence and the original stones still surround the Green, the crowns which originally ornamented the tops of the pillars having been broken off.

At the breaking out of the Revolution, to celebrate the news of the Declaration of Independence, this statue was dragged from its pedestal, and drawn through the streets. It was then sent to Litchfield, the residence of Oliver Wolcott, Governor of Connecticut, by whose wife and daughter it was run into 42,000 bullets, "to assimilate with the brains of the adversary." Subsequently, during the invasion of Connecticut by Governor Tryon, over four hundred British soldiers were killed, probably by this very lead. The pedestal of the statue remained standing for some time longer, as is shown in a contemporaneous print of the Bowling Green at the time of the Revolution.

On August 26, 1776, the city was captured by the English. Shortly after the occupancy of the British a great fire occurred, destroying four hundred and ninety-two houses, nearly one eighth of the entire city. The houses at the lower end of Broadway, facing Bowling Green on the west side, were saved.

The Green again welcomed the joyous and exultant crowds who there gathered to see the final evacuation of the city by the British on November 25, 1783. Before leaving, the English had nailed their defeated colors to the flag-pole which stood near, and in the hope of preventing the immediate raising of the stars and stripes, had thoroughly greased the pole. Captain John Van Arsdale, however, quickly managed to climb the pole, and in sight of the departing troops flung our flag to the breeze. Ever since then it has been the custom for one of his descendants, on the morning of Evacuation Day, to raise the flag on the present liberty pole in the park.

A map of Brooklyn, drawn by General Jeremiah Johnson about this time, is curious,

Bowling
Green
Leased to
Chan=
cellor
Livingston

as indicating a fact which probably is unknown to most New Yorkers: that Governor's Island was at one time used as a race-track.

On the adoption of the new constitution by the State of New York, the event was celebrated by a "wonderful" procession, which was reviewed by Washington and other notables, from the ramparts of the Fort, as it circled around the Bowling Green. One of the principal floats in this procession was an enormous ship named *Hamilton*, which at the close of the procession was deposited in the Green. This required, in 1789, the appointment of a committee "to remove the Federal Ship out of the Bowling Green, to have the fence repaired, and to let out the Bowling Green."

Three years before this, in 1786, there is recorded a request of Mr. Daniel Ludlow.

"That he may be permitted to have the care and use of the Bowling Green, at the lower end of the Broad Way, for two years, he being willing, at his own expense, to manure the ground, and sow the same with proper grass seed, and have it well laid down as a green; and a request of Mr. Chancellor Livingston, that the direction and use of the said Bowling Green may be granted to him, were respectively read. *Ordered*, That the direction and use of the said Bowling Green, be granted to Mr. Chancellor Livingston, on the terms offered by Mr. Ludlow." Evidently, Mr. Chancellor Livingston had "a pull."

In 1791, the street committee reported "That in their opinion the Bowling Green, in front of the Government House, ought to be preserved, and that it will be necessary the fence should be raised in proportion to the regulation of Broadway. Agreed to." In 1795, it was "*Ordered,*—that the inclosed ground, commonly called the Bowling Green, in front of the Government House, be appropriated to the use of the Governor, for the time being." Notwithstanding the fact that it had been thus set aside for the use of the Governor, in this same year, on July 18, the sanctity of the Green was invaded by a tumultuous crowd of citizens who had just held a public meeting to express their opposition to the treaty with England, which had recently been concluded by John Jay. At this meeting, which had been addressed by Aaron Burr and Chancellor Livingston, some one moved that they should adjourn to the Bowling Green and burn the treaty. This was done, the band playing the "Carmagnole,"—the French and American flags being bound together,—the treaty having been considered by many as a repudiation of our indebtedness to France.

The Governor did not seem to appreciate the advantages of the Bowling Green, or perhaps he was not able to preserve its privacy, for, in

1798, we find that it was ordered "That Mr. John Rogers may have the use of the Bowling Green, on condition that he keep it in good order, and suffer no creatures to run in it."

In a map of 1797, the Bowling Green has assumed its present shape, the fort has disappeared, the Government House, above referred to, occupying its site, the Battery has been extended, but even yet the "order" given seventy years before for the laying out of additional streets, had not been complied with except as to Greenwich Street, showing that municipal progress was not much more rapid at that time than now. The destruction of the Fort seems to have been determined upon in 1789, when, by act of the Legislature, "The ground at the Fort and the Battery was reserved for the public use and for continuing the Broad Way through to the river." This last was never done.

In 1790, it was "Ordered, that Messrs. Torboss, Van Zant and George Janeway, be appointed commissioners to superintend the taking down the stone and removing the earth of the Fort." The earth thus removed was used to enlarge the area of the Battery "from Eli's corner to the Flat Rock." When the Fort was torn down, a vault, which had been sealed up under the chapel, was uncovered. In this were the remains of Lord Bellamont, members of his family, and some others.

Lord Bellamont's family was distinguished by the silver plates bearing the family escutcheon, let into the lead coffins. The coffins and bones were buried in an unmarked grave in St. Paul's churchyard. Mr. Van Zant, one of the commissioners, secured the silver plates, intending to preserve them, but after his death they were converted into spoons.

The Battery, which has retained nothing whatever suggestive of its warlike origin except the name, owes its beginning to the following order. In 1693, the then Governor made the following proclamation:

"Whereas there is actual warr between our Sovereign Lord and Lady the King and Queen, and the French King; and I am informed of a Squadron of Ships and land forces, intended from France to invade this Citty and Province; and whereas, for the safety and preservation thereof, I finde itt of absolute necessity to make a platforme upon the outmost pointe of rocks under the Fort, whereon I intend to build a battery to command both rivers; I have therefore thought fitte, and doe hereby require you, the Mayor, Recorder and Aldermen of the Citty of New York and Manning and Barnes Island, to cut down 86 cordes of stockades, of 12 feet in length, and to have them in readiness to be conveyed to New York.

(Signed) "BENJ. FLETCHER."

The rocks upon which the Battery was built were called Capske Rocks. These works were then known as the Whitehall Battery, and from this time on, until the close of the Revolutionary War, various additions were made thereto, and later, somewhere about the beginning of the present century, there was built what was known as the Southwest Battery, some three hundred feet or more from the shore, the approach to which was by means of a bridge with a draw. This later was called "Castle Clinton." In the year 1822, upon the Federal government taking possession of Governor's Island, Castle Clinton was ceded to the city. It was then proposed that this and the former Battery, and the grounds included between, should be made into a public park, Castle Clinton being turned into a public assembly-room, and called Castle Garden, afterwards to be made famous by Jenny Lind's first concert, September 12, 1850.

On Lafayette's return to America, in 1824, "a splendid fête and gala was given to him at Castle Garden, on September 14, which for grandeur, expense, and entire effect was never before witnessed in this country. About six thousand persons were assembled in that immense area, and the evening being clear and calm, the whole passed off happily, owing to the excellent arrangements of the committee."[18]

On December 5, 1851, the Hungarian hero, Louis Kossuth, arrived, and was received at Castle Garden, after which he was escorted to his hotel by a procession, which for years was famous for its size and enthusiasm. For nearly forty years, beginning in 1855, this building was used as the emigrants' landing-place and depot, and later was transformed into a public aquarium.

For many years the Battery was the city's parade-ground. Here, in the heyday of their popularity, the Pulaski Cadets, the Light Guard, the red-coated City Guards, and the Tompkins Blues went through their elaborate manœuvres, before the admiring gaze of the citizens grouped in surrounding windows and on the walks. Here, also, the Blue Stockings and the Red Stockings vied for championship in the national game.

In his Diary, Philip Hone writes:

"*April 15, 1834.*—This was the day of the Great Fête at Castle Garden, to celebrate the triumph gained by the Whig Party in the late Charter election in this city, and it went off gloriously. Tables were spread in a double row within the outer circumference. Three pipes of wine and 40 barrels of beer were placed in the centre under an awning, and served out during the repast." [19]

"*Monday, October the 27th, 1834.*—The Jackson men marched down to Castle Garden, where a feast (not of reason) was prepared, and a flow of whiskey (not of soul) was served out gratuitously to the well drilled troops of the Regency. They fired guns and exhibited fire works, and all in the way of rejoicing for victories *not* won, or rather 'to keep their spirits up by pouring spirits down.'"[20]

"*April the 10th, 1835.*—The weather being fine and spring-like, I walked for an hour with my wife on the battery. Strange as it is, I do not think that either of us had done such a thing in the last seven years, and what a wonderful spot it is. The grounds are in fine order. The noble bay, with the opposite shores of New Jersey, Staten and Long Islands, vessels of every description, from the noble, well-appointed Liverpool packet, to the little market craft and steamers arriving from every point, give life and animation to a prospect unexcelled by any city in the world. It would be well worth travelling 100 miles out of one's way in a foreign country to get a sight of, and yet we citizens of New York, who have it all under our noses seldom enjoy it. Like all other enjoyments, it loses its value from being too easily obtained."[21]

In a very rare book of letters, written in 1793, by Governor Drayton, of Carolina, he writes: "At the lower end of Broadway is the Battery, and public parade; . . . between the guns and the water is a public

walk, made by a gentle decline from the plat-
form; . . . some little distance behind
the guns two rows of elm trees are planted;
which in a short time will afford an agreeable
shade; . . . the back part of the ground
is laid out in smaller walks, terraces, and a
bowling green."

"Overlooking this prospect, is the Government House; plac'd upon an handsome elevation, and fronting Broadway, having before it
an elegant elliptical approach, round an area of
near an acre of ground, enclosed by an iron rail-
ing. In the midst of this is a pedastal, which formerly was pressed by a leaden equestrian statue
of the King of Great Britain; but having been
dismantled of that, for the use of the continental army, it now remains ready, in due time I
hope, to receive the statue of the President of
the United States of America. When that period shall arrive, in addition to the many daily
occurrences which lead the mind of the pas-
senger to pensive reflection; this monument
of his country's gratitude shall call his attention; and while deeds of former times, shall
pass in sweet review before him, the tear
shall lament the loss of an hero—but the heart
collected within itself, shall urge him by so
bright an example, to call forth his powers
and to pursue the steps of virtue and of
honor."

" . . . The Government House is two

stories high. Projecting before it is a portico, covered by a pediment; upon which is superbly carved in basso relievo, the arms of the State, supported by justice and liberty, as large as life. The arms and figures are white, placed in a blue field; and the pediment is supported by four white pillars of the Ionic order, which are the height of both stories."

The Government House herein referred to was built upon a part of the land occupied by the Fort. As we have already seen, it was in 1790 that the Fort was taken down, and shortly afterward this house was erected for the use of Washington. Afterward, Governors Clinton and Jay both lived in it, and at one time it was used as a Custom-House.[22]

We can find no record showing when the Fort and the adjacent land passed from under the control of the City to that of the Province, and thence to the State. It was by an act of the Legislature, not of the City Council, that, in 1790, the Fort was destroyed and the Government House built. On May 26, 1812, an act was passed:

"Be it enacted by the people of the State of New York, represented in Senate and Assembly, that the Comptroller is hereby authorized to sell and convey in fee simple, all the right, title and interest of the people of this state in and to the Government House and the grounds adjoining, in the city of New York, to the mayor, aldermen and commonalty of the said city, for a sum not less than fifty thousand dollars, and to receive in payment therefor, the bond of the said mayor, aldermen and commonalty, payable in ten years, with interest annually, at the rate of six per centum:

"*Provided always*, That the said corporation shall not have the right of selling the said grounds for the erection of private buildings, or other individual purposes."

The city authorities evidently did not propose to be limited in their rights, nor to pay a round sum of money for land which they could not realize upon, however cheap it might seem. They refused to avail themselves of the option to purchase, so on April 13, 1813, another act was passed: "Be it further enacted, That the proviso to the enacting clause of the act entitled 'An act to authorize the sale of certain public property in the city of New York,' passed the 26th of May 1812, be and the same is hereby repealed, and that if the mayor, aldermen and commonalty of New York shall not, by the first day of November next, purchase the Government House and lands adjoining, then the authority given to the comptroller in and by said act to sell the said house and land shall cease."

This threat seems to have supplied the necessary fillip, and suggested a chance for speculation, for under date of August 2, 1813, the Comptroller of the State "conveyed to the said Mayor, &c., all the certain messuage and lot of ground situate in the First Ward of the city of New York, commonly known by the name of the Government House and lot. Subject to a lease of the Government House to DeWitt Clinton and others, made pursuant to section 34 of the act of 29 March, 1809, which does not expire until the 1st of May, 1815." As soon as the lease expired, the city hastened to "bag its profit," selling the land and giving title thereto on June 19, 1815, for about double what they were under bond to pay, and before they had paid out anything whatever. Some time during this year the Government House is said to have been destroyed by fire.

The land facing on the Green was sold in seven parcels or lots, each being about thirty-one feet front and one hundred and thirty feet in depth, except the one on the northeast, at the corner of Whitehall Street, which was only four feet on the front and twenty-three feet wide in the rear. The original grantees were:

Lot 1. (*Northwest corner.*)

Deeded to Noah Brown.

1825 to 1861, owned by Stephen Whitney.

1888 " present, " " U. S. Trust Company.

Lot. 2. Deeded to Abijah Weston.

1834 to 1887, owned by Elisha Riggs.

1887 " present, " " J. L. Cadwalader.

Original
Grantees

Lot 3.   Deeded to Elbert Anderson.
1821 to 1829,   owned by Samuel Ward, Jr.
1829 " 1853,   "   " Andrew Foster.
1854 " present, "   " Cornelius Vander-
    bilt, *et al.*
Lot 4.   Deeded to Elbert Anderson.
1823 to 1829, owned by Herman Le Roy.
1829 " 1852,   "   " Lewis Curtis.
1862 " present, "   " A. Hemenway, *et al.*,
    trustees, etc.
Lot 5.   Deeded to James Byers.
1838 to 1883,   owned by Ferdinand Suydam,
    et al., trustees, etc.
1883 to present, owned by Theodore Chiches-
    ter.
Lot 6.   Deeded to Peter Remsen.
1840 to 1855,   owned by W. E. Wilmerding.
1871 " present,   "   " Herman C. Von Post.
Lot 7.   (*Northeast corner.*)
    Deeded to John Hone.
Hone was the only original owner who retained his lot more than a year or so. He
sold it in 1860 to W. B. Cooper, in whose family it still remains.

From the earliest days of the city, when the
Governor lived within the Fort, later, when
the Government House occupied this same
site, and afterwards, when this land became
private property, this locality, and the immediate neighborhood, was the most select and
fashionable part of the city. As the natural

growth of the city and the encroachment of business drove private residences farther and farther northward, this particular row of houses facing the Green preserved their individual characteristics, and were used as dwellings. They still retain their exterior appearance, though they have ceased to be so used. They are now occupied by the offices of the large foreign steamship companies, which has given them the name of "Steamship Row." Some years ago it was ordered by Congress that this land should be bought and the United States Custom-House be built here. Opposition and litigation have until now prevented, but at last it seems likely that this project will be accomplished, and this land, which had always been public property until 1815, and upon which the old Custom-House had been for a time, will again become the property of the public, and in place of a Fort—emblem of strife and distrust among nations—a Custom-House, suggestive of peaceful intercourse and friendly commerce, will be built, worthy of the nation and of the city.

The land on the east of the Green, where the Produce Exchange now stands, was first granted to individuals about 1646. Among the first owners were Jonas Barteltzen and Frerick Arenzen. The latter owned the land on the southwest corner of Whitehall and what was then Marketfield Streets. Allard Anthony, one of the most prominent citizens of his day, lived on the opposite corner. Roelof Jansen Haas owned the land to the corner of Beaver Street." The southern portion of the Produce Exchange land was forfeited to the people of the State at the time of the Revolution, by the attainders of Beverly Robinson and Frederick Philipse. The Legislature, on May 12, 1784, passed "An Act for the speedy sale of the confiscated and forfeited estates within this State." Isaac Stoutenburg and Philip Van Cortlandt, the commissioners appointed under this act, sold the land. In 1880, the Legislature passed a special act authorizing the closing up of Marketfield Street, and deeding it to the Produce Exchange.

We have already referred to some of the earlier occupants of the properties now known as numbers 1 to 11 Broadway. In the house standing on what is now 9 Broadway, Benedict Arnold, after the capture of André and the exposure of his treachery, had his quarters." It was while here that Sergeant John Champe attempted to capture him. The garden at the rear of the house sloped down to the river, and a party of patriots were to land here from a boat, and, having secured, carry him away. The very day of the attempt Arnold moved his quarters, it was never known whether simply by accident, or from disclosure of the plot. Washington Irving lived around the corner, on State Street, and near him Mr. Howland, long one of the most prominent shipping-merchants of the city.[26] James K. Paulding, a descendant of one of the captors of Major André, and who afterward became Secretary of the Navy under Van Buren, one of the authors of *Salmagundi*, lived on the same block, at 29 Whitehall Street.

While all these changes have been going on around it, the Green has quietly, and with the proud conservatism of age, preserved its own dignified existence. Always ready to give itself to the public, whether for play or rest, in peace or war, it has been the centre of the busy life of the village, of the fashionable life of the town, and now of the commercial activity of the city. The Produce Exchange, controlling the grain trade of a continent, looks down upon it. The offices of the largest steamship companies of the world surround it. The Custom-House, registering the commerce of the Western Hemisphere, will face it. Some of the greatest modern office buildings, overtopping the spire of "Old Trinity," hem it in. Broadway, the longest street in the world, starts from its oval. In this year of grace, 1898, New York has greatly enlarged its borders; the city of Brooklyn and many of the surrounding townships having united in the one city now called colloquially "Greater New York." Of this new city our little friend, the Bowling Green, has become the heart.   It is the geographical centre of the enlarged metropolis.

REFERENCES.

1. PETER FAUCONNIER'S *Survey Book*, 1715–34.
2. *Documents relating to Colonial History of New York* (edited by E. B. O'Callaghan), i., p. 74.
3. BOOTH'S *History of New York*, p. 122.
4. *Records of New Amsterdam*, i., p. 65.
5. *Ibid.*, i., p. 90.
6. *Ibid.*
7. VALENTINE'S *History*, p. 161.
8. VALENTINE'S *Manual*, 1857, p. 498.
9. English Records.
10. VALENTINE'S *History*, p. 287.
11. English Records.
12. VALENTINE'S *History*, p. 285.
13. BOOTH'S *History*, p. 490.
14. LAMB'S *History*, p. 98.
15. VALENTINE'S *History*, p. 98.
16. VALENTINE'S *Manual*, 1856, p. 381.
17. English Records, 1693.
18. VALENTINE'S *Manual*, 1853, p. 467.
19. PHILIP HONE'S *Diary*, p. 101.
20. *Ibid.*, p. 115.
21. *Ibid.*, p. 137.
22. WASHINGTON IRVING, *Salmagundi*, p. 319. N. Y., 1897.
23. VALENTINE'S *History*, pp. 96, 127.
24. BOOTH'S *History*, p. 562.
25. WILSON'S *History of New York*, 1893.

NEW AMSTERDAM FAMILY NAMES
AND THEIR ORIGIN

Half Moon Series

Published in the Interest of the New York
City History Club.

VOLUME II.   NUMBER VI.

NEW AMSTERDAM FAMILY NAMES AND THEIR ORIGIN.

By BERTHOLD FERNOW.

Nomen=
clature in
Greece
and
Rome

"WHAT 'S in a name?" and "That
which we call a rose, by any
other name would smell as sweet," said
Shakespeare, three hundred years ago, *mais
nous avons changé tout cela*, and to-day we are
more or less proud of the name derived from
our forefathers, no matter how it was first
acquired.

The study of proper names of persons and
places is not only a matter of curious interest,
but also of some historical importance, when
we look into the names of the people who
were the first settlers of New Netherland.
For in many cases we learn thereby where
they came from, although, to a great extent,
they were not far above the savages, whose
system of nomenclature was only changed
by the rite of Christian baptism, giving each
child a *permanent* "call-name," to which the

father's name was added. This did away with the change of appellation which took place in, say, a Mohawk Indian's name at different periods of his life. Born on a stormy day, the babe would be called "Lightning," or "Thunder," or "Rain," and the boy was known as such until he accomplished his first daring feat in the hunting-field or the chase, by which he possibly acquired the name of "Cinnamon Bear," because he had killed one. Then he went out as a warrior, killed and scalped a noted enemy, and was henceforth, to the end of his life, known as "He who scalped Tom Noddy." To all was added the totem name,—the name of the clan to which the youth belonged,—in reality a family name, to wit, the Bear, the Turtle, the Wolf, etc. We find something similar in the Greece and Rome of antiquity, after social institutions had become so permanent that male kinship and paternity were recognized, for then the custom of patronymics, differing from the Mohawk totem only by not being tattooed on the bearer's breast, was introduced. The totem name became a gentile name, and in Greece gave place to a local one, derived from the "$\delta\acute{\eta}\mu\eta$": thus, a Greek is called Thukydides, a name given him after his grandfather; he is the son of Olorus of the deme of Halimusia; while a Roman has received at his birth the name of Marcus, he belongs to the

Tullian clan, and is therefore entitled to the name of Tullius; and because he requires a special designation, to distinguish him from a cousin or uncle, he becomes known as Cicero, from the large pea-shaped wart on his nose.

This system of nomenclature answered the purposes of Greek and Roman civilization. Among the Teutonic races, the earliest and most widely spread class and family names were totemistic, and frequently derived from animals and plants. This tendency to use the objects surrounding man or his favorite occupation in the choice of a name is inherent in the human race. Up to the first quarter of this century the Jews in Prussia observed the biblical way of calling themselves Isaac, the son of Abraham, or Abrahamson, and Isaac's son Moses became Moses Isaacson, so that great confusion, especially in legal cases, occurred; to obviate this the government ordered them to adopt permanent family names. Then, as a sarcastic old gentlemen of the writer's acquaintance used to say, "the characteristics of the men came out": the poetically inclined called themselves after flowers, as Lilienthal, Rosenthal, Rosenberg (dale of lilies, of roses, hill of roses) ; the ferocious took the name of wild beasts, as Wolf, Bear, Fox, combining them also with the dale or hill or stone, whence we have the names Loewenthal,

Loewenstein, Loewenberg (lion's dale, stone, hill). The Hebrew, fond of money and other values, became a Silverstein, Goldstein, Rubinstein ; a small number adopted the names of their trades and occupations, as Schneider (tailor), Kaufman (merchant), or retained the names of their fathers, as Mosesson, Jacobson, or called themselves after the place of their birth, Berliner, Stettiner, Hamburger.

The same system as adopted by the Jews in Prussia prevailed among the early settlers of New Netherland, who added a new difficulty for the genealogist by often calling a person after the mother's baptismal name, not because it was a case of illegitimacy, but because the mother had become a widow with young children and it was easier to designate these children that way. In regard to married women among the Dutch, it must be said that only in a few instances we find the woman called by her husband's family name; she may occasionally be called Annetje *Dircks*, the wife of Dirck Smitt, but she is as often designated as Annetje *Meinders*, when, after her first husband's death she marries Abel Hardenbroeck, Meinders meaning the daughter of Meindert.

As the HALF-MOON SERIES is principally devoted to the history of Manhattan Island, the writer considers it appropriate to speak only of the names found in the Index of the lately published *Records of New Amsterdam*, and begins the inquisition into the origin of names with that of the island.

Somebody tells that Manhattan, in its various spellings, means the "Big Drunk"; because, according to Indian tradition, which, by the way, is as reliable as if graven in stone, the first meeting of red and white men resulted in the utter stupefaction of a young Indian, who courageously dared to drink the goblet filled with wine which the white men offered as a token of friendship and which the older men of his tribe had suspiciously refused. He fell on the ground, completely overpowered by the hitherto unknown beverage and the place was called the "Big Drunk," or, in colloquial Spanish (the first white men coming here having been Spaniards), *Moñado* or *Monhado*, meaning the same. This Spanish word passed, like a great many others, into the Indian dialects and is now considered an Algonquin Indian word.

In treating names of the first settlers of New Netherland, it must not be forgotten, first, that they belonged to probably almost every nationality in Europe and secondly, that during the Eighty Years' War with Spain the United Provinces had been overrun by soldiers born in every corner of the Old World, and carrying with them names of their localities.

The first name in the Index used as a patronymic is the father's baptismal name with the addition of an *s*, when a woman is to be designated, or of the syllable *sen* or *zen*, for a man, meaning Aart's or Aarend's daughter or son respectively, and had the father been an Englishman they would, in this case, have been called Arthur's or Arthurson. In the same way originated Aarnoutsen, the son of Arnold, and Abelsen (the intervening Abbesen being probably an orthographical error for Abelsen of the clerk who recorded the proceedings of the Court); and going through the whole Index we find Abrahams and Abrahamsen; Adams, Adamsen; Albers, Albertsen (also Elbert and Elbertsen); Andries, Andriesen (*Anglice,* Andrews); Anthony, Antonissen, with the Greek form of Antonides; Arians and Ariaansen, which is a misspelled Adrian; Barens, Barentsen, Bernard's daughter and son, respectively; Bartelsen, the son of Bartholomew; Bastiansen, the son of Sebastian; Carelsen, the son of Charles; Carstensen, the son of a Sleswig Christian; Caspersen and Gaspersen, son of Caspar; Claasen, son of Nicolas; Cornelissen, also Corsen, son of Cornelis, a name which is often abbreviated into Cors; Flipzen for Philipsen; Fransen, the son of Francis; Frericksen standing for Fredericksen; Gerritsen from Gerard; Gillisen, Jelissen, and Jillisen from Giles or Julius, in its French form, Jules; Hansen, the son of Johannes, in its abbreviation,

Hans; Harmensen, Harmsen, Hermsen, the son of Herman; Hendricksen, the son of Henry; Huybertsen, the son of Hubert, or, in old English spelling, Hobart; Jansen, like Hansen, a shortened Johannessen; Jochemsen, the son of Joachim; Jorissen and Juriansen, the son of George; Leendertsen, the son of Leonard; Lodewycksen, the son of Lodowyck, which is the old German form of Louis or Lewis; Paulisen, Pauluzen, and Poulissen, the son of Paul; Reinoutsen, the son of Reinold; Roelantsen, the son of Orlando or Roland; Roelofsen from Ralph, Rolph, or Rudolph; Sandersen from the Scotch form of Alexander; Stoffels and Stoffelsen, daughter and son of Christopher, in Dutch, Christoffel, and abbreviated Stoffel; Teunissen from the Dutch form of Anthony; Woutersen, the son of Walter. In all these cases the genealogist will have to discover what family names the descendants adopted.

Coming to names which are still used to-day, we have in Lysbet Ackermans the daughter or the wife of a tiller of the soil, or a husbandman. As the first English name we find Ackleton, perhaps intended for Hackleton, with the *H* dropped, and meaning a place where the people hackle, or clean, hemp and flax; another English name, that of Addison, is derived from some connection with an adze, in obsolete English, *addice*, and in Saxon, *adese*.

Jan Adely, sailor, may have been a Scandinavian, whose name, a slight corruption of the Swedish word *adelig*, (*Anglicé*, noble,) may refer to his birth; but it may also be the corrupted Dutch word *Adelaar*, the eagle. Whether Leendert (Leonard) Aerden derived his name from Mother Earth (*Aerde* in Dutch) generally, whether it came from his occupation as a worker in earth, making earthenware, or whether he came from Shakespeare's Forest of Arden, cannot be decided here. The writer suspects William Aest to have been an Englishman named East, which name the recording clerk fancifully wrote Æst. He was probably an ancestor of the still flourishing family of Ast, and if the clerk's spelling was correct according to the standard of his day, William came from Germany and was, as his name suggests, a branch of a tree. The name of Richard Airy, also an English one, explains itself.

Alders, the daughter of Aldert or Aldart: this Aldert is a baptismal name occasionally found among the Dutch of the eastern, more purely Saxon, Provinces, and means " of all," while Aris is evidently the Bible name Ares. The next name to be considered, Aldrix, is so variously spelled, *i. e.*, Alrichs, Aldrighs, Alricx, etc., that it is impossible to say to what nationality the first of this name in America belonged; but we find in Swedish the name of Alarich, the great chief of the Huns, spelled Alrik, and this fact, combined with the appearance of the first of this name in the Swedish-Dutch colony on the Delaware, points to him as a Swede.   François Allard suggests, by his baptismal name, French nationality, but we come further on to Allard Anthony, supposed to have been an Irishman; François had, therefore, only taken his father's first name. Henry and John Allen were Englishmen, deriving their patronymic from the old Norman Allan, but *allen* in Swedish means "alone."

Isaac Allerton is to-day claimed by collateral descendants as an Irishman, notwithstanding the ending of the name with the English *ton*, an abbreviation of *town*, taken from the Dutch *tuyn*, an enclosure.   All possible sources may be called upon for this name; beginning with the English *alert*, we come to the Spanish *alerto*, but the single *l* is against this supposition.   Allerton having been an Irishman, it behooves us to look for a Celtic origin, and we find that perhaps the first two syllables of the name are a contortion of the word *allod*, ancient, and the whole means "old town."   In Amy we have the old spelling of the French *ami*, friend. Appel, Appelgate (modern Applegate) explain themselves, but they may have taken their names from their native place, Appel, in the Province of Guelderland.

Asdalen;
Bancker

Asdalen suggests by its combination of the Swedish *as*, carrion, and *dalen*, the dale, or valley, a Scandinavian origin, while John Ashman's name came from the same occupation which Colonel Waring's "White Angels" now pursue. The first of the Atwater family who assumed the name took it because he was born or lived at the water, and so did the first Bach, as the name, a German one, refers to a small stream.

Backer, Baker, Becker, took their names from their occupation as bakers; Badger, if that was the name, because he was allowed to deal in grain from place to place, or if he spelled it Badgard, because he was the guardian of a bathhouse ; while Baeck had something to do with a beacon, or he may have been a very tall man, whose head was always to be seen in a crowd.

Bagyn, Baguyn : among the many religious societies of the fifteenth, sixteenth, and seventeenth centuries there was one in Flanders whose members were called Beguins, not restricted, however, by monastic vows, and our Anthony was so nicknamed because of his connection with the order. Bamboes is evidently also a nickname, perhaps given to Hermen Jacobsen of the Index, because he dealt in, or in some other way had something to do with, bamboo. Bancker is not a banker, unless we use the word in the Dutch sense of sitting long on a bench or bank.

Barfort : Webster explains *bar* as a piece of wood or iron used as an obstruction, or as the shore of a sea, and we can, by translating the other, the French, part of the name, give it the meaning of a strong bar of wood, or a fort on the shore. Bartelott is a French diminutive of Bartholomew; Barton, a town on the sea; and Barwick, a village on the sea, the syllable *wyck* having been taken into the Saxon from the Latin *vicus*.

Whether Baxter is another spelling of the Dutch word *Bakster*, a woman baker, we leave to the decision of etymologists.

The name Bayard is probably one of the oldest among the New Netherland names, but it is doubtful whether its bearers of to-day would be willing to accept the first being called by it as their ancestor. For, in the *Geste de Doon de Mayence* we read "*Renaud, li fils Aymon est en Baiart montez.*" Baiart was the war horse of Renaud, eldest son of Aimon de Dordone or Ardenne, which at a dangerous moment develops a human intelligence and awakens its master by striking the shield with its hoof, and at another time carries Renaud and his three brothers. It is not told of this first Bayard that it could bark, and yet there seems to be no other derivation of the name possible than from the Italian *baiare*, to bark, unless we go farther afield and say Bayard was one who stood around gaping, deriving it from the French *bayer*, or a crier, from the significance given to the word in the Loir et Cher ; but it is possible that the name comes from the Swedish word *Boyort, Boyert*, a species of small Dutch vessel, which appears later on as Boyer.

Beaulieu and Beauvois are distinctly French, meaning " handsome place " and " handsome sight."

Beck is the Dutch for the mouth of an animal, the English *beak*, but it may also be an abbreviation of the Dutch word *bekken*, a basin; while on the other side we have the Swedish *beck*, for pitch, and as Father Isaac Jogues of the Society of Jesus reports that when he passed through New Amsterdam on his way to France, in 1643, he found seventeen different nationalities represented here, Joannes Beck may have been a Swede, who for some reason called himself Pitch.

Beekman, or the Man of the Brook : this interpretation of the name was recognized by King James I. of England when he granted to the Reverend Mr. Beekman, grandfather of Willem, as a coat of arms a rivulet running between roses.

Been, a bone, a leg, Beer, a bear, Beetman if not a misspelled Beekman, the man of the beet, the man who has a bite or bait, Benhem, the basket home, Berck, the birch tree, Besem, the broom, need no further explanation, nor does, properly, Bestevaar, the old man, the grandfather, were it not that we have two juniors of this name; hence we must suppose that it had ceased to be a nickname and had become a well-established patronymic.

Blau, blue, Blauvelt, the blue field, may also be translated into English as foolish, false, instead of blue. Seeing how the name of Blommert is differently spelled, we must conclude that the first of the name was a florist and, therefore, was called Bloemaert. Blyenberg, or, as now spelled, Blidenberg, is a glad hill; Bode, a messenger; Boeckstat, probably meant for Boeckstaf, a letter or character; Bogaart, Bogardus, an orchardist, and Boheem, a Bohemian.

It seems that Claas Bordingh came from the neighborhood of Danzig on the Baltic, and that his name was derived from his occupation as a lighterman, like the father of Marryat's hero in *Jaçob Faithful*, for in this East Prussian dialect *bording* means a boatman or lighterman.

Bos comes from *bush*, meaning a wood, and Cornelis Boshuyzen from a bush house; Botsen had kicked or run against something; Bottelaar is the original of the English Bottler, now Butler, the man who has charge of and fills the bottles; Boulter would seem to be a corruption of the English Bolter; Bout is in Dutch a bolt, a shoulder of mutton, a bold man, a quill, or a duck, and from these definitions we must apparently choose the origin of this name, as the English word does not lend itself for use as a patronymic. Bowers is probably a misspelled Bouwers, the builders, and Brackenbury, the borough of the ferns. Dirck Classen Braeck, or his ancestor who assumed this family name, came either from a *braak*, a pond, or from untilled land.

The name Braidley is only once spelled Bradley, and might be translated as a deceitful meadow, Chaucer using the Saxon word *brede* as "to deceive," but it is more likely that the name came from the Irish *braid*, broad, or that the clerk spelled it phonetically, or thought the English *a* had to be written as the diphthong *ai*; in both cases it would be a broad meadow, while Brandley is a burned-over sward or meadow. Bredenbent offers an opportunity to speculate in the construction of names; were it spelled Breedenbent we could say the first two syllables meant broad; but as it never occurs with two *e*'s we cannot suppose this the usual carelessness in the spelling of names and must assume that the name had something to do with the former barony and present fortress of Breda. But the principal difficulty lies in the last syllable of the name, for we cannot accept the explanation given by G. R. Howell in his paper on *Origin and Meaning of English and Dutch Surnames* that Bent means "a frame" and Benthuysen "a frame house," for there is no word *bent* in the Dutch language and the English word of that spelling would not have been used to make a Dutch name. We must therefore fall back on the Dutch *bende*, a troop or company, or on the equally Dutch *Bend*, the name of a society of German and Dutch painters in Italy two hundred years ago, so that Bredenbent had probably something to do with a painter from Breda belonging to the society.

Bremer is a native of Bremen; Breser, a breacher, or a man who made a breach by shooting; Mr. Breun is Mr. Brown. Briant is evidently an Irishman, though he is often called Bruyn, the name given to the bear in the old German epic of *Reinard the Fox;* but the two ways of spelling the name leads to the supposition that both are meant for Bruyant, a noisy fellow.

Charles Bridges took it easy with his name. An Englishman, coming to New Amsterdam from the West Indies in 1639, he was sent to Curaçao as Member of the Council under Stuyvesant in 1644, and translated his name into van Brugge, which means " of the bridge." He returned to New Amsterdam with Stuyvesant in 1647, continuing in the service of the West India Company, but when the English took New Netherland he called himself again Bridges, changed once more to Van Brugge for a short time in 1673, and died as Bridges at Flushing, L. I., in 1682.

Bridnell, in other records spelled Brudenell, is again hard to explain, for *bru*, the French for daughter-in-law, or in old French, the string, *de*, of, and *neille*, or *nelle*, in French, the edge or rim of a hoop, give no sense; yet we must call this an old French name, for its device, *En grace affie* (trust in grace), is old French; it was later changed to the English "Think and Thank." Briel and Bryel have taken the name of their native town, Briel, on the island of Voorn, in the Delta of the Rhine, without the usual *van* or *from.*

Broeders and Broerzen are a brother's daughter and son. The only word at all like the name Bronk is the Greek βρογχος, the windpipe, but it is not likely that any one would have adopted this as a patronymic; but it is possible that the name grew from *bron*, the spring or well, into Bronck, to become our modern Bronx. Brouwer is now a brewer. Bruinsen, Bruynen, and Bruynsen have been explained before, and in Bruyver we have a misspelled obsolete Swedish word for brewer. Bryn is a Swede, who lives at the edge or on the surface, and John Bugby probably came from the village (*by* in Swedish, *bye* in Danish) of the sprites (*buka* in Russian).

Bullaine, Bolline, Bolleyn, offers, by its various spellings, a chance of being derived from the Latin *bulla*, meaning "a bubble," "a trifle," "a pinhead," or of having something to do with "a bull"; in its forms Bolline and Bolleyn it points to the Latin *Bolanus*, an inhabitant of the town of Bola, now Poli, in Italy. But the form Bullaine may also be derived from the old English word bull, meaning large, to which the other English word, boll, the pod of a plant, is closely related.

Caleb Burton, or one of his ancestors, appears to have been a seaman, who took his name or was nicknamed, from the top-burton-tackle of his ship.

The Dutch call a gust of wind *buy*, hence the first Buys was probably an irascible man ; but if the name is spelled Buis it comes from a tube or from a herring-fishing vessel, a *buss*. Byswyck may be translated as "bees' village."

Caarber is probably a misspelled Caarder or Kaarder, a man who cards wool, while Calder seems to have some relation to the Spanish *caldera*, a caldron. Calebuys becomes in one entry Kalckbuys, which seems to be the more correct, or at least is easier to explain, as *halch* is the Dutch for limestone. Campen took his name, which also appears as van Campen, from his native place, so called, in the Province of Overyssel.

Has Canidal anything to do with Canidia, the witch, spoken of by Horace, or with Canidius Crassus, the general under Lepidus and Anthony, whom Octavius put to death ?

Capito comes evidently from the Latin *caput*, the head, and Capoen is our modern capon. Capps may have been a dealer in caps (Dutch, *kap*), and Cardel (Kardeel), one in ropes, a ship-chandler.　Carelsen was the son of a Charles, or of somebody called a *kaerel*, a stout fellow.　In Carmer we have the Old Swedish word for coachman, and Carpenet, with Carpesy, seems to be derived from the French *carpeau*, a small carp ; so perhaps also Carpyn ; but its other form, Corbyn, which nowadays has become Corwin, points to the Latin *corvus*, the raven, which they carry in their coat-armor.　Whether Cartwright, the maker of carts, is an English form of the Dutch name *Kortreght*, short law, or *vice versa*, the genealogist has to decide.　Casier is the French for a maker of Parmesan cheese, which the clerk spelled phonetically Casige, the *g* being strongly aspirated in Dutch.　Cattoen is woven cotton, and Cawyn strongly reminds us of the crow's caw ; but it sounds also like the Dutch *kawaan*, a coarse turtle-shell.　Ceely, and later on Sely, have evidently some connection with the obsolete English word *seely*, meaning lucky or silly, although there is a suspicious resemblance to the German word *selig*, happy, blissful.　Cees is an odd abbreviation of Cornelis, and is pronounced Kees.　Chartier, the old French form of Cartier, makes paper and cardboard ; Chatlin is a misspelled French chatelain, or guardian of a castle; while the Latin *castrum* has become an English Chester. Claarbout and Claarhout may have both been intended for one or the other, but as the recording clerk made two names of it we must accept it so, and say that Claarbout is an evident or ready bolt, and the other such timber. *Clabboard*, the Dutch way of spelling the English clapboard, or shingle, was a nickname occasionally given to Thomas Chambers, one of the first settlers of Kingston, New York. Clein, Cleyn, Clyn, Kleyn, de Cleyn, is the little one; Clock and Clocq, "a bell" in Dutch, but "clever" in Swedish. Jan Cloet is said to have come from Nuremberg, in Germany; if he did so, he did not bring his patronymic along, for only in vulgar German is there a word spelled like his name. If he assumed his name here he called himself after a bowl, or globe; but if he was of Swedish origin, and the name is spelled Cluet, it may come from the Swedish word *klut*, a sail, or generally, a rag. There is, however, the possibility of a French origin of the name, a French maker of nails, a *cloutier*, having abbreviated the designation of his trade to Clouet, and spelled it Cloet. The already quoted *Origin and Meaning*, etc., says that the Dutch *Kluit* is the English "lamp," but we cannot find a verification of this assertion; on the contrary, the Dutch *Kluit* is the English "clod." Clof, Klof, was suspiciously like the Swedish *Klofvc*, a log; but it may be that Richard Clof lived somewhere in a cleft or gap (*Kloof* in Dutch), and was called after his dwelling-place. Clomp is our English "lump," Clopper, a knocker or beater, and Cloppenborgh may have been sent about the country to alarm the boroughs. Colfex, or, as now spelled, Colfax, seems to be a mingling of Swedish and Saxon, for we have in Swedish *Kol* for coal, and in Saxon *feax* for hair: probably the first man so called had coal-black hair, a rarity among the Northern races.

The name Cregier is again so variously spelled, that is, Crigier and Krigier, Crugier and Krygier, that it is hard to say to which tongue it belongs. It may originally have been the French *crechier*, guardian of a *crêche* on a fortified bridge ; it may have been a nickname for a man who obtained (Dutch, *kreeg*) everything he asked for; it may have been a corrupted German *Krieger*, the warrior, or an equally corrupted East Prussian *Krueger*, the keeper of a village tavern, a *Croeger* in Dutch.

With the names beginning with a *de*, the Dutch for *the*, we come mostly to nicknames, pure and simple, adopted as patronymics. De Backer is the baker; de Boer, the farmer; de Bruyn, the bear; de Caper, the privateersman; de Carman and Kerman, the carter; de

Conninck, usually written without the *de*,
King; de Coster, the sexton; de Cromp, the
bow-legged; de Cuyper and Kuyper, the
cooper; de Decker, the roofer; de Drayer,
the turner; de Goyer, one who casts; de
Graaf, the count; de Groot, the tall man;
de Haan, the cock; de Haart, the heart,
but probably misspelled for de Hert, the
deer; de Haas, the hare; de Hagenaar, the
hedger; de Hooges, the high one; de Ja-
ger, the hunter; de Jardin, of the garden;
de Jongh, the young; de Kersausvaarder,
the canal boatman, or, literally translated,
the seaman going through the daisies; de
Kleuse, the close one; de Looper, the runner;
de Meyer, the house or farm steward; de
Milt, properly de Mild, the liberal man; de
Peyster, the shepherd, from the old French
form of *paistre*, for *paître;* de Pottebacker,
the maker of earthenware; de Potter, the
merry jester; de Riemer, the saddler; de
Ruyter, the rider; de Ryck, the rich man;
de Sterre, of the star; de Visser, the fisher;
de Vos, the fox or the sorrel horse; de Vries,
the Frisian; de Waart, Waert and Waard,
Waerd, the tavern-keeper; de Weerhem,
probably misspelled for Weerhan, the weath-
er-cock; de Witt, the white one; de Wys,
the wise man; de Yonge, the young.

But there are a number of names beginning
with *de* of French origin, in which case it

means *of*, as de Foreest, or Forêt, as written to-day, of the forest; de la Montagne, of the mountain; de la Motthe (Motte), of the soil; de la Nooy, of the nut; de la Plyne, of the plain; de la Chair, of the flesh, but possibly this is meant for de la Chaire, of the chair; de la Vaal or Val, of the valley; de Marée and Mareest, either "of the salt fish" or "of the tide"; de Neufville, of the new city.   Some of these French or Walloon names go farther afield and require more explanation: in de Hondecoutrie we have in the syllable *hon*, according to Valois's *Notice des Gaules*, the English "ham" or "hamlet," while *coutrie*, or *coutrerie*, is the office of a sexton, so that the whole name would signify the place where the sexton has his official quarters.

As it would become tedious to the reader to wade through the surmised, apparent, or obvious origins of names, we give henceforth only the explanations most evident: Davenport, has its origin from the French *D'avant port*, before the port; Doesbury, Doesburg, now Dusenberry, from the city of Doesburg, on the eastern branch of the Rhine, in the Province of Gueldern; Draek, the dragon; Droogestradt, the dry street; Dubo (Dubois), of the woods; du Four, of the oven; du Mont, of the hill; du Puys, now Depew, of the well, or from the town of le Puy, in the French Department of the Loire; Duyckingh, a diving-man; Duyts, a German; Duyvelant, the land of pigeons, or he came from the island of Duivelant, in the Province of Zeeland; Fullewever, the fuller, weaver; Gaaljaard, the French *gaillard*, a merry fellow; Gaineau (Gano) had something to do with a scabbard; Gansevoort, from the geese ford; Hackins, in its various spellings, shows that it is the English Hawkins.

Although neither of the two Robert Livingstons appear in the *Records of New Amsterdam*, it may interest the reader to know that the name was originally von Linstow and that the family came from the Grand Duchy of Mecklenburg, whence, some time in the sixteenth century, a Linstow had emigrated to Scotland. Thence he was sent by the king as ambassador to the German Emperor Matthias, in 1612, and when the last of the Linstow family in Mecklenburg died, about twenty years ago, there was discovered among his papers the copy of a letter written to his cousin, the Ambassador Livingston, inviting him to pay a visit to the home of his ancestors.

Keteltas was a bag for the kettle, and Kettelhuyn was a chicken ready for the pot.

At a time of great monetary depression in Germany, some people took advantage of the uncertain laws of coinage and of the multitude of foreign coins in circulation to decrease the value of the coins by cutting the rim; these were called *Kippers* and *Wippers*, and possibly the name of Kip came from this nefarious practice; but it is more likely derived from the Dutch word *Kip*, a pack or a bundle, or from the colloquial Dutch word *Kip*, a hen. On the other hand, there is the German word *Küpe*, *Kiepe*, the coop or wicker basket. A French origin of the name, as claimed, seems impossible.

Loockerman was the man who dealt in or liked leeks; Meersman, a triton ; Megapolensis, the Latinized name of van Mecklenburg, the man from Mecklenburg ; Menist, the Mennonite; Metselaer, the mason; Meutelaer, the mutineer; Middagh, mid-day ; Moesman, the porridgeman; Mol, the mole (also a sort of beer), but as the device of the Mol family in Europe is *Laet de Mol in t'hol* (leave the mole in the hole), we must accept the first explanation ; Molegraaf, the mill count; Molenaer, the miller, from the Italian Molinari, a family name still in existence in Europe ; Naber, the neighbor; Nagel, the nail; Naghtegael is the nightingale, but the bearer of this name did not show herself as a mellifluous female in the *Records;* Op Dyck lived on a dyke; Pluyvier, who himself spelled his name Pluvier, perhaps did not know enough to come in when it rained, or he liked the plover; Steenwyck took his name from the village of that name in the District of Drent,

Overyssel, and Sterrevelt, from the field around
Sterre, a place in the fork of the Waal and
the Rhine.   There is in the Department of
Côte du Nord, France, a river, the Trieux, from
which the name du Trieux, Truy, etc., was
taken.

We come now to the peculiarly Dutch names
with *ten, ter, van, van der,* and *ver,* the *ten* and
ter meaning *at the,* the *van, van der,* and *ver*
(a contraction of van der), *of.* Thus we have:
ten Eyck, at the oak; ter Heun, at the hedge;
while the *vans* have mostly adopted the names
of their native places, some of them so small
that no geographical hand-book mentions
them, but in probably no case has the Dutch
van become, like the German *von,* the nobil-
iary prefix, for in the Netherlands noble birth
was always indicated by a title; besides, in
those days of almost constant war, the noble-
man found always a chance to occupy himself
profitably in the army, and under no condition adopted a mercantile life.   The places
where the *vans* came from, and which are
found in gazetteers, are :

Aalst: Terwen, in *Het Koningrijck der
Nederlande,* describes two places of the
name of Aalst, one a village near Waalre, the
ancient Waderlo, in the Province of North
Brabant, the other in Guelderland.   Besides,
there is an Aalst, or Alost, near Ghent, Belgium.

Aarnhem, Province of Guelderland.

Aachen, Aecken, Aix-la-Chapelle, in the Prussian Province of the Rhine.

Baal, Basle, in Switzerland.

Beeck, near Nimeguen.

Berckelo, in Guelderland.

Bergen, in Holland.

Bolsward, in Friesland.

Bommel, an island formed by the Waal and a branch of the Rhine.

Breeste, Brestede, Bredstede, in the District of Flensborgh, Denmark.

Bremen, the well-known city in Germany.

Blockzyl or Brocksel, in Friesland.

Broutangie is either meant for the French Bretagne, or an oddly spelt Bourtang, the name of a marsh on the eastern frontier of Groningen and Drent.

We have already disposed of one van Brugge under the name of Bridges. Whether the others also came from Bridges, or from the Belgian city of Bruges, in Dutch spelled Bruggen, cannot be decided here.

Campen lies in Overyssel; Ceulen is the Dutch for Cologne; Cleef is the Duchy of Cleves.

It is claimed for the van Cortlandt family that their first ancestor in America, Oloff Stevensen, was a descendant of the dukes of Curland. There are several objections to this theory. Curland, the country of the Kures, a branch of the Lithuanian people, was an in-

Van
Cortland

dependent possession of the Knights of the Teutonic Order, who Christianized that part of the world in the twelfth, thirteenth, fourteenth, and fifteenth centuries. Upon the overthrow of this order by Poland, in 1561, it became part of that kingdom, and was only created a duchy, to be given as such to Biron, the favorite of Empress Anna of Russia, in 1710, more than fifty years after the name van Cortland appeared here. The second objection is based on the social conditions of the seventeenth century, which would have prevented the scion of a noble family from becoming a trader; he could always find service with his sword in the various armies of the Thirty Years' War. Then the first part of the name of Curland, or Kurland, the *Kur*, is too much like the Dutch word *Keur*, the choice, to have been changed into *Cort*, short. Cortland is simply "short land."

The name of van der Bilt, or van de Bilt, is taken either from the village of de Bilt, a suburb of Utrecht, or from the parish of Het (the) Bilt, in Frisia, or, possibly, from one of the *Bilts*, or narrow passages of the sea, between the peninsula of Denmark and the island of Fuenen; van de Linde, from a town in Guelderland; van der Heyden, from a place in Holstein, or it may mean "from the heath"; van der Eyck, Kuil, Perck, Ree, Schel, Schuyr, Sluys, Smisse, Spiegel, Veen, Veer, Vorst, are purely local designations, from which the names were taken, as from the oak, the cave, the park, the sail-yard, the bell, the barn, the sluice, the forge, the looking-glass, the fenn, the ferry, the forest. Van der Stighelen may have some connection with the Dutch *Sticht*, or *Diocese*, and van der Vin is from the fin of a fish. Van Dincklagen comes from Oldenburg; van Deventer, from the place of that name in Overyssel; Elsland is the country around Elsinore, on the island of Zeeland; Hasselt, a town in Overyssel; Hagen, Hattem, and Harderwyck, in Gueldern; Huesden, in North Brabant; Imbroecken lies near the Zuyder Zee; Iselsteyn, in Utrecht; Laar (Lahr) is a town in the Grand duchy of Baden; Loon lies on the Maas River, in Brabant; Meppel, in Drent; Naerden, in Utrecht; Wyck is a fortified town on a branch of the Rhine, the Vechte or Wechte. Malte-Brun says, in his *System of Geography*, that this river in the Netherlands is of less importance than the Yssel, Issel, or Isel, to-day the branch of the Rhine called the Vechte.

Some names of Dutch towns have changed since natives of them came to America: thus, there is in Belgium the city of Tirlemont, as the French call it, which is called by the inhabitants Theenen, and was the Tienhoven from which Secretary Cornelis van Tienhoven took his name.

To close this article, it is only necessary to repeat that *ver* is an abbreviation of *van der*, and the meaning of the names Verbeeck, Verbraack, Verbrugge, has already been explained. Verhage is van der Hage, of the bush or from the Hague ; Vermeulen, from the mill; Verplanck, of the plank; and we add the few names which require translation, to wit: Visser, the fisher; Vogel, the bird; Vogelsang, bird's song; Vos, the fox, and Joncker Vos, the son of a Baron Vos; Vredenburgh, borough of peace ; Vries, the Frisian; Waecker, the watchman ; Waldman, the man of the forest; Wandel, probably an abbreviated Wandelaar, the walker; Wantenaar, the rigger; Webber, the weaver ; Wisselpenningh, change the penny ; and finally, Wyt Straat, either a wide street or a badly written Uyt Straat, outside street.

References

REFERENCES.

TERIVEN, *Koningrijck der Nederlande.*

MALTE-BRUN, *Système de Geographie.*

OWEN, *Welsh Dictionary.*

BALBI, *Atlas ethnographique.*

DUMONT, *Voyage sur les bords du Rhin.*

OLD TAVERNS AND POSTING INNS

Half Moon Series

Published in the Interest of the New York
City History Club.

Volume II.   Number VII.

OLD TAVERNS AND POSTING INNS.

By ELISABETH BROWN CUTTING.

THE uncertain temper of Director-General
William Kieft was the indirect occasion
of the building of the first recorded tavern
upon Manhattan Island. His predecessors had
opened their doors to the "stranger within
the gates" with Leyden hospitality, but the
almost daily passing of ships trading between
New England and Virginia brought many
guests, and "in order to accommodate the
English, from whom he suffered great annoy-
ance, Kieft had built a fine inn of stone."
"It happened well for the travellers," was the
appreciative comment of De Vries, who was
wont to dine with Kieft.[1]

This Stadt Harberg, or the City Tavern, was
the property of the West India Company, and
was erected on the site of the warehouses now
occupying the building 71–73 Pearl Street, and
facing Coenties Slip.[2]   On the seventeenth of
February, 1643, Director Kieft leased this tav-

The
Stadt
Harberg

ern to one Philip Gerritsen, at a rent of three hundred guilders, or one hundred and twenty dollars, "with the right to retail the Company's wine and brandy, on which he is to be allowed a profit of six stivers (or twelve cents) a gallon." The lease specified further, that a well and brew-house might be erected in the rear of the inn.

What the rates of the tavern were is not known, but in November, 1643, Joannes Winckleman, agent of Meindert Meindertson Van Keren, gave his note to Philip Gerritsen for one hundred and thirty-two guilders, four stivers (or fifty-two dollars and eighty-eight cents), "for board, etc. for the people of the colonie of Achter Col," (Hackensack, New Jersey).[1] The people of Achter Col, had been driven to seek the doubtful protection of Fort Amsterdam after the destruction of the colony by the Indians; but the number of guests, or the length of their stay, is not given, so we have no basis on which to compute the charges. The inhuman treatment of the Indians was a characteristic of the Kieft administration, and had the speedy effect of causing a general uprising on the part of the savages, and the serious threatening of the annihilation of New Amsterdam. The necessary expedient of procuring a considerable number of soldiers, with other expenditures, which were met only partially by the Company, drove

Kieft to fix an excise on beer, promising that it should cease "on the arrival of a Company's ship or new Director, or at the end of the war."[4]

In June, 1644, the first excise law was passed, and in August of that year, the Fiscal, or roughly speaking, the sheriff, obtained a judgment against Host Gerritsen of the Harberg, for payment of the excise. The beer, according to De Vries, was as good as that brewed in the Fatherland, and the entertainment at the Harberg was not to be questioned. Certainly, Host Gerritsen was supported by Church and State, for in the previous March he invited "the minister, City magnates, and their wives to sup with him," but the feast came to an untimely and disorderly end through the "outrageous attack" led by the Indian fighter, John Underhill, and the English Secretary, George Baxter.[5]

Little more is known of Host Gerritsen, but the Harberg continued as a place of entertainment until 1653, when their Honors, the Burgomasters and Schepens of the then incorporated city, informed "every body" that from this time on all their meetings would be held in the "house hitherto called the City Tavern, henceforth the City Hall." So ended the career of the Harberg as a public-house, though entertainments may have been held there on occasions, as when the Burgomasters and Schepens voted to provide "a gay

First Ordinances

repast" in the Council Chamber of the City Hall for Peter Stuyvesant as he was about to take "a gallant voyage" to the West Indies for trading purposes, in December, 1654.

The number of taverns and tap-houses increased constantly with the growing population, so that in 1648 one fourth of the buildings of New Amsterdam had been turned into taverns for the sale of brandy, tobacco, and beer. Peter Stuyvesant, who succeeded Kieft in 1647 as Director, in the following year issued a proclamation demanding that all tavern-keepers and tapsters should present themselves in person within eight days to give their names to the Director-General and Council. Twelve men obeyed the summons, and promised, as true men, to live up to the regulations for tavern-keepers and tapsters. The list included Daniel Lithscoe, Abraham Pietersen, Jan Snediger, and Martin Cregier, whose tavern was situated near that of Peter Kochs, another Dutch tapster, on the present site of the Washington Building, 1 Broadway.

The ordinances passed by the Director-General and Council declared that the men already established as tavern-keepers were to be allowed to continue in their business for four years at least, but only on condition, that they should not "transfer their former occupation of tapping and selling liquor by the small measure nor let their houses and dwellings to another party, except with the previous advice and full consent of the Director-General and Council." In the future no new tap-room, tavern, or inn could be opened without the unanimous consent of the Director and Council.

Tavern-keepers and tapsters were not to be allowed to sell to the Indians, and if any fight or mishap should occur at their houses, they were to be heavily fined for every hour during which they concealed the fact from the officers. "Unseasonable night tippling," viz., drinking after nine o'clock, when the bell was rung, and "intemperate drinking on the Sabbath," that is, drinking by anyone not a traveler or table-boarder on Sunday before three o'clock, when divine service was over, were infringements to be met by heavy penalties.

These ordinances left as favorable means of evasion as some of the Raines Law provisions, so a year later it was found necessary to order that no inhabitant who made it a business to brew, should be allowed "to tap, sell, or give away, beer, wine, or strong water by the small measure, excepting at meal times, not even to table-boarders, who they may pretend to board, under which pretext we have seen many frauds perpetrated." Later, an ordinance was passed to prohibit "the sitting of clubs" at taverns on any night after the ringing of the bell or on the Sabbath, since it was found that there were those who frequented such places more on that than on any other day, the intention not being, so the record says, "to prevent the stranger or citizen from buying a drink of wine or beer for the assuaging of his thirst, but that the privilege of resorting to divine service might not be hindered." The boarding-house keepers were obliged to pay the Collector half the tapster excise if wines, brandy, distilled waters, or beer were to be consumed by the guests. Further, no tavern-keepers or tapsters could receive in pawn any goods as pay, and the lodging of savages over night between the Fort and the Fresh Water (Centre Street, near the site of the Tombs) without a pass signed by the Director-General or the Secretary, involved a fine of twenty-five florins or ten dollars. Licenses for taverns were required to be renewed quarterly, and could be obtained from the City Treasurer; but later the retail sellers were allowed to take them out annually.[6]

The taverns most frequently mentioned in the Dutch period are the Stadt Harberg, the resort of the traders, and the houses of Martin Cregier and Peter Kochs, the resorts, doubtless, of the soldiery, for both Cregier and Kochs had won distinction in the Dutch service, and had located themselves near Fort Amsterdam. To these must be added the tavern in Pearl Street, near Broad, kept by Mettje Wessels, whose son, Warnaer Wessels, is a familiar figure in New Amsterdam, as farmer of the Tapster's Excise, later farmer of the Burgher's Excise on wine and beer, and attaining, in 1669, the high office of Constable. On November 22, 1656, the Burgomasters and Schepens granted the request of Neeltie, or Mettje, Wessels, to be allowed "to follow the trade of an eating house and to bring in and tap out beer." Judging from the number of times her name appears in the Court proceedings, her career as an inn-keeper must have been tempestuous. It was at the house of Mettje Wessels that William Bogardus, doubtless the son of Dominie Bogardus, possessing the traditional character of a minister's son, engaged in a fight. This little diversion, on the complaint of Schout Peter Tonnemann, cost the said William, according to the rule of the Court, the sum of fifty guilders, or twenty dollars, with costs.' All through the records, however, are to be found accounts of disturbances and scuffles in the taverns, and the house of Mettje Wessels should not be considered as exceptional in this particular.

When, in September, 1664, the Dutch colors were lowered, and the Red Cross of St. George floated over Fort Amsterdam, the city becoming New York, the inference might well have been made, that under the English a distinctive change in the taverns would immediately appear. Later, the English did make their impress, and the inns became political and educational, as well as social centres, but for the moment tavern life continued much the same as under the Dutch, necessitating similar laws and ordinances. The tavern-keepers were compelled to take out their licenses annually from the Mayor, he having the sole power to grant them, and anyone selling wine, brandy, or rums at retail, or by the small measure, without a license, did so under a penalty of five pounds. As late as 1748, no inn-keeper, victualer, or ordinary keeper was allowed to receive company into his house, and sell to them any sort of liquor on the Lord's Day in time of divine service or preaching, unless to strangers, travelers, or those who lodge in such houses for their necessary refreshment, and the sale of strong liquor to Indian or negro was prohibited.[8]

It would be impossible, in limited space, to give a history of all the taverns and posting inns in New York during the eighteenth century, however alluring such signs as The Blue Boar, St. George and the Dragon, Dog's Head-in-the-Porridge-Pot, The Three Pigeons, in Smith (William) Street, The Fighting-Cocks, next door to the Exchange Coffee-House, in Broad Street, where Eastham promised to show to his customers "a curious portable microscope with several different magnifying lenses." Other attractive hostelries were The Thistle and Crown, near Spring Garden, where the old gardener of the old Bowling Green sold seeds at reasonable rates,[9] to be distinguished from The Crown and Thistle on the Whitehall, near the Half-Moon Battery, the starting-point for the stage line to Burlington, New Jersey, and kept by "Scotch Johnny"; The Sign of the Spread Eagle, near the Whitehall, at which place Host Hamilton Hewetson announced would be seen "Punch's Opera, *Bateman, or the Unhappy Marriage*, with a fine dialogue between Punch and his wife Joan, acted by a set of lively figures late from Philadelphia;" The Duke of Cumberland, opposite the Merchants' Coffee-House, kept by Thomas Lepper, who made an ordinary or *table d'hôte* a feature of this house, advertising that dinner would be served at the sign of the Duke of Cumberland every day at one o'clock; The Bunch of Grapes, near the Fly (Fulton) Market, distinguished in having as a guest "a Person" who provided "a very warm and commodious room for scholars," and agreed to teach the three R's and "fit youths for a Counting House, or to carry on any business."[10] From these, and many others, it is necessary to turn and seek for a more detailed account of tavern life among those historic taverns and inns that were centres from which radiated plans of civic business, schemes of privateering, projects for education, exhibitions of patriotism, and social entertainments.

One of the early records of the use of an inn for purposes of civic business is in 1701, when a committee of the Council was appointed to meet with a committee of the Assembly, to confer in regard to the public accounts, and the meeting was to take place "at the house of Mr. Roger Baker at three of the clock in the afternoon."[11] The "house of Mr. Roger Baker" was the tavern known as the King's Head, situated on the northwest corner of the present Pearl Street and Maiden Lane.[12] Baker himself appears in the list of freemen in 1695, as Roger Baker, victualer, and later he is met in the celebrated trial of Colonel Bayard, leader of the anti-Leislerian party. Here he was charged with having said "the king is made a nose of wax and no longer king than the English please," and being found guilty was made to pay a fine of four hundred pieces of eight. The White Lion, kept by Gabriel Thompson, shared with the King's Head the honor of entertaining the Committee of Council and Assembly. The location is not certain, but its frequent mention in the Journal of the Legislative Council indicates it to have been a favorite resort of the Conference Committees.

After 1704, the Coffee-House seems to have

been a popular place of meeting for conference. A Coffee-House was in existence as
early as 1701, for the son of Colonel Bayard
states that it was at the Coffee-House, in the
presence of his father and himself, that the
addresses which led to the conviction of
Colonel Bayard for high treason were signed.[13]
The site of the Coffee-House cannot be absolutely proved; but the publication of a map
made by Lyne during Governor Montgom-
erie's rule, 1728–1732, together with an advertisement in the *New York Gazette* of March
1, 1730, give some clue. The map indicates
that the Exchange (a building erected in 1691–
92 as a market-house) was at the foot of Broad
Street, between the East and West Docks.
The advertisement announced the sale of land
at public vendue at the Exchange Coffee-
House, and probably this Coffee-House was
in the neighborhood of the Market-House, or
Exchange.[14] If, however, its location may be
questioned, it is certain that on October 5,
1705, a Conference Committee was called "at
the Coffee House at nine of the clock," and
again at four o'clock the following afternoon
at the same place. In 1708–9 the Committees
met again at the Coffee-House, although there
was a Council Chamber in the new City Hall
completed in 1700, and situated on Wall and
Nassau Streets, the site of the present Sub-
Treasury Building.

Later we meet with other coffee-houses like that of the New, or Royal, Exchange, erected in 1752, at the lower end of Broad Street, near the Long Bridge, and so "laudable an undertaking" was this considered to be, that one hundred pounds was voted by the Common Council for its construction. It was completed in 1753, and leased to Oliver De Lancey for fifty pounds.[16] It is described as having a long room raised upon brick arches, and generally used for public entertainments, concerts, balls, and assemblies. Keen and Lightfoot opened it as a coffee-room, February 4, 1754.[16]

On the southeast corner of Wall and Water Streets was the Merchants' Coffee-House, which for many years was the centre of mercantile transactions. The files of the newspapers abound with advertisements of lands, houses, ships, cargoes, and negroes offered for sale at public vendue at the Merchants' Coffee-House. Such an advertisement as the following is to be seen in any of the provincial papers: "A parcel of likely negroes to be sold at public vendue to-morrow at ten o'clock at the Merchants' Coffee House." In 1759, the Old Insurance Office advertises that at this coffee-house "all risques whatsoever are underwrote at very moderate premiums, and due attendance given from twelve to one and six to eight, by Keteltas and Sharpe, clerks of the office." [17] The Merchants' Coffee-House attained its highest historic interest when, in 1789, upon the arrival of President-elect Washington at Murray's Wharf, the procession which was to escort him to his new home formed before its doors.

From 1742 to 1748, and from 1756 to 1763, England was at war with France, and seizures upon the high seas were frequent. Undoubtedly, plans for privateering were matured around the tables of the different inns. The wealthy merchants of New York had been interested in such enterprises, and many were owners of ships engaged in the business. The war gave a suitable pretext for such undertakings, hence it was that an advertisement like the following may be read in the newspapers of the time:

" To all Gentlemen, Sailors and others who have a mind to try their fortunes on a cruising voyage against the enemy. That the Brigt. *Hester* and Sloop *Polly* are now fitting out at New York in the best manner under the command of Captain Francis Rosewell, and the owners of said vessels being to find everything necessary for such an undertaking. The Brigt. is a fine, New Single Deckt Vessel of one hundred and fifty tons. The Sloop is also New Burthen one hundred tons, to mount twenty-six Guns and to be Manned with eighty men, being both Prime Sailors and to go in Company." [17]

The articles of agreement were to be seen at the sign of the Pineapple, kept by Benjamin Kiersted, on the New Dock. [18] From the Jamaica Arms, on Cruger's Wharf, and the Griffin Tavern on the New Dock, were advertised equal facilities for engaging in privateering. When a prize was brought into port, the goods which it carried would be sold on shore, and an inventory of the cargo could always be seen at the coffee-houses or taverns. Sometimes differences would arise among the owners of privateers, and arbitrators would meet at the taverns to agree upon a settlement, as for example, in 1745, when four privateers arrived with six French prizes, the Black Horse Inn, the patrician house of Mr. Robert Todd, was fixed upon by the arbitrators as the meeting-ground for settlement.[19]

The art of letter-writing was taken so seriously by our amiable forbears, that a regularly established post-office in New York was not found a necessity until 1775. In 1659, under the Dutch, provision was made by the Director-General and Council for a box to be placed in front of the Secretary's office for the reception of all letters, and where, if one so wished, he could register his letter on the payment of three stivers.[20] In the English days various inns served as places of distribution and reception of mail matter, and the date of departure and arrival of the post-riders would be announced in the papers. "The Albany Post arrived last night and proposes to set out again from hence on Wednesday next. Per-

sons are desired to send their letters to Sergeant Younge at the Hartfordshire and
Yorkshire near the Fort." This tavern was
on Marketfield Street, commonly called Petticoat Lane (site now covered by the Produce
Exchange), and directly opposite the Secretary's office, which was on Whitehall Street
close by the Fort. It was by the Albany
Post that the news in regard to Indian affairs,
and, during the war with France, the news
from Quebec, was brought, so the selection
of an inn near the Fort, where the army and
navy congregated, was natural. The Hartfordshire and Yorkshire has also a picturesque
interest, in that it was selected as a place of
enlistment for the Louisburg expedition of
1745, under Admiral Warren.[21] But Louisburg was lost and won again after the Warren expedition, and when, in 1758, news was
received that a powerful fleet under Admiral
Boscawen had retaken it, a grand official dinner was given, not at the Hartfordshire and
Yorkshire, where the brave men of thirteen
years before had recruited, but at the Province
Arms, the then favorite resort of loyal Englishmen. The cannon of Fort George responded to every toast, and the city was
illuminated, as was customary.

The coffee-house was a favorite place for
the reception of letters, especially with sea-
faring people. On August 27, 1744, the fol-

lowing spirited notice appeared in the weekly *Post Boy:*

"Whereas about a Fortnight ago three or four letters directed to the Printer of this paper were left at The Merchants' Coffee-House in this City, among many other letters, by Captain Romar from South Carolina; which letters have been by ill-minded persons either destroyed or conveyed away unknown. This is to notify, that if any Person will give sufficient Information whereby the Offender may have justice, he shall have twenty shillings reward. The Keeper of the said Coffee House late usage of me obliges me to have no more Sentiments of him than the Case will allow."

In 1752, one William Wood was the carrier between New York and Albany, and he gave the public notice that letters would be "taken in at his house on Thurman Dock on the North River or at Benjamin Pain's, who at this time was keeping the Gentleman's Coffee-House and Tavern on Broad Street, near the Old Slip." Some of the inn-keepers advertised as a special feature of their houses, that they would "take in the newspapers." When George Burns took the Cart and Horse, in 1750, he promised his patrons that they should always find the Boston, Philadelphia, and New York newspapers; and in 1774, when Edward Bardin was again keeper at the sign of the King's Arms, he announced that the "public prints" were taken for the gentlemen's amusement. Four years later, when John Adams was stopping a few days in New

York on his way to the Continental Congress, he visited, under the escort of the "disinterested patriot," Alexander MacDougall, the coffee-house, "which," says Adams, "was full of gentlemen and where we read the newspapers."[23]

In the early half of the last century, the house most frequented by the gentry was Mr. Todd's, at the sign of the Black Horse, located, in 1735, in Smith (William) Street, near the Old Dutch Church. The Black Horse was the centre of the social life of the city; balls, concerts, and dinners were given there, and the Ancient and Honorable Society of Free and Accepted Masons was accustomed to hold its meetings at this fashionable inn. The *New York Gazette* of January 6, 1786, announces

"a Concert of Musick, Vocal and Instrumental for the Benefit of Mr. Parchebell, the Harpsicord Part performed by himself. The Songs, Violins and German Flutes by private Hands. The concert will begin at six precisely In the House of Robert Todd, Vintner. Tickets to be had at the Coffee House, and at Mr. Todd's at 4s."

It was at the Black Horse that "a very splendid entertainment was provided by the principal Merchants and other Gentlemen of this City for His Excellency Governor Crosby in order to congratulate him upon his safe return from Albany!" The fête for which this house is famous, however, is that given in honor of the birthday of the Prince of Wales, on January 19, 1736. During the day there was the usual celebration at the Fort, where the healths of the Royal Family and the Governor and Council were drunk, and "in the evening the ball at Mr. Todd's at which there was a very great appearance of ladies and gentlemen and an elegant entertainment made by the gentlemen in honor of the day."[24] Another newspaper account says: "The ball opened with French dances and then the company proceeded to country dances, upon which Mrs. Norris led up two new country dances, made upon the occasion, the first of which was called the Prince of Wales, and the second the Princess of Saxe-Gotha." It comments further upon the "most magnificent appearance" of the ladies, which may be well believed, for Mr. Smith, the discriminating historian, has much to say of the social life in New York at that time, and speaks of the ladies as "comely and well-dressed, very few having distorted shapes."[25]

Nine years later the host of the Black Horse had died, and his widow, Margaret Todd, advertised for sale fine old Madeira wine, Canary wines, etc., and also playing-cards, all at reasonable rates. When Jonathan Ogden bought the sign he moved it to Queen Street, and in 1750, the Boston Post made this tavern its stopping-place. After his death, in 1753, it was purchased by John Halstead, and he agreed to keep it as formerly, but from this time on little more is known of the Black Horse Inn.

The sporting element in New York could give vent to its feelings at the Drover's Inn, kept by Adam Van Der Burgh, and occupying the ground covered by the present Astor House; here horses were run over a race-course laid out, somewhat incongruously it would seem, on the Church Farm. Entries were required to be made the day before the race, and all spectators in chaises or on horseback, except those having racing-horses, were charged sixpence each upon going into the field.[20] Ten years later the same element was to be found at the old Bull's Head Tavern, on the Bowery (the site of the Thalia Theatre), whose presiding genius in 1755 was one George Brewerton. This was the last halting-place for the stages before entering the city. From this tavern started the procession which escorted General Washington in his triumphal march through the city on November 25, 1783. Governor Clinton, the Lieutenant-Governor, and the members of the Council accompanied him under an escort of a party of horse eight abreast; after passing down Queen Street and the line of troops up the Broadway, their Excellencies alighted at Cape's Tavern, the familiar Province Arms, or State Arms, as it was then called.[21]

Between the old Bull's Head, of sporting proclivities, and the quiet inn at Kingsbridge were two or three taverns of more or less note. Five miles out from New York, on the old post-road, at about the present Sixty-fifth Street, was the sign of the Dove, which is described in an advertisement in 1770, as having "a commodious kitchen, garden, barn, stable, and small tract of land." The Half-Way House, at the foot of Harlem Lane, marked by its name the distance between the City Hall, in Wall Street, and the King's Bridge. The inn at Kingsbridge, Hannah Callender, a Philadelphia lady, visiting New York in 1759, describes in her diary as being very prettily situated at the foot of a hill, the little river meandering through a meadow before it. On one side were highlands of woods, and in another direction cattle could be seen grazing on the plains. A Dutchman was the host, and a very good one, so she says, who "insisted upon having their names and promised to send them some sweethearts!" Washington makes mention twice in his diary of stopping here when on his way to and from Boston.

On Broadway, between Stone (Thames) Street and Little Queen (Cedar) Street, stood the mansion owned by Lieutenant-Governor James De Lancey, and built by his father, Etienne De Lancey, shortly after 1700. This was one of the fine residences of the city. From its windows could be seen life and death, in marked contrast, for the Mall, where fashionable folk walked, and the Trinity Churchyard, where fashionable folk lay, were close at hand. In the rear was a broad piazza, which commanded a fine view of the North River, and a garden sloping down to the water's edge. The picturesque and central location of the house commended itself to Edward Willet, and in 1754 he opened a tavern there under the sign of the Province Arms."

This house was destined to become one of the famous taverns of the century. It began its brilliant career by two public dinners of note. The first was given to Sir Charles Hardy, who came out in 1755, to succeed, as Governor, Sir Danvers Osborne, whose suicide in the previous year had created great excitement. The second took place a year later, upon the occasion of the laying of the corner-stone of King's College. The arrangements for this last function provided that the Lieutenant-Governor, Governors of the College, and students should assemble at Mr. Willet's, and from there proceed to the college grounds. After the ceremony of the laying of the stone "they returned to Mr. Willet's, where there was a very elegant dinner, after which the usual loyal healths were drunk and Prosperity to the College, and the whole was conducted with the utmost decency and propriety."[30]

In May, 1763, Mr. George Burns, of Cart and Horse fame, who had followed the itinerant career of an inn-keeper, moved from the King's Head, in the Whitehall, to the Province Arms, where, he assured his customers, they might depend upon the best treatment. He advertised further in the newspapers, that he had "two Excellent Grooms to attend his stables, and take in travellers and their horses; and will stable town horses by the Month, Quarter or Year on Reasonable Terms."[31] A month after Burns took possession, a lottery was drawn at the Province Arms to raise money for the building of the lighthouse at Sandy Hook.

In April, 1761, Cadwallader Colden, at that time President of His Majesty's Council, recommended to the House, for its consideration, a memorial which he had received in regard to the erecting of a lighthouse at Sandy Hook, " so essential is it to the welfare of our commercial interests and the preservation of a very useful part of the community." The location for such a building was chosen on land belonging to New Jersey, so Colden suggested that the House act at once upon his recommendation, in order that he might communicate their resolution to both branches of the New Jersey legislature then in session. A month later, on a motion of Alderman Philip Livingston, a law was passed authorizing a sum not exceeding three thousand pounds, to be raised by way of a lottery, to build the lighthouse.[32] A year later it was found that the sum would not be sufficient, and as the colony was then overtaxed by reason of the long war with France, it was voted to raise the money by lottery again, and this time there were to be two lotteries of three thousand pounds each.

The scheme was as follows: "The lottery is to consist of two thousand tickets at forty shillings each, whereof sixteen hundred and eighty-four are to be fortunate, subject to fifteen per cent deduction."[33] The drawing of the lottery was advertised to take place on June 14, 1763, at the City Hall, where lotteries were usually drawn, but a change of place was made necessary by the fact that the City Hall at that time was undergoing repairs, and so the numbers were drawn in Mr. Burns's Long Room at the Province Arms.[34] The lighthouse was built, and in the August number of the *New York Magazine* for 1790 is a picture and description of the building. The interesting but fanciful statement is there made that the light could be seen at a distance of ten leagues! The Sandy Hook light of to-day is officially registered to be seen at just one half that distance, fifteen miles!

Perhaps what has largely contributed to

The
Province
Arms

make the Province Arms historic is that its walls were witness to more than one outburst of patriotic sentiment during the Stamp Tax excitement. The first was the famous Non-Importation Agreement, which was signed by two hundred merchants on the night of October 31, 1765,[16] the eve of the day the law was to take effect in the colonies. Again, on November 26, in the afternoon, between three and four o'clock, a meeting of the "Freeholders, Freemen and Inhabitants of the City and County of New York" was held, in order to agree upon some instructions to be given to their representative in the General Assembly in regard to their refusal to have anything to do with the Stamp Tax. The day after the meeting Peter De Lancey made himself illustrious by resigning from the office of Inspector of Stamps, to which he had been appointed while away.

In the following February it was discovered that two bonds had been executed in New York with the detested stamp, and so great was the excitement that these, together with some blanks not yet distributed, were secured, and the whole burned before the Coffee-House in the "presence of a multitude of spectators." This was no doubt the effective work of the Sons of Liberty, and one of the incidents that Philip Freneau wished to commemorate in the following lines:

" When a certain great King whose initial is G
  Shall force stamps upon paper and folks to drink tea;
  When these folks burn his tea and stamp paper like stubble
  You may guess that this King is then coming to
    trouble."

The English people themselves appreciated, if royalty did not, how obnoxious the tax was to their fellow-countrymen in the Colonies, and the common wager in the London coffee-houses had been one hundred guineas to ten that the Stamp Tax would be repealed as soon as Parliament met in the middle of November. It was March, 1766, however, before the Act was repealed, and May before an authentic report of its repeal reached the Colony. A day of celebration was speedily appointed. The Sons of Liberty, after listening to " an elegant sermon " at Trinity Church in the morning, spent the rest of the day in more or less turbulent rejoicing, and concluded the festivities with a dinner at the Province Arms, where twenty-eight toasts were drunk, the two most worthy of note being one to Pitt, the other, " Perpetual Union between Great Britain and her Colonies." Every year, on the anniversary of the repeal of the Act, there was a celebration in honor of the day; the firing of cannon, a procession, and the illuminating of the city were the usual features, and it always concluded with dinner at various taverns.

In 1770, a dinner took place at Hampden Hall, a corner house at Broadway and Ann Street, opposite the lower end of the Fields. Forty-five toasts were drunk, the last one being "The Day." Dinner was served at two o'clock, and the bill was called for precisely at six. Colors were displayed on the liberty pole and on Hampden Hall. On the same occasion, a dinner was given at the King's Arms, which at that time was kept by De La Montayne, in the Fields, near which the famous battle of Golden Hill was begun; two hundred and thirty guests were present, and the liberty colors, inscribed with "G. R. III. Liberty and Trade," were hoisted. But the Province Arms, or City Arms, as it was frequently called, was used for other purposes than celebrations. In January, 1770, a sacred oratorio or concert of music was given, the tickets for which were eight shillings. It was the favorite meeting-place of different societies, St. Andrew's and the like, and the Governors of King's College found that educational problems could be solved more successfully in its genial atmosphere than elsewhere.[36]

Burns, after seven years' tenure of this famous house of entertainment, was succeeded in 1770 by Bolton, for some time host at the Queen's Head, the famous Fraunces's Tavern, and he, in turn, was shortly succeeded by Hull, who had the honor of entertaining John Adams and his friends on their way to Philadelphia. In 1777, a duel was fought at the Province Arms, or City Arms, between Captain Tollemache, of His Majesty's Ship *Zebra*, just arrived, and Captain Pennington, of the Coldstream Guards, one of the passengers on the same ship. Captain Pennington had written a sonnet which Captain Tollemache unfortunately fancied reflected on the supposed wit of his lady; swords were the weapons, and a few days afterwards Captain Tollemache was interred in Trinity Churchyard." From now on host succeeds host in rapid succession. During Cape's proprietorship the tavern was a favorite meeting-place of the gentlemen subscribers to the dancing assembly, who met there to discuss plans and to make arrangements for this amusement, which was to be the feature of the winter of 1783. It was not until 1792 that the Province Arms property passed out of De Lancey ownership; then Peter De Lancey sold it to the Tontine Association, who tore down the famous old mansion, and in its place erected the City Hotel, which acquired a reputation in the early part of this century as great as that of its predecessor. On the Boreel Building, which now covers the site of this historic tavern, is a commemorative tablet, placed there in 1890, by the Holland Society.

Another tavern which had the prestige of

De Lancey ownership before it became a public-house was Fraunces's Tavern, still standing on the southeast corner of Broad and Pearl Streets. The firm of De Lancey, Robinson & Co. used this house as a store from 1757 to 1761, when the partnership was dissolved. In January, 1762, the property passed into the hands of Samuel Fraunces, known to history as "Black Sam," and the steward of President Washington's household after his inauguration. Fraunces swung out a sign with the device of the head of Queen Charlotte, and the tavern was known as the Queen's Head. From then till now the building has always been used as a public-house, with, however, varying degrees of excellence, and in later years with none of its early distinction.[38] In April, 1763, Fraunces announced that he had opened an "Ordinary" at the Queen's Head, and dinner was to be served every day at half-past one.

After a three years' stay Fraunces withdrew, and John Jones succeeded him. Jones, however, remained only a year, and then opened the Ranelagh Gardens, where he promised to have "Band Concerts during the summer season on Monday and Thursday evenings, beginning precisely at seven." For the convenience of the gentlemen, tickets were to be had at the Queen's Head, which was near the Exchange.

Bolton and Sigell were the hosts next in succession, and they promised "Dinners and Public Entertainments at the Shortest Notice." They advertised further the comfortable breakfast hours of 9–11. It was in the reign of Bolton and Sigell that the New York Chamber of Commerce was established in the Long Room, and here the meetings of the Chamber were held until it moved to the new Royal Exchange. In 1770 they dissolved partnership, and Bolton "solicits the continuance of the public favor." Fraunces, in the meantime, had assumed the proprietorship of the Vauxhall Gardens, which were situated on the southwestern corner of the Bogardus farm, at about the junction of Greenwich and Warren Streets. Hannah Callender, the Philadelphia lady already referred to, tells of a visit to these Gardens about ten years before Fraunces kept them.

The diversion, in her day, was to stop at one of the mead houses, which were in the Gardens, "inside the Palisadoes," and imbibe that eminently feminine tipple of the same name. She very carefully describes mead to be a "sort of liquor made of honey, which is weak and has a pleasant taste." On another occasion when she visited the Gardens, she sat in a bower where she had "a fine view of the North River down as far as Sandy Hook," and was served to "sangaree," another mild beverage consisting of red wine sweetened and flavored with nutmeg and diluted with water.

When Fraunces had the Gardens he established a museum, the humble progenitor of the Eden Musée, where could be seen a series of wax works, "seventy figures in miniature representing the Queen of Sheba bringing presents to King Solomon, with a view of his Palace, Courtyard and Garden." Tea, coffee, and hot rolls were served morning and evening, and the place became a favorite resort for the world and his wife on their afternoon drive.[39] When Bolton, in 1770, left the Queen's Head to take the Province Arms, Fraunces again became host, still continuing, however, his interest in the Vauxhall Gardens. In his advertisement announcing his return to the Queen's Head he "flatters himself that the public are so well satisfied as to his ability to serve them as to render the swelling of an advertisement useless." He agreed to "send out dinners and suppers to lodgers and others who lived at a convenient distance."

Fraunces apparently wished to pose as a patron of science, for shortly after his return two lectures on "That Part of Philosophy which tells of the Nature, Use and Effects of the Air" were given at the Queen's Head. It was presumed that these lectures would be considered "a polite and rational amusement," for which you paid a half dollar, and tickets were on sale at the tavern and the publishers'.[40] This famous old inn had its share of patriotic celebrations, due perhaps, in part, to the fact that the host was a patriot. His name is to be found in the roster of State troops as private in Colonel Malcolm's regiment, one of the sixteen officered by General Washington. On this old building—that for more than one hundred years has continuously stood—"that Temple of true liberty, an Inn," is painted in letters so large that he who runs may read, the following:

> Washington
> Long Room,
> 1768
> The Oldest
> Landmark
> in the City.

History supplies the interesting fact that it was in this Long Room that Washington, on December 4, 1783, bade farewell to his officers when starting for Annapolis, a circumstance which led to the inn being known as Washington's Headquarters. Ten days earlier, the evacuation of the city by the British had been joyously celebrated, and a public dinner given by Governor Clinton to General Washington, and the other officers at the Queen's Head concluded the festivities of the day."[41] After the dinner thirteen toasts were drunk,—a significant number in those days,—the first to the " United States of America," and the last to our cherished Monroe Doctrine—in embryo —"May this Day be a Lesson to Princes!"

REFERENCES.

1. D. P. De Vries, *Voyages from Holland to America,* 1632–44, p. 148.
2. *Records of New Amsterdam,* New York, 1897, ii., p. 49, note.
3. E. B. O'Callaghan's *New York Calendar Historical Manuscripts,* ii., pp. 45, 89.
4. *New York Colonial Documents,* i., pp. 189, 190, 300.
5. E. B. O'Callaghan's *New York Calendar Historical Manuscripts,* iv., p. 200 ; ii., p. 101.
6. *Records of New Amsterdam,* i., pp. 5–8, 13, 22, 28, 34 ; iii., p. 159, note ; vi., pp. 364, 403, 405.
7. *Ibid.,* ii., p. 233 ; v., p. 43.
8. *Charter of the City of New York,* 1735, p. 11 ; Appendix, p. 53.
9. *New York Weekly Journal,* September 18, 1738 ; March 10, 1740.
10. *New York Gazette,* October 1, 1753 ; May 28, 1750 ; December 3, 1750 ; *Weekly Post Boy,* August 31, 1747, Supplement.
11. *Journal of the Legislative Council,* August 29, 1701.
12. John Austin Stevens, *Harper's Monthly,* 80, p. 844.
13. *New York Colonial Documents,* iv., pp. 946, 957.
14. John Austin Stevens, *Harper's Monthly,* 64, pp. 483, 484.
15. T. F. De Voe's *The Market Book,* 1, p. 279.
16. *New York Gazette,* February 4, 1754.
17. Gaine's *Mercury,* November 5, 1759.
18. *New York Weekly Journal,* October 10, 1743.
19. *Weekly Post Boy,* September 10, 1744 ; January 28, 1745.
20. E. B. O'Callaghan's *Laws and Ordinances of New Netherlands,* p. 380.
21. *New York Weekly Journal,* July 18, 1743 ; *Post Boy,* January 7, 1746.

References

22. *New York Gazette,* May 13, 1751.
23. *Life and Works of John Adams,* ii., p. 346.
24. *New York Gazette,* June 30, 1735 ; January 20, 1736 ;
    Weekly Journal, July 4, 1737.
25. *New York Historical Society Collections,* 1829, p.
    277.
26. *New York Weekly Journal,* September 6, 1742.
27. *New York Gazette,* November 26, 1783.
28. *Pennsylvania Historical Magazine,* xii., p. 445.
29. *New York Gazette,* April 15, 1754.
30. *King's College,* of this series, p. 35.
31. *New York Gazette,* May 16, 1763.
32. *Journal of the General Assembly,* 1764, ii., pp. 655,
    659.
33. Gaine's *Mercury,* April 25, 1763.
34. *New York Gazette,* June 13, 1763.
35. *Post Boy,* November 7, 1765.
36. *Mercury,* February 17, 1766 ; May 26, 1770 ; January 7, 1771.
37. *New York Gazette,* September 28, 1777.
38. *Colonial Records of the Chamber of Commerce,* p.
    307.
39. *Mercury,* March 19, 1770.
40. *New York Weekly Journal,* October 5, 1770.
41. *New York Gazette,* November 26, 1783.

THE DOCTOR IN OLD NEW YORK

Half Moon Series

Published in the Interest of the New York City History Club.

VOLUME II.   NUMBER VIII.

THE DOCTOR IN OLD NEW YORK.

BY F. H. BOSWORTH, M.D.

The Seventeenth Century Doctor

NEW YORK had its beginnings in the early part of the seventeenth century, and the first doctor who made his appearance on Manhattan Island was a seventeenth-century doctor. The world at this time, as we know, had not fully emerged from that long era of darkness which we call the Middle Ages. While the arts, letters, and the amenities and luxuries of life had developed in a remarkable way, science can scarcely be said to have made any progress; and the doctor, if we are to regard his calling as a science, still followed the traditions which had been handed down from remote ages.

We can perhaps best understand the status of medicine at this period when we recall the fact that the works of Hippocrates, who lived in the second century before Christ, and those of Galen, who lived in the fifth century of the Christian era, were still the standard authorities on physic for the practitioner of the seventeenth century. This condition of things seems most curious to us in the present progressive age, when the teachings of twenty or thirty years ago are so often set aside as obsolete. The doctor's conception of disease processes, and of the action of remedies, was a confused and shadowy theory of humors, sympathetics, and antagonistics. As Culpepper, one of the standard authorities of the day, writing in 1657, says: "The whole ground of physic is comprehended in these two words, sympathy and antipathy. The one cures by strengthening the parts of the body afflicted, the other by resisting the malady afflicting."

The seventeenth-century doctor affords a curious and interesting study both in his personality and his practice. His armamentarium consisted of certain simples and compounds, together with a few mineral remedies. These were made up into unguents, plasters, liniments, pills, boluses, and decoctions, while his herbs required to be gathered in certain phases of the moon or conjunctions of the planets. Above all, however, his lancet was his main reliance, and he seems to have used it on all occasions, and oftentimes continuously and most vigorously. Of this we have a quaint and striking illustration in the letter of the good Deacon and Doctor Fuller of Plymouth, who, writing to Governor Bradford, on June 28, 1630, says: "I have been to Matapan (Dorchester) at the request of Mr. Warham, and let some twenty of these people's blood. I had conference of them till I was weary."

Of the doctor, as met with in the early days of New Amsterdam, we have but brief and fragmentary records. Perhaps we can form some estimate of him by a brief glance at his English confrère of the day. At this time the most prominent medical man of London was Sir Theodore Mayerne, physician to Henry IV. and Louis XIII. of France, and James I. and Charles I. of England. He was probably the most eminent physician of his time in Europe, and was a somewhat extensive writer on medical topics. With a shrewdness which has found many imitators, even in our own time among fashionable physicians, he made a specialty of the treatment of gout. Dr. Mayerne, however, recommended a most clumsy and inordinate administration of violent drugs. Calomel and sugar of lead, as well as pulverized human bones, were among his favorite remedies. The principal ingredient in his famous gout-powder was raspings of a human skull unburied. But his sweetest compound, as Jeaffreson tells us, was his Balsam of Bats, strongly recommended as an unguent for hypochondriacal persons, into which entered adders, bats, sucking whelps, earth-worms, and the marrow of the thigh-bone of an ox.

Another distinguished doctor of this period also was Sir Thomas Brown, the erudite and famous author of *Religio Medici*. Another was the "eccentric, gallant, brave, credulous, persevering, frivolous" Sir Kenelm Digby, courtier, cook, lover, warrior, political intriguer, and finally doctor. By means of his famous sympathetic powder some of the most marvellous cures in the history of medicine were accomplished. Curiously enough, the composition of this powder was revealed after the Doctor's death, by his chemist, and consisted merely of sulphate of lime which was obtained by a rather unusual but unnecessarily complicated process. Among others of this time were William Harvey, who, unlike those we have mentioned, left to the world a bequest of incalculable value in his great discovery of the circulation of the blood, and Sydenham, one of the first to make available to his own and subsequent generations the value of intelligent clinical observation.

We refer casually to these gentlemen as throwing a certain light on the seventeenth-century doctor whose advent on Manhattan Island is the subject of the present paper. For while none of them, with the exception of Sydenham and Harvey, made any permanent contribution to the world's progress, their personality and practice afford us an interesting subject for study. They certainly did not treat disease with any intelligent conception of the pathological process they intended to counteract, or of the true action of drugs; yet they undoubtedly thought they cured disease. Was it by their practice or their personality? Something of the practice we have seen. Their personality was a curious picture.

On the continent at this time the doctor was decked out in long black gown and skull-cap, a modification of the robe of his priestly predecessor. There seems to have been an evident attempt to make himself impressive and decorative. His gold-headed cane was absolutely essential, and we have, preserved in the College of Physicians in London, to this day, the cane carried successively by Radcliff, Mead, Askin, Pitcairn, and Bailey. His wig was adorned with two and even three tails, and so elaborately dressed that he often went bareheaded through the streets of London lest it should become disordered. His silk coat and stockings and silver buckles appear to have been essential parts of his dress, and even a muff to preserve the softness and delicacy of the hands was carried by many. Up to the days of Charles II. he made his visits on horseback, riding sideways after the fashion of women, but after that time he rode in his coach, drawn by two, and sometimes four and even six horses.   This, then, is the prototype of the physician who, compelled by the stress of home surroundings to emigrate, or led by the hope of gain, made his advent on Manhattan Island in the early beginnings of New York.

Although the West India Company's directors in their original charter enjoined upon the colonists to find ways and means whereby they could support the minister and schoolmaster to attend to the mental and spiritual needs of the people, they seem to have been content in ministering to the physical ailments with directing that comforters of the sick (*Zieckentroosters*) be appointed.   I trust that this was not a reflection on the medical men of the day, although one can easily understand how a comforter of the sick might under some circumstances be a safer attendant than the seventeenth-century doctor, to whom we have before referred.   We find recorded as officially serving in the capacity of *Zieckentroosters* and receiving pay from the Company under the first Governor, Eva Pietersen Evertsen and one Molenaer.

After the great commercial value and promise of the settlement of the New Netherlands had been recognized, and the Dutch West India Company was organized for establishing a post here and carrying on trade, it is probable that in each ship's company a barber-surgeon was included, who was competent to bleed and perform minor operations, for we find that Harman Mynderts Van den Bogaerdet visited the province in 1631, as surgeon to the ship *Eendraght*, while in 1633 William Deering, surgeon to the ship *William* of London, visited the island. These good gentlemen seem to have been birds of passage who left no abiding record on the pages of history, and it is not until twenty-eight years after Hudson's discovery, and fourteen years after the arrival of the good ship *New Netherlands*, sent out by the Dutch West India Company, that we find the record of a regularly educated medical man making his appearance in the settlement. Previous to this, however, midwives seem to have been established in the colony in an official character, for we find Lysbert Dircksen, wife of Barent Dircksen, was the town midwife of New Amsterdam in 1638, and that a house was erected for her at the public expense by the direction of Governor Van Twiller. In 1644, Tryntje Jonas, the mother of Annetje Jansz, was the midwife of the town. She died in 1646, and the daughter had some difficulty in collecting from the West India Company certain monies due for the mother's services to the colony. In 1655, Hellegond Joris was appointed midwife to the town, and in 1660, the Council voted her a salary of one hundred guilders a year for attending the poor.

The first educated medical man who made his appearance in New Amsterdam was Dr. Johannes La Montagne, a learned Huguenot gentleman, who arrived in the spring of 1637. He was born in 1595, and received his degree from the University at Leyden, where he married his first wife, Rachel De Forest. After practising in Leyden a number of years, he determined to follow his wife's family, who had previously emigrated to America. He is styled "*een wel gestudient man*" and his reputation as a physician immediately gave him a certain prominence in the village. His first wife dying a few years after his arrival, he married again, in 1647, Agritha Fillis, widow of Arent Corson. By the latter he had no family. By the first wife he had five children, of whom his daughter Rachel married Dr. Gysbert Van Lintroch. Dr. La Montagne's ability was early recognized by Governor Kieft, who appointed him to a seat in his Council in 1638, a position he retained under Governor Stuyvesant. Again, when the Council voted that a public school should be established, if practicable, in the City Tavern, La Montagne was for the time appointed schoolmaster. He is said once to have saved Governor Kieft from assassination. At one time he was sent with an expedition of fifty men to defend Fort

New Hope (New London) against the Massachusetts colonists. At the time of the English occupation he was in command of Fort Orange as Vice-Director and surrendered the fort to the newcomers. La Montagne held, moreover, at different times various positions of trust, in which he seems always to have acquitted himself with credit. It is believed that he accompanied Governor Stuyvesant on his return to Holland in 1665, and that he died there in 1670.

On March 28, 1638, there arrived the third Governor of the Colony, William Kieft. He was accompanied by two surgeons, who apparently came in an official capacity: Gerrit Schult and Hans Kierstede. Of Schult we have no further record; but Kierstede, who came from Magdeburg, Saxony, seems to have settled down to practise his profession in the colony permanently. He is described in the old records as "surgeon," and received various grants of land on the Strand, now Pearl Street, from the Company, in 1647, 1653, and 1656. In 1642, he married Sarah Roelofs, the daughter of the famous midwife, Annetje Jansz, by whom he had ten children. In one of the letters from the Director in Holland he is spoken of as having served the Company "long and faithfully." He died in 1666. Henry T. Kierstede, who kept the drug store on Broadway near its junction with Seventh Avenue, some thirty years ago, was the great-great-grandson of Surgeon Hans, and sold a famous unguent, Kierstede's ointment, which was said to have been made after a formula of his ancestor.

In the same year, 1638, Dr. Peter Van der Linde came over in the ship *Lore*, accompanied by his wife, Elsje. His wife dying, he married, in 1644, Martha, the widow of Jan Menje. In 1640 he appears in the records as inspector of tobacco, and in 1648, as schoolmaster and clerk of the church. He seems to have been harshly treated by Stuyvesant, and left the colony. Apparently the colonists had not learned the art of specializing in occupations, and professional men, as well as others, had to take their turn at whatever opportunity suggested or necessity compelled, as in the case of Roelofsen who added to the slender salary of a school-teacher the probably larger emoluments which accrued from taking in washing.

The Indian War of 1643, so rashly brought on by Governor Kieft, necessitated the bringing to the colony from Curaçoa a company of soldiers, and with them came Surgeon Paulus Van der Beeck. At the close of the war he married the Widow Bennet, who owned a farm of nine hundred and thirty acres in Gowanus. The farm had been devastated and the house burned. The site was about what is now the corner of Third Avenue and Twenty-eighth Street, Brooklyn, and there the newly married couple rebuilt the house and reclaimed the farm. Van der Beeck, dividing his time between farming and the practice of his profession, thus became the first medical man of Brooklyn. He seems to have been a man of enterprise, acting also in later years as tithe-collector and ferry-master. He was at one time severely reprimanded by the Council for keeping would-be passengers waiting "half the day and night before he would carry them across the river." He seems to have prospered and grown rich, for in 1675 he was assessed "two polls, two horses, four cows, three ditto of three years, one ditto of one year, and twenty morgens of land of the value of £133, 10 s."

In 1647, William Hayes and Peter Brucht are recorded as having practised in the colony, and between 1649 and 1652 we find notices of John Can, Jacob Mollenaer, Isaac Jansen, and Jacob Hendrichsen Varvanger. The former of these were probably ship surgeons who practised upon the colonists while their vessels were detained in the harbor. The latter seems to have settled here permanently, and is one of three men whom we find recorded as regularly established physicians in 1658, the other two being Hans Kierstede and one L'Orange. Dr. Jacob Hendrichsen Varvanger came over to New Amsterdam in 1646, and served the Company faithfully until the English occupation, when he took the oath of allegiance. In 1654, we find him petitioning the Director-General and Council for payment "for the use of his medicament," which he had been importing from Holland at his own expense for several years. He was promptly paid and his salary increased. In 1674 his property was valued at 8000 florins.

Among the physicians who landed in New York and settled in the outlying colonies was Dr. Abram Staats, who came from Holland in 1642, and settled at Fort Orange, immediately taking a somewhat prominent position in the colony, for he became a member of the Council and aided in making an important treaty with the Indians. His house at Claverack was burned by the savages and his wife and two sons perished in it. He was a large fur trader and for many years commanded a sloop plying between Albany and New Amsterdam. He had a son, Samuel Staats, who was born in the village of New Amsterdam and was subsequently sent to Holland for an education, returning to practise his profession in New York, where he arose to a considerable degree of eminence, dying in 1715. Another son, Jacob, was a surgeon in Albany.

Another physician at Fort Orange was Jacob

D'Hinnse, who appears to have made a considerable reputation as a teacher of medicine. A number of medical students from the various settlements studied with him. The records of a lawsuit are still extant at Albany between the doctor and a patient, one Thos. Powell. The doctor sues for his fees. The plaintiff pleads the existence of a contract for yearly attendance at two beavers ($6.40) per annum. The doctor responds that the contract was for medical attendance alone, not for surgical treatment. The case was not decided.

In 1660, Jacob De Commer is said to have been the leading surgeon of New Amsterdam, but later he removed to one of the outlying colonies, New Amsdel (Newcastle), Delaware, and in 1661, Dr. J. Hughes practised his profession in the city. Between 1658 and 1680 we find recorded the names of Doctors Peter Johnson Vandenburg, Cornelius Van Dyke, Henry Taylor, and Herman Wessels, together with Samuel Megapolensis. This latter was a son of the Rev. Johannes Megapolensis, who came to New Amsterdam in 1642. He was sent to Harvard College in 1657, and afterwards to the University of Utrecht where he graduated in theology and also received the degree of Doctor of Medicine. On his return to this country he was appointed pastor of the church but continued to practise medicine also during his life. He was one of the Dutch

Commissioners to negotiate terms of capitulation with the English in 1664. Among other professional men of whom we have brief record as connected with the Colony at this period were Girardus Beekman, Michael de Marco Church, and Giles Gaudineau. Beekman was a son of William Beekman, who was a member of Governor Leisler's Council. After the overthrow and execution of Leisler, Beekman was tried for treason, convicted, and sentenced to be hanged. He was subsequently pardoned and filled a number of prominent positions in the councils of different governors. Gaudineau, who signed himself *chirurgo-physician*, was a Huguenot and a man of considerable ability. He became a citizen of New York in 1686, and took an active part in the affairs of the settlement. He was from Sigournay in Low Poictou, and had two daughters, Suzanne and Helene. Suzanne returned to France, but Helene remained in America and was married, October 18, 1702, to Jacques DesBrosses. Gaudineau was a lieutenant under Dongan in the war against the French and Indians, and in 1708 was a vestryman of Trinity Church.

At the time of the Dutch surrender, Johannes Kerfbyle, a Hollander and a graduate of Leyden University, came to the Colony, where he arose to a considerable eminence as a practitioner of medicine. In 1691, he performed what was probably the first *post-mortem* examination made in America, when under the direction of the authorities he made an autopsy on the body of Governor Slaughter, whose sudden death it was suspected had been due to the administration of poison.

During Governor Kieft's administration a moderate immigration seems to have set in, and the village was filling with people not in the employ of the Company ; hence the question arose in the minds of the Directors, whether they should still maintain a surgeon at their own expense, or allow all those who wished, to practise their profession independently. As we have already seen, medical practice at this day was not restricted by diplomas and licenses, but, to a certain extent, every one deemed himself competent to practise along certain lines, and large numbers were accustomed to avail themselves of the privilege. Three such practitioners were well known to have made pills and sold Vienna drinks, *i. e.*, a concoction of rhubarb, senna, and port wine, to the people of New Amsterdam in 1652. Pieter Le Feber, a French Huguenot, petitioned the Council in 1653 for permission to sell certain waters prepared by him for medicinal uses. The desired permission was given, but the Council were in doubt as to the legality of their action under the laws of the Company, since brewers and wholesale

Barber-
Surgeons

dealers, including distillers, were not permitted to keep a tavern, or sell beer or wine at retail.   Le Feber seems to have discoursed so eloquently before the Directors of the many virtues of his decoction, that an exception was made in his favor on humane grounds, and he was permitted to sell his marvellous water at both wholesale and retail.

We have seen that one of the doctors of the early colony called himself a chirurgo-physician.   This was an irregular title, for the doctor of the seventeenth century was either a chirurgeon (contracted into surgeon at the beginning of the eighteenth century), physician, or barber-chirurgeon, the designation of doctor not coming into use in America until about 1769.   This association of the surgical and tonsorial art seems very curious to one living in the nineteenth century, but it arose in a very simple and natural way.   Physicians have been known in history from the earliest recorded times.   A chirurgeon (from the Greek words, $\chi\epsilon\acute{\iota}\rho$, hand, and $\acute{\epsilon}\rho\gamma o\nu$, work) seems to have been at first merely an assistant of the physician, performing for him various minor duties. This condition existed through the days of Greek and Roman civilization, but during the Dark Ages the practice of medicine in Europe fell almost entirely into clerical hands, and the duties of both physician and surgeon were performed by the priesthood.   Certain abuses

crept in which led the ecclesiastical authorities to interfere and forbid the clergy from practising outside their monasteries.   And again,
as we find recorded in various Councils of the
Church during the ninth and tenth centuries,
the shedding of blood by the clergy, as in
surgical operations, was absolutely interdicted.
In order to retain their practice they were in
the habit of sending out their barbers to perform blood-letting and other of the minor operations in surgery.   By that time the shaven
priesthood had come into being, and the bar-
ber was an *attaché* of every monastic institution.   As we can readily see, these monastery
barbers very soon began to practise independently.   As they grew in number and strength
they became incorporated into special crafts,
that of the barber-surgeons of England being
regularly chartered in the fourteenth century.
This institution became one of the wealthy
corporations of London, and flourished for
four centuries, and it was not until 1745 that it
became separated into two crafts, that of the
barbers on the one hand, and the surgeons on
the other.   Of course, there resulted from the
condition of things during this period a bitter
and persistent rivalry between the barber-
surgeons and the chirurgeons.   This spirit of
rivalry was early manifested in New Amsterdam, where we find that the surgeons of the
colony seemed to consider themselves entitled

to the exclusive right to practise on shore. But it also seems evident that they desired to include in this practice the art of shaving, while the barbers of ships visiting in these waters claimed also the right to practise on shore while their ships were lying in harbor. It appears that the ships' barbers had committed a number of mistakes in treatment while on shore, although there was no reflection cast on their proficiency with the razor. Hence, as a result of this, the surgeons of the colony sent a petition to the Directors, asking them to forbid these intruders from shaving people on shore. The action of the Directors in this matter is the first ordinance, I believe, ever passed to regulate the practice of medicine in New York. It is a curious document, and I copy it in full, as embodied in the Dutch Records of the island, February 2, 1652 :

" On the petition of the Chirurgeons of New Amsterdam, that none but they alone be allowed to shave, the Director and Council understand that shaving doth not appertain exclusively to chirurgery, but is an appendix thereto ; that no man can be prevented operating on himself nor to do another the friendly act, provided it is through courtesy and not for gain, which is hereby forbidden. It is further ordered that ship barbers shall not be allowed to dress any wounds nor administer any potions on shore without the previous knowledge and special consent of the petitioners, or at least of Dr. Montagne."

During the latter years of Stuyvesant's incumbency, the Company's surgeon was the before-mentioned Master Jacob Hendrichsen Varvanger. He was a man of somewhat broader humanity than his fellows, and conscientious in the performance of his duty. He was in the employ of the Company for a number of years and seems to have become considerably exercised over the fact that the soldiers and other employees of the Company, when sick, could not have that care and attendance which was necessary to a proper treatment of their diseases. He says in a report to the Director and Council, December 12, 1658,—

"He is sorry to learn that such sick people must suffer much through cold, inconveniences, and the untidiness of the people who have taken the poor fellows into their houses where bad smells and filth counteract all health-producing effects of the medicaments given by him, the surgeon. Death has been the result of it in several cases and many deaths will follow.

"He requests, therefore, that by order of the Director and Council a proper place may be arranged for the reception of such patients, to be taken care of by a faithful person, who is to assist them bodily with food and fire and allow soldiers to pay for it out of their wages and rations, Company's negroes to be attended at Company's expense or as thought most advisable."

He was directed to look up such a place and person and report.

The first hospital on Manhattan Island, and probably the first hospital in North America, was thus established, and on the twentieth

Dr.
Varvanger

day of December, 1758, Hilletje Wilbruch, the wife of Condil Tubias Wilbruch, was appointed its matron at a yearly salary of 100 florins. It became known as the Old Hospital. It was sold by the Governor, in 1680, for £200, after it had become unserviceable, and better buildings were supplied.

The first coroner's inquest of which I find record in the Colony was held in February, 1658, by this same Master Varvanger, with his colleagues, Kierstede and Jacob N——. It seems that one Bruyn Barentsen had gotten into a brawl with Jacob Eldersen and had received a severe beating at his hands, of which, apparently, he subsequently died. Eldersen was acquitted, however, as they found that the beating had nothing to do with the death, for after receiving it Bruyn had been able to row across to Breuckelen.

Some suggestion as to the social position of the doctor at this time is found in the enrolment of the citizens of New Amsterdam in 1657, when Dr. Varvanger's name is absent from the "Great Citizens," numbering twenty, but is found in the list of "Small Citizens," numbering 204.

The first attempt on the part of the authorities to regulate the practice of medicine by official enactment we have noticed in the matter of the barber-surgeons in 1652. In 1657, we find an effort made to enroll the doctors or to compel them to do detective work. An ordinance passed by the Schout and Burgomaster and Scheppens gives notice to all chirurgeons of the city, that when they are called to dress a wound they shall ask the patient who wounded him, and that information be thereby given to the Schout. If these gentlemen were as jealous of their professional privileges as the doctor of the nineteenth century, they probably took a firm stand in this matter and declined to reveal professional secrets. These two enactments are the only ones which we find recorded as having been instituted under the Dutch régime. Immediately after the British took possession of the Colony, a curious law was promulgated by the Duke of York for the government of all the lands included within the Duke's patent, as follows :

" That no person or persons whatever employed about the bodys of men, women, or children for the preservation of life or health as chirurgeons, midwives, physicians, or others, presume to put forth or exercise any act contrary to the known approved rule of art in each mystery or occupation, or exercise any force, violence, or cruelty upon or towards the body of any, whether young or old, without the advice and consent of such as are skilful in the same art (if such may be had) or at least of some of the wisest and gravest then present, and consent of the patient or patients if they be mentis compotes, much less contrary to such advice and consent, upon such severe punishment as the nature of the fact may deserve ; which law, nevertheless, is not intended to discourage any from all lawful use of their skill, but rather to encourage and direct them in the right use thereof, and to inhibit and restrain the presumptious arrogance of such as, through confidence of their own skill or any other sinister respects, dare boldly attempt to exercise any violence upon or towards the body of young or old, one or another, to the prejudice or hazard of the life or limb of man, woman or child."

The fees collected by the doctors of this day were probably very small, and yet, undoubtedly, the laity were oftentimes subjected to extortion at the hands of quacks and ignorant pretenders, and while we have no legislative enactment recorded in the Dutch colony to counteract this, the following act, passed in the Colony of Virginia in 1645, is interesting, as bearing upon the point :

" Whereas by the 9th act of Assembly, held the 21st of October, 1639, consideration being had and taken of the immoderate and excessive rates and prices enacted by practitioners in physick and chirurgery, and the complaints made to the then assembly of the bad consequence thereof, it so happening through the said intolerable exactions that the hearts of divers masters were hardened rather to suffer their servants to perish for want of fit means and applications than by seeking relief to fall into the hands of griping and avaricious men ; it be apprehended by such masters, who were more swayed by politick respects than Xian [Christian] duty or charity, that it was the more gainfull and saving way to stand to the hazard of their servants than to entertain the certain charge of physitian or chirurgeon, whose demands for the most parte exceed the purchase of the patient ; it was therefore enacted, for the better redress of the like abuses thereafter, untill some fitter course should be advised on, for the regulating physitians and chirurgeons within the Colony, that it should be lawful and free for any person or persons in such cases where they should conceive the acc't of the physitian or chirurgeon to be unreasonable, either for his pains or for his drugs or medicines, to arrest the said physitian or chirurgeon either to the quarter court or county court where they inhabitt, where the said physitian should declare upon oath the true value, worth and quantity of his drugs and medicines administered to or for the use of the plt. [patient] whereupon the court where the matter was tryed to adjudge, and allow to the said physitian or chirurgeon such satisfaction and reward as they in their discretions should think fitt.

" And it was further ordered that when it should be sufficiently proved in any of the said courts that a physitian or chirurgeon had neglected his patient, or that he had refused, being thereunto required, his helpe or assistance to any person or persons in sickness or extremity, that the said physitian or chirurgeon should be censured by the said court for such his neglect or refusal, which said act, and every clause therein mentioned and repeated, this present grand assembly to all intents and purposes doth revive, ratifie, allow and confirme, with this only exception that the plts. [or patients] shall have their remedy at the county courts respectively, unless in case of appeal."

And how much the fees were at this time may be judged from the fact that this same colony only a hundred years later passed an act making the highest fee for every visit or prescription in town, or within five miles, five shillings, and for every mile above five, sixpence. Curiously enough, it was further enacted that any person who had studied physic in the university, and had taken a degree therein, be allowed to charge double the above amounts.

The first burial-ground in New York was situated on the west side of Broadway, on the rise of ground above the Bowling Green, and not far north of the present Morris Street. This ancient churchyard had become very full in 1665. In 1656, Governor Stuyvesant had proposed to abandon it as a place of burial, and desired instead to tear down houses south of the fort, (the first was the plot bounded by Bowling Green, Whitehall Bridge, and State Street,) and make a burial-place there. The citizens suggested the establishment of a place on the hill west of the fort, near a windmill (part of the present Battery), which they described as a good hill, clear of timber. Nothing was done till 1665, when a new fence was put up, and the old graveyard, which had for some time prior lain quite open to the encroachment of animals along the streets, was enclosed.

"In 1676 or 1677 the old church yard was divided up into four lots each 25 x 100 and sold at auction, the new burial place being established near Trinity Church."

As the colony grew in numbers and prosperity under the English administration we find at the beginning of the eighteenth century a flourishing village of five thousand inhabitants and its doctors becoming men of more liberal education and wider culture. It is unnecessary to enumerate all who practised here at this time, but certain names stand out more prominently and are worthy of note. John Van Buren, a native of Buren, near Amsterdam, came to New York early in 1700, having studied under the celebrated Boerhave and taken his degree at Leyden University. He occupied a prominent position in the colony, and his son, Beekman Van Buren, who was born in 1727, succeeded him in his practice, becoming the progenitor of the large family of that name scattered throughout the United States. Another prominent physician of the day was Dr. Cadwallader Colden, who was born in Scotland, and graduated at the University of Edinburgh in 1705. Having studied medicine, he spent ten years in practice in Philadelphia, when he was appointed by Governor Hunter to the position of Surveyor-General of the New York Colony. He was not only an accomplished physician and writer, but also an eminent naturalist, his writings on botanical subjects showing a remarkable familiarity with this science. He moreover is said to have collected and described between three and four hundred new plants in America. He wrote a history of the Five Nations, besides various papers on medical subjects, and held the position of Lieutenant-Governor in 1761, and again in 1765. He died in 1766. .

Dr. Isaac Du Bois, also a graduate of Leyden, practised here in the earlier part of the century. He is notable, I think, in having contributed an excellent paper on the subject of blood-letting, in which he discoursed rather vigorously upon its abuse, as well as its use. Another practitioner of the day was Dr. John Nichol, who died in 1745, after having practised in this city for nearly half a century. He divided his duties to his patients with occupying a position on the Bench in Governor Leisler's time. Dr. John Dupuy, who died in 1745, at the age of twenty-eight, seems to have attained a somewhat enviable position in the Colony for so young a man, if we may believe the following notice outlined in *The Weekly Postboy* of that year: "Last night, Sunday, July 21st, died in the prime of life to the almost universal regret and sorrow of the City, Mr. John Dupuy, M.D., and man midwife, in which loss it may be truly said, as of Goliah's sword, 'there was none like unto him.'"

Among others of this period were Frank Brinley, who was surgeon to the New York troops during the French and Indian War; Ebenezer Crosby, a surgeon in the Continental Army, who settled in the city after the close of the war and became a professor in Columbia College; and Charles McKnight, another surgeon in the Continental Army, who graduated from Princeton in 1761, and settled in the city after the close of the war, and also became a professor of anatomy. It is said that Dr. McKnight was the first physician who ever made use of a carriage in his round of visits to patients.

Dr. John Bard, a native of New York, who was born in 1716, attained notable eminence in the profession in his day. He studied under Dr. Kearsley, a prominent English physician, and settled in New York in 1746. He practised his profession here for fifty-two years, and was the first president of the Medical Society of New York, which was organized in 1788. He was a warm personal friend of Benjamin Franklin, and in connection with Dr. Middleton, in 1750, performed the second dissection of a human cadaver recorded in America. His son, Dr. Samuel Bard, who was born in 1742, after graduating at the University of Edinburgh commenced the practice of medicine in this city in 1765. In 1769, Dr. Bard started the first agitation in favor of the erection of a public hospital, which was finally successful, and was also one of the professors and associated in organizing the first medical school in the city of New York in 1757. He was Washington's physician during the General's residence in this city.

Richard Bailey practised in the city until his death in 1801. He published a number of interesting essays on yellow fever, which had devastated the city on so many different occasions during the seventeenth century, and is said to have been one of the first physicians to make a specialty in this city of obstetrical practice. Dr. Nicholas Romaine, who was born in 1766 and died in 1817, was one of the presidents of the New York City Medical Society, and is said to have been a fine scholar and an active promoter of all educational measures. Dr. Samuel Colossy, an Irish physician who settled for a time in New York, has left a name behind him as one of the organizers of the first medical college in the city, in which he held the chair of Professor of Anatomy. Another of the professors of this college was Peter Middleton, a Scotch physician, already referred to as having assisted Dr. Bard in his dissection.

In looking over the brief records of the eighteenth-century doctors of New York, I find no one who has inspired in me a warmer personal interest and admiration than Dr. John Jones, the son of Dr. Evan Jones. His father and grandfather were physicians before him. He studied medicine with Dr. Cadwallader Colden, of Philadelphia, and subsequently went to London and from thence to France, where he obtained the degree of doctor of medicine from the University of Rheims, and still later studied at the Universities of Leyden and of Edinburgh. On returning to New York he was made a professor of surgery in the College of New York. His life seems to have been an extraordinarily busy one. He built up a large practice, which necessarily occupied much of his time, and yet he was a large contributor to medical as well as general literature, and was a busy lecturer and clinical demonstrator. He became a warm personal friend of both Washington and Franklin. He died at the age of sixty-two. An event in the early part of his career is interesting as throwing a certain light on the times in which he lived, as well as showing the essential dignity of his character. Some of the physicians entered into a compact to distinguish themselves from the rest of their fellow-citizens by a particular mode of wearing their hair. Among the rest, it was proposed to Dr. Jones, who indignantly and very properly declined to enter into any such arrangement, declaring that he considered that and every similar means to impose upon the weakness or credulity of others, as unworthy the members of a liberal profession, and as intended to enforce that attention and respect which their own conduct and abilities should always command. While the other doctors in the town, therefore, were strutting about in the new-fashioned bob, Dr. Jones could not be distinguished from any well-bred gentleman of any other profession. Of course an attempt was made to boycott Dr. Jones by a plan not altogether unfamiliar to physicians now living, namely by refusing to consult with him. The result was as might have been expected: on the first occasion in which this plan was brought into practice the physician who refused to consult with Dr. Jones was promptly dismissed, and Dr. Jones installed in his place.

This brief review of the New York doctor of this day, I think, gives us a fair estimate of his personality, abilities, and practice. But we have referred only to the regular practitioner. That the country was overrun by ignorant pretenders, we have ample evidence by the numerous diatribes against them in the secular press. One writer, speaking of this condition, tells us that " quacks abound like locusts in Egypt." But these arise in all communities and possess no especial points of interest in this connection, except that their existence led to legal enactment for their suppression, for with the exception of the Duke of York ordinance of 1664 (already quoted), no attempt was made to protect the community from these irregular practitioners until 1760, when the following law was passed:

" An Act to regulate the practice of Physick & Surgery in the City of New York, June 10, 1760.

" Whereas many ignorant and unskilful Persons in Physick and Surgery in order to gain a Subsistence do take upon themselves to administer Physick and practice Surgery in the City of New York to the endangering of the Lives & Limbs of their Patients; and many poor & ignorant persons

inhabiting the said City who have been persuaded to become their Patients have been great sufferers thereby ; For
preventing such abuses for the future,

"Be it Enacted by his Honor, the Lieutenant Governor,
& the General Assembly, and it is hereby Enacted by the
Authority of the same, That from & after the Publication
of this Act, no Person whatsoever shall practice as a Physician or surgeon in the said City of New York before he shall
first have been examined in Physick or Surgery and approved
of and admitted by one of His Majesty's Council, the
Judges of the Supreme Court, the King's Attorney General
and the Mayor of the City of New York for the time being,
or by any three or more of them, taking to their assistance
for such Examination such proper person or persons as they
in their discretion shall think fit.   And if any Candidate
after due Examination of his learning and Skill in Physick
or Surgery as aforesaid shall be approved and admitted to
practice as a Physician or Surgeon, or both, the said Exam-
iners, or any three or more of them, shall give under their
Hands and Seals to the Person so admitted as aforesaid, a
Testimonial of his Examination & Admission in the form
following, to wit—

*" To All To Whom These Presents Shall Come Or May
Concern Know Ye*

"That We whose names are hereunto subscribed in pur-
suance of An Act of the Lieutenant Governor, the Council
and the General Assembly, made and published at New York
the ——— day of ——— in the year of our Lord One thousand
seven hundred and ——— Entitled **AN ACT** to regulate the
Practice of Physick & Surgery in the City of New York,
have duely Examined ——— of ——— Physician [or] Surgeon [or] Physician and Surgeon [as the case may be] and
having approved of his Skill have admitted him as a Physician [or] Surgeon [or] Physician and Surgeon, to practice in
the said Faculty [or] Faculties throughout this province of
New York.   **IN TESTIMONY** whereof we have subscribed
our Names and affixed our Seals to the Instrument at New

York this ———— day of ———— Anno Domini One Thousand ————.

"AND be it further Enacted by the Authority aforesaid that if any Person shall practice in the City of New York as a Physician or Surgeon or both as Physician and Surgeon without such testimonial as aforesaid he shall for every such offence forfeit the sum of five pounds, One half thereof to the use of the Person or Persons who shall sue for the same, and the other Moiety to the Church Wardens and Vestrymen of the said City for the use of the Poor thereof, the said Forfeiture to be recovered with costs before the Mayor, Recorder or any one of the Aldermen of the said City who are hereby empowered in a summary way to hear try and determine any suit brought for such forfeiture, and to give Judgment and to award Execution thereupon.

PROVIDED that this Act shall not extend to any Person or Persons administering Physick or Practicing Surgery within the said City before the Publication hereof; Or to any Person bearing His Majesty's Commission and employed in His Service as a Physician or Surgeon."

The fees of the doctor in the eighteenth century do not appear to have increased proportionately to the growth of the town, if we may judge from the following account rendered by Dr. William Laurence in the latter part of the century:

	£	s.	d.
To inoculating a child	2	8	
To a visit and a Calomel bolus		4	
To a bottle of Black Water		16	
To a visit, sewing up ye boy's lip and to sundry dressings in the cure of it		10	

	£	s.	d.
To rising in the night, a visit and dose of Calomel ye child		1	12
To five visits dressing gave ye head and bleeding		1	4
To a puke			1
To drawing a tooth			4

A writer in the *Independent Reflector* in 1753, referring to New York, says: "That place boasts the honor of above 40 gentlemen of the faculty, and far the greater number of them are mere pretenders to a profession of which they are entirely ignorant." That this latter statement is a grossly unjust charge, I need not affirm, for while one cannot always regard the seventeenth-century doctor as seriously as he seems to have taken himself, we find in his successor of the eighteenth century a broader culture, a deeper appreciation of the essential dignity of his calling, and a far better preparation and equipment for his duties. When we remember that at the end of the second third of the eighteenth century New York was a somewhat rude little town of about twenty thousand inhabitants, we cannot but accord respect to the doctors of the period, and admiration for the great foresight and broad-minded humanity which characterized the enterprises inaugurated by them for the public good.

We have already spoken of Dr. Bard. In

1768, there was organized in connection with King's College, now Columbia College, the second medical college in the New World, the first having been organized in Philadelphia in 1765. It arose apparently by a voluntary combination on the part of a number of gentlemen who had already been engaged in giving private instruction. Its faculty consisted of Drs. Middleton, on the Theory of Physic, Colossy on Anatomy, Bard on the Practice of Physic, James Smith on Chemistry and Materia Medica, J. V. B. Tennant on Midwifery, and J. Jones, Professor of Surgery. In 1769, Columbia College had conferred the degree of Bachelor of Medicine upon Samuel Kissam and Robert Tucker, but in 1770 the first degree of Doctor of Medicine conferred in New York was given to Kissam, while Tucker received his Doctor's degree in the following May. These were the first medical degrees ever conferred in America, antedating by a few weeks only those which were given at Philadelphia. On the delivering of Kissam's and Tucker's degrees in 1769, Doctor Samuel Bard made a popular address, in which he advocated the utility and necessity of a public infirmary. So "warmly and pathetically," as Dr. Middleton tells us, was the need set forth, that a subscription was immediately started, headed by Sir Henry Moore, then Governor of the Province, and the sum of £800 sterling was collected for the furtherance of this purpose, £300 being added by the corporation of the city.

The establishment of the New York Hospital was thus assured and its corner-stone was accordingly laid, on July 27, 1773. It had just reached its completion in 1775, when it was destroyed by fire. The Revolutionary War coming on prevented any attempt to re-establish it until later years. Many of those still living will recall its sequestered court, and ivy-covered walls, into which one cast a restful glance while passing through the crowded streets of lower Broadway a few years ago. Its destruction to make way for the encroachment of business, and its removal to 15th Street are of comparatively recent date. The medical and anatomical instruction which was given in that old building, was the direct cause of an event, which, for a time, seriously interrupted that cordial good-feeling which, in a notable degree, has always existed between the medical profession and the laity, as the doctor usually calls the non-medical "rest of the world." The event referred to was the Doctors Riot, in 1788, the third great riot which had occurred in the history of New York, the first being the Negro Riot in 1712, and the second being the Stamp Act Riot in 1765. The following account is the more interesting, perhaps, as being contemporaneous:

" During the last winter, some students of physic, and other persons, had dug up from several of the cemeteries in this city, a number of dead bodies for dissection. This practice had been conducted in so indecent a manner, that it raised a considerable clamor among the people. The interments not only of strangers, and the blacks, had been disturbed, but the corpses of some respectable persons were removed. These circumstances most sensibly agitated the feelings of the friends of the deceased, and wrought up the passions of the populace to a ferment.

" On Sunday, the 13th inst., a number of boys, we are informed, who were playing in the rear of the Hospital, perceived a limb which was imprudently hung out of a window to dry ; they immediately informed some persons—a multitude soon collected—entered the Hospital ; and, in their fury destroyed a number of anatomical preparations ; some of which, we are told, were imported from foreign countries —one or two fresh subjects were also found—all of which were interred the same evening. Several young doctors narrowly escaped the fury of the people ; and would inevitably have suffered very seriously had not his Honor, the Mayor, the Sheriff, and some other persons interfered, and rescued them, by lodging them in gaol. The friends to good order, hoped that the affair would have ended here ; but they were unhappily mistaken.

" On Monday morning a number of people collected, and were determined to search the houses of the suspected physicians. His Excellency, the Governor, His Honor, the Chancellor, and His Worship, the Mayor, finding that the passions of the people were irritated, went among them, and endeavoured to dissuade them from committing unnecessary depredations. They addressed the people pathetically, and promised them every satisfaction which the laws of the country can give. This had considerable effect upon many ; who, after examining the houses of the suspected doctors returned to their homes. But, in the afternoon the affair assumed a different aspect. A mob, more fond of riot and confusion than a reliance upon the promises of the Magistrates, and obedience to the laws, went to the gaol, and demanded the doctors who were there imprisoned. The Magistrates finding that the mild language of persuasion was of no avail, were obliged to order out the militia, to suppress the riot, to maintain the government, and protect the gaol. A small party of about 18 armed men assembled at 3 o'clock, and marched thither—the mob permitted them to pass through with no other insult than a few volleys of stones, dirt, &c. Another party of about 12 men, about an hour afterwards made a similar attempt, but having no orders to resist, the mob surrounded them, seized and destroyed their arms. This gave the mobility fresh courage—they then endeavoured to force the gaol, but were repulsed by a handful of men, who bravely sustained an attack of several hours. They then destroyed the windows of that building with stones, and tore down part of the fence. At dusk another party of armed citizens marched to the relief of the gaol ; and as they approached it, the mob, huzzaring, began a heavy fire with stones, brick-bats, etc.; several of this party were much hurt, and in their own defense were obliged to fire ; upon which three or four persons were killed, and a number wounded. The mob shortly after dispersed.

"On Tuesday morning the militia of General Malcom's brigade, and Col. Bauman's regiment of artillery were ordered out ; and a detachment from each were under arms during that day, and the subsequent night. But happily the mob did not again collect, and the peace of the city is once more restored.

"It must give pleasure to every good citizen to observe, by the charge of our worthy Chief Justice to the Grand Jury, that 'our laws are competent to punish any degree of guilt.' This being the fact, every friend to the State will patiently wait their operation ; and obedience to the laws, are their principal securities for the safe and quiet enjoyment of life, liberty and property. But, from mobs,

riots, and confusion, 'may the Good Lord deliver us.'"
—*New York Packet*, Friday, April 25, 1788.

Among the injured on the second day of the rioting were old Baron Steuben and John Jay, who were struck by missiles while attempting to pacify the rioters.

We have reviewed briefly the practice and personality of the seventeenth-century and of the eighteenth-century doctor. The nineteenth-century doctor, with his various activities and acquirements, comes so closely within the memory and knowledge of the present generation that we refrain from entering upon any discussion of his many virtues. This we do mainly because it is not within the province of this paper ; but were it so, it would surely be a most pleasing task to record the marvellous changes which have taken place in the latter half of the nineteenth century, building so well upon the foundations which were laid by the many earnest workers of the eighteenth, and which have gone so far towards creating out of the old mass of ignorance and superstition a true science of medicine.

REFERENCES.

American Medical Biography. JAMES THACHER, M.D., Boston, 1828.

Contribution to the Annals of Medical Progress. JOSEPH M. TONER, M.D., Washington, 1874.

Old New York. Historical Discourse. JOHN W. FRANCIS, M.D., New York, 1866.

A Book about Doctors. J. C. JEAFFRESON, London, 1860.

Curiosities of Medical Experience. J. G. MILLINGEN, M.D., London, 1839.

Historic Tales of Olden Times. J. F. WATSON.

American Medical and Philosophical Register.

BRODHEAD'S *History of the State of New York.*

VALENTINE'S *Manual of the Common Council of New York.*

New York Independent Reflector.

HENING'S *Statutes at Large.*

Ancient Charter and Laws of Massachusetts Bay.

E. B. O'CALLAGHAN'S *History of the New Netherlands.*

Documentary History of New York.

Medical Repository.

LAMB'S *History of the City of New York.*

STONE'S *History of New York City.* New York, 1872.

New York Gazette.

New York Packet.

New York Journal.

Daily Advertiser.

New York Gazeteer.

EARLY SCHOOLS AND SCHOOLMASTERS

Half Moon Series

Published in the Interest of the New York City History Club.

VOLUME II. NUMBER IX.

EARLY SCHOOLS AND SCHOOLMASTERS OF NEW AMSTERDAM.

By EMMA VAN VECHTEN.

DURING the first few years after the founding of New Amsterdam little attention was paid to the education of the children. The West India Company regarded the settlement in the light of a trading-post rather than of a colony and was bent on receiving rather than giving privileges.[1]   Although it had made vague promises guaranteeing to settlers many advantages, spiritual and material, it was in no haste to redeem its pledges.   The settlers for their part were so much occupied with planting grain, raising their thatch-roofed cottages, and repairing their rickety old fort, that the children were neglected and roamed unvexed of schoolmasters, in ignorance and bliss, along the banks of the broad canal, or clambered across the rocks of the Capske at low tide.

So things went on for seven years ; then came a change.   The spring of 1633 opened propitiously for the little colony. Surely it promised great things that the same year should bring to the settlement a new governor, a new minister, and a new schoolmaster, the first who had ever set foot in the colony. Yet it was but a very short time before the new Governor had earned his title of "Walter, the Waverer," before the new domine, Everardus Bogardus, proved himself a quarrelsome shepherd, and the new schoolmaster had shown his unfitness to train the youthful burghers of New Amsterdam either in wisdom or virtue.

The career of Adam Roelantsen, this first pedagogue of New Amsterdam, was a checkered one, and hardly bears inspection, if we wish to believe in the worth of the founder of our schools. Valentine gives a sad account of his misdoings, and though that Froissart of our city chronicles is generally to be taken with many grains of caution, in this instance he is so reinforced by the court records that his testimony must be accepted as in the main fair and just.

Roelantsen was born in Dokkum, a city of Northern Holland, in 1606,[2] and was therefore twenty-seven years old at the time he landed in New Amsterdam. Within a few years after his arrival he had entered upon his turbulent and litigious experiences. On September 20, 1638, we find a suit before the court in which Roelantsen figures as plaintiff against Gillis de Voocht, on a demand for payment for washing defendant's linen. The defendant made no objection to the price asked ; but claimed that Roelantsen had agreed to do the washing by the year, and that time being not yet expired, the payment was not due. The court held with the defendant, and Roelantsen was compelled to subsist till the end of his contract upon his professional stipend, which was unquestionably meagre. In the same year the schoolmaster appeared again in the courts, making affidavit this time against Grietje Reyners for misconduct. He soon had occasion to prove the truth of the proverb of his race—*Wie zijn buren beledigt maakt het zich zelven daarna zuur* (He who slanders his neighbors makes it sour for himself), for when he undertook to circulate evil reports touching Jochem Haller's wife, that angry burgher haled him before the court on a charge of slander. Roelantsen in his turn accused various people of slander, though it is hard to see what fiction worse than truth could have been invented about him by his neighbors.

No wonder the old record states that "people did not speak well of him." In spite of his reputation, however, he succeeded in marrying a widow presumably possessed of some property, as we hear no more of his taking in washing, and in 1642, after his return from a temporary sojourn in Rensselaerswyck, we read of the following contract made by him for a house to be built on the north side of Brouwer Street, between Whitehall and Broad, and next door but one to Van Courtlandt's brewery. By the terms of the contract "John Teunison agrees to build the same of the following dimensions : In length thirty feet, in width eighteen feet, in height eight feet ; the beams to be hewn at four sides, the house to be well and tight clapboarded and roofed with substantial reed thatch ; the floors tight and made of clapboard ; two doors, one entry, a pantry, a bed-stead, a staircase to go to the garret ; the upper part of the chimneys to be of wood ; one mantelpiece ; the entry to be three feet wide with a partition. The house to be ready by 1st of May next."

For the building of this house Roelantsen agreed to pay three hundred and fifty guilders ($140), half payment to be made when the timber was brought, and the rest when the house was finished.

This appears to have been the most prosperous period of Roelantsen's life. He had a daughter, Tryntje, baptized in the old church, and as a husband, a father, and a landholder he seemed to have given hostages to fortune, and engaged to comport himself as a good and thrifty citizen. In 1643, he was made "Weighmaster "[3] and added to his possessions by the

Adam
Roelant-
sen

purchase of another lot of land. In 1644, a son was born to him, and baptized Daniel. Two more children were added to the household before the death of his wife (spoken of in subsequent records as Lyntje Martens), and then the prosperity began to suffer eclipse.

In 1646, he set sail for Holland; but made only a short stay, for in the fall of that year we see him once more in litigation in the New Amsterdam court. The skipper of the vessel in which he returned had endeavored to collect passage money; Roelantsen refused payment, and claimed that the skipper had agreed that he should cross the ocean "free of passage money and freight of his trunk provided he would work as one of the sailors, and the skipper had also said repeatedly that he should ask no pay from Roelantsen because he said the prayers." Apparently the worth of Roelantsen's prayers was accepted by the court as an equivalent for the passage money, since it is recorded that the skipper was non-suited.

A month later Roelantsen was brought before the court as a malefactor charged with an offense so flagrant that the court declared such deeds "may not be tolerated in a country where justice is revered; therefore we condemn the said Roelantsen to be brought to the place of execution and there flogged and banished forever out of this country." In consideration of the defendant having four motherless children the sentence was delayed ; though it is difficult to see what benefit was to accrue to the little half-orphans from the guardianship of such a father. This singular vagabond seems to have had some peculiar charm for the staid burghers of New Amsterdam, for, in spite of his misdeeds, I find it stated on excellent authority that in 1647, he was appointed Provost, and in 1653, was a member of the Burgher-Corps of New Amsterdam.[4] With this date this strange figure in our early history vanishes from the records, to give place to a long line of pedagogical successors, often worthier, but seldom either so picturesque or so clearly etched out against the background of the past.

His career is the more amusing in the light of the duties of the Parochial Schoolmaster, as set forth in his commission ; these were " to promote religious worship, to read a portion of the Word of God to the people, to endeavor, as much as possible, to bring them up in the ways of the Lord, to console them in their sickness, and to conduct himself with all diligence and fidelity in his calling so as to give others a good example as becometh a devout, pious, and worthy consoler of the sick, church-clerk, Precenter and Schoolmaster."[5] The form of this commission shows how closely State, Church, and School were bound together in Old Holland, and New. The old

Dutch records expressly declare that "School-keeping and the appointment of Schoolmasters depend absolutely from the *Jus patronatus* and require a license from the Director-General and Council."* The offices of teacher and preacher were closely allied and the duty of consoling the sick equally devolved upon both domine and schoolmaster.

The requirements for the office of schoolmaster in all its capacities were severe. At one time the Consistory stated them as follows :

" First : That he be a person of suitable qualifications to officiate as schoolmaster and chorister, possessing a knowledge of music, a good voice so as to be heard, an aptitude to teach others the science, and that he should be a good reader, writer and arithmetician.

" Second : That he should be of the Reformed Religion, a member of the church, bringing with him testimonials of his Christian character and Conduct.

" Third : That whether married or unmarried he be not under twenty-five nor over thirty-five."

The duties of this official were as varied as his qualifications, since he was expected to keep the books for the Consistory, to read and pray with the sick, and in every way to supplement the work of the minister, even to turning the hour-glass during church service as a reminder that the sermon had continued beyond the allotted time. This semi-ecclesiastical character belonged only to the official schoolmaster, appointed by the West India Company and acting under the direction of the church. Other teachers independent of such control, though requiring a license from civil and church authorities, appeared in the colony from time to time and sought to earn a livelihood by tuition fees ; but these fees seem to have proved discouragingly small, and the schoolmaster generally tried to combine school-keeping with some more remunerative occupation.

One Arien Jansen Van Ilpendam opened a school in New Amsterdam a year before the sentence of banishment was passed upon Roelantsen.[1] His terms of tuition were two dried bear skins *per annum*. His school was so successful that it continued for over a decade.

The official successor of Roelantsen was Jan Stevensen, whose school-keeping is set down in the Register of New Amsterdam as dating from 1643, the year in which Roelantsen was made Weigh-master. The Company granted Stevensen a patent of a lot of land located on Broadway, then the "Heere Straat," adjoining the old churchyard. The question of a public schoolhouse was by this time seriously agitated. There was talk of building a schoolhouse when the stone church in the Fort was begun; but that edifice used up all the funds available, and the children found themselves with no better accommodation than a room in a private house, and those who have studied the conditions of life in the New Amsterdam of Stuyvesant's day, and appreciate how small were those private houses, built of mud and reeds,[*] will understand how inadequate a single room in one was likely to prove. In 1647, public education was entirely suspended, owing to the lack of suitable accommodation. The Director appealed to the Commonalty for aid, saying: "Whereas, for want of a school house, no school has been kept here during three months, by which the youth are spoiled, it is proposed to consider where a convenient place may be fixed upon so as to keep the youth from the streets and under strict subordination." Contributions for erection of the school-building were called for, and some response was made; but still without result, for a petition addressed to the States-General by the New Netherlanders in October, 1649, sets forth that

"the bowl has been going round a long time for the purpose of erecting a school house and it has been built *with words* [observe the fine sarcasm] for as yet the first stone is not laid, some materials only are provided. The money, nevertheless, given for the purpose has found its way out and is mostly spent so that it falls short and nothing permanent has as yet been effected for that purpose."[*]

To this remonstrance the West India Company made rather tart answer that "the Director hath not the administration of the

Jan
Cornelis-
sen

money that was taken up on the plate; but
Jacob Couwenhoven who is one of the petitioners, hath kept account of it in his quality
of churchwarden." These bickerings and
recriminations continued for several years ;
meanwhile Stevensen was succeeded, in 1648
or 1649, by Jan Cornelissen, reputed to have
been lazy, and much given to the use of "hot
and rebellious liquors." Perhaps the Directors of the Company began to perceive that
such service was worse than none, and that
it was hopeless to secure better without both
assured income and a suitable place of instruction, for in the spring of 1652 we find them
writing to Stuyvesant:

"We give our consent that a public school may be established, for which one schoolmaster will be sufficient, and
he may be engaged at 250 florins [$100] annually. We rec-
ommend you Jan de la Montagne whom we have provision-
ally favored with the appointment. You may appropriate
the city tavern for that purpose, if practicable."

The city tavern herein noted was no other
than the old inn which later gained greater
renown as the Stadt Huys. It raised its
quaint "crow-step gables" far above the
lowly thatched roofs of the village that clustered around it, and its walls and chimneys
of substantial brick and stone were built to
withstand wind and weather and, like the old
church, to bear enduring testimony to the

greatness of Director William Kieft, who ordered it erected, in 1642, at the head of Coenties Slip.

The Burgomasters perhaps found it not "practicable" to oust the loungers who had so long smoked their pipes in the cozy corner by the great chimney or tippled their beer over the wooden tables standing close to the roadside on the brick-floored, vine-shaded stoop. No doubt these frequenters of the old tavern were loath to give place to schoolboys with puffed breeches and plastered hair, sitting solemnly on the benches which ran along the wall, or standing in disgrace, *zotscap* on head, in the corner allotted to dunces. Just how they settled the question does not appear; but several years later, in 1656, the schoolmaster, then Harmanus Van Hoboocken, sent the following urgent appeal to the Burgomasters and Schepens on the occasion of the burning of the schoolhouse :

"The reverential request of Harmanus Van Hoboocken, Schoolmaster of this city, is that he may be allowed the use of the hall and side chamber of the City Hall for the use of his school and as a residence for his family, inasmuch as he, petitioner, has no place to keep school in, or to live in during the winter, it being necessary that the rooms should be made warm, which cannot be done in his own house from its unfitness. The petitioner further represents that he is burthened with a wife and children and moreover his wife is expected shortly to be brought to child-bed again, so that he is much at a loss how to make accomodation for his family and school children.   The petitioner therefore asks that he may use the chamber wherein Gouert Coerten at present dwells." [10]

The answer to this petition set forth that "Whereas, the room which petitioner asks for his use as a dwelling and schoolroom is out of repair and moreover is wanted for other uses, it cannot be allowed to him.   But as the town youth are doing so uncommon well now, it is thought proper to find a convenient place for their accommodation, and for that purpose petitioner is granted 100 guilders yearly."

Before the coming of Hoboocken, the office of pedagogue and *Ziekentroster*, or "consoler of the sick," had been filled by William Verstius, "a pious, well qualified and diligent schoolmaster," "who served for several years to the satisfaction of the community, and was only parted with on his own urgent solicitation to be permitted to return to Holland.

When Harmanus Van Hoboocken came over in 1655, to take the place of Verstius, he found New Amsterdam a thriving village, numbering over a hundred cottages, and sheltering about a thousand inhabitants.   He followed the traditions of his office by marrying a widow, and conducted the school so satisfactorily that, when at the end of several years he was replaced by Evert Pietersen, he was engaged as *Adelborst* (something above a common

soldier) in the Company's service, at a salary
of 10 guilders a month, and his board, and
was also employed on Governor Stuyvesant's
bouwery as clerk and schoolmaster.   As this
bouwery was located in the region of what is
now lower Third Avenue, in the neighborhood
of Twelfth Street, this second school, being at
that time far out of town, did not conflict with
the school in the little village near the Fort.
There is some evidence to show that this
lower school was held at one time within the
walls of the Fort itself ; but this is only vaguely
touched upon in the records, though it is a
constant source of wonder to me that the
great stone church raised by Kieft and of no
use except o' Sundays, was not utilized be-
tween-times for educational purposes.

Now that the colony was growing so fast
it was found that there was room for more
than one school and schoolmaster ; but the
church and the Company were very tena-
cious of their rights of control, and looked
with a jealous eye upon every effort to establish schools outside their jurisdiction.   A
very lively controversy took place between
the city magistrates and the colonial authorities on the occasion of the granting of a school-
keeping license by the magistrates to Jacob
Van Corlaer.   Straightway the Governor and
Council directed the Attorney-General to go
to the house of van Corlaer, "who has for

some time past arrogated to himself to keep school," and warn him that his arrogance and his school-keeping must cease, under pain of the displeasure of the Director and the Council.

At this juncture the Burgomasters and Schepens presented a petition in Van Corlaer's favor, and the delinquent himself humbly begged the privilege of continuing what seems at this remove his harmless calling ; but all efforts were in vain. The record states that "for weighty reasons influencing the Director General and Council the apostille [marginal note] was '*nihil actum.*'" Meanwhile the restlessness of the burghers under their limited educational privileges was increasing. Their "*Vertoogh,*" or remonstrance to the home government, had set forth that

"There should be a public school provided with at least two good masters, so that first of all, in so wild a country, where there are many loose people, the youth be well taught and brought up, not only in reading and writing but also in the knowledge and fear of the Lord. As it is now, the school is kept very irregularly, one and another keeping it according to his pleasure, and so long as he thinks proper."

As time went on and the population steadily increased, the ideas of the colonists expanded in this direction as in every other. Moreover, their local pride was touched by the advance of New England and the establishment in Massachusetts of the academy destined to become the first college planted in the Western hemisphere. In 1658, this righteous ambition found vent in a petition of the Burgomasters and Schepens to the West India Company.

"It is represented," the petitioners say, "that the youth of this place and the neighborhood are increasing in number gradually and that most of them can read and write, but that some of the citizens and inhabitants would like to send their children to a school the principal of which understands Latin; but are not able to do so without sending them to New England; furthermore they have not the means to hire a Latin schoolmaster expressly for themselves from New England, and therefore they ask that the West India Company will send out a fit person as Latin schoolmaster, not doubting that the number of persons who will send their children to such a teacher will from year to year increase until an Academy shall be formed whereby this place to great splendour will have attained, for which, next to God, the Honorable Company which shall have sent such teacher here shall have laud and praise. For our own part we shall endeavor to find a fit place in which the Schoolmaster shall hold his school."

It must always be borne in mind that the "children" for whom these educational privileges were to be provided were boys only. Nothing would have more surprised the burghers than the prediction of the classical schools and normal schools, the college and university opportunities now open to the daughters of Manhattan. In those days the domestic training of the home, or, at most,

Alexander
Carolus
Curtius

the dame-school, with its very rudimentary instruction in reading and writing, was enough to content the educational ambition of the colonial maidens.

The Directors in Holland looked with favor upon the petition of the Burgomasters and Schepens ; but they did not allow their enthusiasm for education to run away with the thrift which throughout the history of Dutch rule marked their dealings with the colonists. They wrote to Stuyvesant :

"The Rev. Domine Drisius has intimated to us more than once that in his opinion it might be serviceable to establish a Latin School for the instruction of the youth, and as we do not disapprove of the plan we have thought it proper to communicate it to you that if you consider it proper to make the experiment you may advise us in what manner it can be effected to the greatest advantage of the Community, *and with the least expense to the Company.*"

As a result of these consultations, the Company, in 1659, despatched a pedagogue, bearing the portentous name of Alexander Carolus Curtius, to be the classical instructor of the new academy at New Amsterdam, which was to bring such "laud and praise" to all concerned. He started out prosperously. The Burgomasters voted him out of the city-chest a very comfortable salary of two hundred guilders, according to one authority, five hundred according to another, with fifty in advance.

Alexander
Carolus
Curtius

Besides this, Valentine fits him out with another advance of one hundred florins where-
with to purchase merchandise to set him up in
business on his arrival in the colony, and, as
if this were not enough, he was granted the
use of a house and garden and given permission to practise medicine. The ingrate still
complained that the compensation was insufficient, and after another anxious consulta-
tion between the Director and the city rulers
it was agreed that he should be allowed to
charge six guilders per quarter for each
scholar. His grasping greed overreached itself in the next year, when he charged several
of his pupils a whole beaver-skin, worth at
least eight guilders. This was too much even
for the long-suffering Burgomasters, and Master Curtius found his salary docked for the
year.

Other causes of discontent had also arisen.
Curtius had brought over with him a fine reputation. He had been a professor in Lithuania,
and no doubt was possessed of a vast stock
of learning, and had the dead languages at his
finger ends ; but unfortunately he had little
knowledge of live human nature, and especially boy nature, which apparently was not
so unlike in New Amsterdam and New York.
The little Dutch pupils laughed to scorn the
authority of the new master, and diverted
themselves, amid the severe application de-

manded for a classical education by beating each other and playfully tearing the clothes from each other's backs. Naturally the parents disapproved, and as naturally they visited their displeasure upon the unfortunate instructor, and we can imagine the contumely they heaped upon "this fine professor who charges a whole beaver-skin and cannot even keep order." Yet we can but feel a thrill of sympathetic commiseration for poor Alexander Carolus Curtius when we read his counter-complaint that he was powerless to preserve discipline, because "his hands were tied, as some of the parents forbade him punishing their children."

Wherever the fault lay, it soon became evident that the children were not being trained up in the way they should go, and it resulted in the return of Curtius to Holland and the substitution as head master in the school, of Ægidius Luyck. This new incumbent, who was established as principal of the Latin School in 1662, proved entirely satisfactory. He was only twenty-two years old, but so staid in character, so firm in discipline, and of such high repute in scholarship that he made the academy well known far and wide. New Amsterdam began to find itself advancing to the front rank in educational advantages among the American settlements, and not only ceased to send youth to New England, but drew to itself pupils from far-away colonies—two at least being recorded from Virginia, others from the settlements on the Delaware, and two, with the promise of more, from Fort Orange.[12]

On the capture of New Amsterdam by the English, Luyck returned to his native land to study theology; but later he came back to this city, then New York, married a relative of Director Stuyvesant, to whose sons he had been private tutor before taking charge of the Latin School, and continued his useful career of teacher in the colony under English rule.[13]

The regular schoolmaster, Evert Pietersen, who taught at the lower school while Hoboocken instructed at Stuyvesant's bouwery and Luyck succeeded Curtius at the Latin School, also continued in office after the English occupation. He made his home on the south side of the *Brouwer Straat*, a section of what is now Stone Street, extending from Whitehall to Broad Street, and gaining its name from the brewery owned by Oloff Stevenson Van Courtlandt.[14] Pietersen was married when he came to this country, but later lost his wife and, following the precedent of his profession, married a widow. His salary when he first came over on the *Gilded Beaver* was fixed at thirty-six guilders ($15) monthly and one hundred and twenty-five guilders annually for his board. The small amount

Influence
of the
Church

was grudingly and irregularly paid and yet such was his thrift that by 1674, he was one of the most substantial citizens of New York, with a property valued at two thousand florins.

The church still held its controlling hand on the official school in Pietersen's time, as for long afterwards, not having withdrawn its sheltering care from the descendant of that old Dutch school even now. This fact its historian proudly points out and indeed we may all take pride in one of the longest-lived educational institutions of our country :

The church influence showed itself in a civil ordinance of New Amsterdam, bearing date March 17, 1664 :

" Whereas it is highly necessary and of great consequence that the youth from their childhood is well instructed in reading, writing and arithmetic and principally in the principles and fundaments of the Christian religion, In conformity to the lesson of that wise King Solomon, ' Learn the youth the first principles and as he grows old, he shall not then deviate from it ' ; so that in time such men may arise from it who may be able to serve their country in Church or in State ; which being seriously considered by the Director General and Council in New Netherland, as the number of children by God's merciful blessing has considerably increased, they have deemed it necessary so that such an useful, and to our God, agreeable concern may be more effectually promoted, to recommend the present school master and to command him, so as it is done by this, that they (Pietersen and Van Hoboocken) on Wednesday before the beginning of the sermon with the children intrusted to their care, shall appear in the Church to examine after the close of the sermon each of them his own scholars in the presence of the reverend ministers and elders who may then be present, what they, in the course of the week, do remember of the Christian commands and Catechism, and what progress they have made ; after which the children shall be allowed a decent recreation." [15]

Under early English rule the schooling of the Dutch children was little interfered with. They were to be instructed in the "Netherlandisch tongue" as of old, and the schoolmaster was still to be under the supervision of the Consistory. The school hours were fixed from nine to eleven A.M. in summer, from half-past nine to half-past twelve in winter, while the afternoon session the year round lasted from one to five o'clock. [16] The schools were opened and closed with prayer, twice a week the pupils were examined in the catechism, and express stipulation was made that teachers should use " none but edifying and orthodox text-books and such as snould meet the approbation of the Consistory."

The control of the schools so wisely conceded by the English continued in the hands of the Dutch long enough to stamp the character which endures to this day in the representative School of the Collegiate Reformed Dutch Church of New York, which with all its fine buildings and elaborate equipments is the direct successor of the little school gathered together by Adam Roelantsen under the shadow of the old Fort.

Those of us of Dutch blood have a special right to look with pride upon this steady growth of the educational institution planted and fostered by our forefathers and bearing perpetual testimony to their energy and perseverance, their just valuation of "the things of the spirit," their respect for learning, and their determination to "learn the youth the first principles" and to make them men " who may be able to serve their country in Church and State." We are compelled to respect their earnestness and their persistence under what might well have seemed insurmountable difficulties, and however we may smile at the limitations of those early days, we must recognize that New Amsterdam has as good a claim as New England to the praise of the poet:

> " And still maintains with milder laws
> And clearer light the good old cause—
> Nor heeds the sceptic's puny hands
> While near her school the church-spire stands,
> Nor fears the blinded bigot's rule
> While near her church-spire stands the school."

The following is a list of the early schoolmasters in their order:

Official.

Adam Roelantsen,
Jan Stevensen,
Jan Cornelissen,
William Verstius,
Johannes Morice de la Montagne,
Harmanus Van Hoboocken,
Evert Pietersen.

Among the unofficial and semi-official teachers, fore-singers, and *krank-besoeckers* were :

Adriaen Jansen Van Ilpendam,
David Provoost,
Joost Carelse,
Hans Steyn,
Andries Hudde,
Jacobus van Corlaer,
Jan Lubbertsen,
Jan Juriaense Beeker,
Frans Claessen,
Johannes Van Gelder.

Latin School.

Alexander Carolus Curtius,
Aegidius Luyck.

End of the Dutch Rule, 1674.

References

REFERENCES.

1. Fisher's *Colonial Era.*
2. Valentine's *Corporation Manual,* 1863, p. 559 *et seq.*
3. *History of the School of the Collegiate Reformed Dutch Church,* p. 17.
4. E. B. O'Callaghan's *History of New Netherland,* ii., p. 569.
5. *Register of New Netherland,* p. 129.
6. *Register of New Netherland,* p. 129.
7. Valentine's *Corporation Manual,* 1863, p. 561.
8. *Holland Documents,* [see letters throughout].
9. *Holland Documents,* iv., p. 300.
10. Paulding's *New Amsterdam in 1647–1659,* p. 40.
11. Tuckerman's *Life of Peter Stuyvesant,* p. 167.
12. Albany Records.
13. Tuckerman's *Life of Peter Stuyvesant,* p. 107.
14. *New Amsterdam Records.*
15. *Albany Records,* xxii.
16. *History of the School of the Collegiate Reformed Dutch Church,* p. 39.

THE BATTLE OF HARLEM HEIGHTS

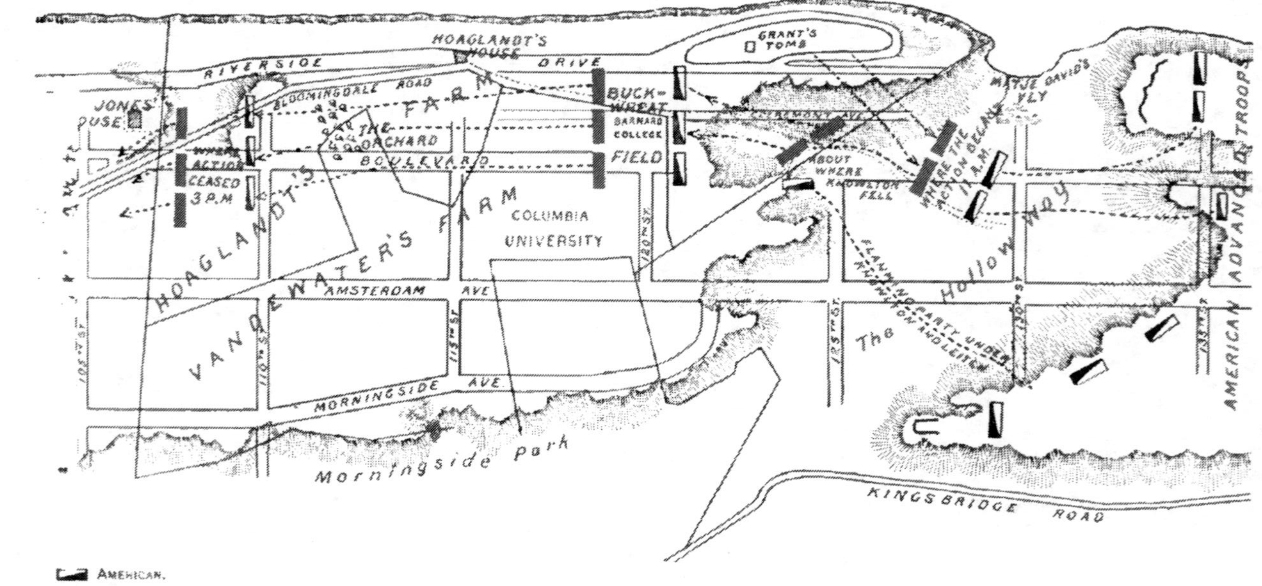

American.
British.

PLAN OF THE BATTLE OF HARLEM HEIGHTS.

(SEE NOTES AND REFERENCES 1.)

Half Moon Series

Published in the Interest of the New York City History Club.

VOLUME II. NUMBER X.

THE BATTLE OF HARLEM HEIGHTS.

By WILLIAM R. SHEPHERD, Ph.D.

ANY event in the Revolution that made a distinct contribution to the establishment of independence has its share of interest to the patriotic American ; but the "affair"' at Harlem Heights has a general importance, colored with a local interest, which specially merits our attention and admiration. Its general importance is attested by the fact that, coming as it did immediately after the calamity on Long Island, it served as a prelude to the brilliant exploits at Trenton and Princeton ; while its local interest is clear, when we remember that it was the only contest within the limits of Greater New York that resulted in a victory for the Americans. The battle of Harlem Heights, therefore, has a peculiar charm to the citizen of the metropolis. Gazing at the very ground on which it was fought, as he traces from one landmark to another the course of the struggle, he may reflect with honest pride that here, within the precincts of his own city, occurred what Washington was pleased to term a " success . . . productive of salutary consequences," [1]—once more a Concord and Lexington which " animated our troops, gave them new spirits," and enabled them " with inferior numbers to drive their enemy, and think of nothing . . . but conquest." [2]

In January, 1776, two months before the British evacuated Boston, the question arose whether an effort should be made to hold New York — probably their next objective point of attack. Although apparent that the insular position of New York with its belt of navigable waters bore out the truth of Charles Lee's assertion that whoever commanded the sea must command the city,[3] still, if a Declaration of Independence was to be issued and its assertion of rights made good, the abandonment of New York, merely on the plea of difficulty in fortifying it, would have been a serious mistake. Even if the city could not be made impregnable, a brave show of resistance might deter the British from attempting its capture, or at any rate "give them," says a blunt patriot, "a scrag which they would not relish very well,"[4] before a capture could be effected.

In order to confine the British water control

to the harbor and the mouth of the Hudson River, the East River—the key of the American position—was fortified along both banks at various points from the Battery to Hell Gate. The water front on the south and west also was protected by batteries on the shore and barricades in the streets ; while to the north of the city other fortifications were constructed along the line of the present Grand Street, to ward off an attack from that quarter. Then to command the Hudson, as well as to cover a possible retreat by way of Kingsbridge, Fort Washington was built a little to the southwest of the Washington Bridge, and connected with Fort Lee on the New Jersey shore by a series of stone-laden boats fastened with chains, and sunk as an obstruction to the enemy's ships. A few hundred feet north of West One Hundred and Ninetieth Street, overlooking the Harlem River, was erected a redoubt which the British later called Fort George. On the mainland also, beyond Spuyten Duyvil Creek, and on what is now Giles' Place west of Sedgwick Avenue, Fort Independence was constructed to hold the approaches to Kingsbridge.

England had regarded the campaign around Boston as a mere preliminary indicative of the resistance likely to be offered by the Americans. Hence it is probable that the British change of base from Boston to New York was prompted as much by motives of strategy as by the pressure of the American besiegers. New York henceforth was to be the centre of British operations, and here the war began in earnest. Late in June, 1776, appeared the first signs of the coming occupation. Within seven weeks over four hundred vessels and thirty thousand troops under the command of General Howe were in New York harbor, the latter being encamped on Staten Island. To oppose this huge array—as mighty a military and naval armament as England had ever sent upon foreign service—Washington had less than twenty thousand effective men. Some of these were fairly armed and equipped, but many of them, farmers fresh from the plough, had hardly any other weapons than a spade or pick-axe, or possibly a scythe made straight and fastened to a pole. Undaunted however by the overwhelming odds, on July 2, Washington addressed to his army the stirring appeal that follows :

"The fate of unborn millions will now depend under God on the courage and conduct of this army. Our cruel and unrelenting enemy leaves us no choice but a brave resistance or the most abject submission. This is all we can expect. We have, therefore, to resolve to conquer or die. Our country's honor calls upon us for a vigorous and manly exertion, and if we now shamefully fail we shall become infamous to the whole world. Let us, therefore, rely upon the goodness of the cause and the aid of the Supreme Being, in whose hands victory is, to animate and encourage us to great and noble actions. The eyes of all our countrymen are now upon us, and we shall have their blessings and praises, if happily we are the instruments of saving them from . . . tyranny." [6]

Not only does this appeal seem to have had the desired effect upon the army in general, but, in particular, "never did people in the world act with more spirit and resolution than the New Yorkers." [7] A part of the enthusiasm was manifested a week later in pulling down the gilded equestrian statue of King George near the junction of Broadway and Bowling Green, and in sending the pieces to Connecticut, where patriotic women converted them into bullets for the American army. [8]

The personality of Washington and the magnetic influence he exercised over his soldiers were well known to General Howe. If he could capture the rebel leader the war would indeed be ended in the single campaign which boastful British officers declared was sufficient. A direct attack on the centre and right of the American position—*i. e.*, Governor's Island, the Battery, and the fortifications facing the Hudson River—would probably be successful ; but, besides entailing serious loss on the aggressive party, might accomplish no more than the withdrawal of the Americans to the heights in the north of Manhattan Island, whence Kingsbridge furnished an easy escape. Several schemes of outflanking, therefore, suggested themselves to Howe's mind, the most feasible being to assail the American left wing, then stationed on Long Island. The defences of Brooklyn once broken through and the forts along the shore silenced, the fleet could sail up the East River and, in conjunction with the army, cut off Washington's retreat on the north. The haughty Virginian rebel, who declined to receive from his Majesty's commissioners any communication addressed simply "George Washington, Esq.," would then be caught like a rat in a trap. Accordingly, on August 22, with fifteen thousand troops the British commander crossed the Narrows to Gravesend Bay, and took possession of the villages on the flatlands where he was soon joined by five thousand Hessians. For several days the armies lay over against each other with no more hostile demonstration than an occasional skirmish. South of the American lines at Brooklyn, and extending eastward from New York Bay, was a low range of densely wooded hills that served as a huge natural barrier to the approach of an enemy, and could be vigorously defended. Four roads led through depressions in this range, three of which were strongly guarded, but at the fourth, known as the "Jamaica Pass," only five mounted pickets had been stationed. On the night of August 26, the British stealthily advanced to the

" Pass," captured the pickets, and ere an alarm could be given fell upon the astounded Americans and routed them with a loss of over eleven hundred. Happily, however, the British had not forced the American lines, otherwise, outnumbering as they did their opponents nearly three to one, the entire patriot army on Long Island must have surrendered. Two nights later, Washington effected his masterly retreat to New York. Leaving his camp-fires ablaze and a few pickets posted so as to lull suspicion, the army of nine thousand Americans marched to Fulton Ferry and crossed in safety, the only accident being the loss of a boat with four stragglers. If the Americans had been outflanked the British had been outwitted, and some consolation at least might be derived from that fact.

Yet, however courageous the resistance and brilliant the retreat, the immediate result of the battle of Long Island was deplorable. No one more than Washington realized it, for in his letter to Congress, September 2, he says:

" Our situation is truly distressing. The check . . . sustained on the 27th ultimo has dispirited too great a proportion of our troops, and filled their minds with apprehension and despair. The militia, instead of calling forth their utmost efforts to a brave and manly opposition in order to repair our losses, are dismayed, intractable, and impatient to return. Great numbers of them have gone off; in some instances almost by whole regiments, by half ones, and by companies at a time."

An absolute disregard of "that order and subordination necessary to the well-doing of an army" made his situation all the more alarming, and evoked from him the sorrowful statement:

> "With the deepest concern I am obliged to confess my want of confidence in the generality of the troops. . . . Till of late I had no doubt in my own mind of defending this place [*i. e.*, New York], nor should I have yet if the men would do their duty, but this I despair of. It is painful and extremely grating to me to give such unfavorable accounts, but it would be criminal to conceal the truth at so critical a juncture." [10]

Indeed it was found necessary to establish guards at Kingsbridge and other points to stop the deserters, especially those with arms and ammunition. One incident will serve to illustrate the simple character of the average militiaman. The guard brought to a halt a ragged fellow who was carrying something in a bag. The something proved to be a cannon ball which, he explained, he was taking home to his mother to pound mustard seed! [11] Yet give these rustic soldiers a little longer time in the army, render them accustomed to the din of warfare, and the skittish militia, for whom the Continental regulars evinced such utter contempt, would soon be found among the bravest defenders of their country. At this moment, however, Washington felt that he could place no reliance on an army

composed largely of such material, and reluctantly began to consider the advisability of
evacuating Manhattan Island, at any rate south
of Harlem Heights. Here an energetic stand
might be made, for Washington had no intention of doing what Lee later proposed,—to
"give Mr. Howe a fee simple"[12] to New
York, without a struggle. From several of
his officers came the suggestion to burn the
city, but fortunately this piece of useless destruction was averted by the prudent modera-
tion of Congress. In reply to Washington's
query on this point, Congress declared that
the city be left intact; for, even "though
the enemy should for a time obtain possession of it," eventual recovery was certain."[13] At length, September 12, it was
resolved to withdraw the army to Harlem
Heights, a sufficient number only of men being
left to keep guard over the approaches from
the East River, while Putnam superintended
the removal of stores and munitions. Hence
at the foot of the present Grand Street (then
Corlaer's Hook), East Twelfth Street, East
Twenty-third Street, and East Thirty-fourth
Street (then Kip's Bay), were entrenched
several brigades of militia. Also at various
points as far north as East Eighty-ninth Street
(then Horn's Hook) was posted a line of sentinels who half-hourly passed along the cheer-
ing watchword, "All 's well," to which the

British sailors, who could distinctly hear the call from their ships in the river, derisively responded, "We will alter your tune before to-morrow night." [14]

Two days later Washington set up his headquarters at the Roger Morris (now Jumel) [15] Mansion, still standing on One Hundred and Sixty-first Street, east of St. Nicholas Avenue, and in one day more the removal of men and munitions would have been complete. Meanwhile several ships of war had forced their way up the East River, in spite of the steady fire from the American batteries on the Manhattan shore ; but it was not until September 11, that the British effected a landing on Montresor's (now Randall's) Island, and on Buchanan's (now Ward's) Island, with the manifest intention of crossing to Harlem and of advancing upon the city from the north. Washington had anticipated this move by the prompt withdrawal to Harlem, and, as the powerful American battery at Horn's Hook had not been silenced, Howe decided to debark his troops at Kip's Bay. On Sunday, the fifteenth, under a furious cannonade from the frigates, the British regulars landed and drove the American militia in wild confusion from their entrenchments. The half-humorous description of the encounter related by a participant on the American side shows the situation exactly :

"At daybreak," he says, "the first thing that saluted our eyes was . . . four ships at anchor . . . within musket-shot of us. . . . They appeared to be very busy on shipboard, but we lay still and showed our good breeding by not interfering with them, as they were strangers and we knew not but they were bashful withal ! As soon as it was fairly light we saw their boats coming, . . . filled with British soldiers. When they came to the edge of the tide, they formed their boats in line. They continued to augment these forces . . . until they appeared like a large clover field in full bloom. . . . It was on a Sabbath morning, the day in which the British were always employed about their deviltry, because, they said, they had the prayers of the church on that day. We lay very quiet in our ditch waiting their motions till the sun was an hour or two high. We heard a cannonade at the city, but our attention was drawn to our own guests. But they being a little dilatory in their operations, I stepped into an old warehouse which stood close by me with the door open inviting me in, and sat down upon a stool ; the floor was strewed with papers which had in some former period been used in the concerns of the house, but were then lying in woful confusion. I was very demurely perusing these papers when, all of a sudden, there came such a peal of thunder from the British shipping that I thought my head would go with the sound. I made a frog's leap for the ditch and lay as still as I possibly could, and began to consider which part of my carcass was to go first. The British played their parts well ; indeed they had nothing to hinder them. We kept the lines till they were almost levelled upon us, when our officers, seeing we could make no resistance, and no orders coming from any superior officer, and that we must soon be entirely exposed to the rake of the guns, gave the order to leave the lines. In retreating we had to cross a level clear spot of ground, forty or fifty rods wide, exposed to the whole of the enemy's fire ; and they gave it to us in prime order ; the grape-shot and langrage

Description of the Encounter at Kip's Bay

flew merrily, which served to quicken our motions. When I had gotten a little out of the reach of their combustibles I found myself in company with one who was a neighbor of mine when at home, and one other man belonging to our regiment; where the rest of them were I knew not. . . . We had not gone far (along the highway) before we saw a party of men apparently hurrying on in the same direction with ourselves; we endeavored hard to overtake them, but on approaching them we found that they were not of our way of thinking; they were Hessians! We immediately altered our course and took the main road leading to King's bridge. We had not long been on this road before we saw another party just ahead of us whom we knew to be Americans; just as we overtook these they were fired upon by a party of British from a cornfield, and all was immediately in confusion again. I believe the enemies' party was small; but our people were all militia, and the demons of fear and disorder seemed to take full possession of all and everything on that day. . . . They did not tarry to let the grass grow much under their feet." [16]

But the ordeal was something which even veteran troops could not have withstood. "The fire of the shipping," wrote General Howe to Lord Germain, "being so well directed and so incessant, the enemy could not remain in their works and the descent was made without the least opposition." [17] This statement of the British commander will go far to extenuate the conduct of the militia, disheartened as they were by the disaster on Long Island, and terrified by the swarms of British troops as well as by the thunderous roar from the frigates. Then, too, the knowledge that their countrymen were safe at Harlem Heights was no small incentive to rapidity in flight. The Americans stationed at East Twenty-third Street soon joined them, and together they hastened along the Kingsbridge road (Lexington Avenue).

As soon as the boom of cannon reached his ears, Washington mounted his horse and sped along the four miles intervening between Harlem and the scene of action. Near Park Avenue and Fortieth Street, what were his horror and consternation to behold the Americans flying in all directions, while scarce a half mile away the dust was rising under the feet of the pursuing British and Hessians. Riding excitedly into the midst of the runaways, he shouted: "Take to the wall! Take to the cornfield!" Beside himself with wrath and mortification at seeing his commands disobeyed, he lashed the fugitives with his riding-whip, flung his hat upon the ground, and cried in accents choked with passion, "Are these the men with whom I am to defend America?" Indeed so blind was he to all sense of danger that, had not one of his attendants seized the bridle of his horse and turned the animal's head in the opposite direction, the Revolutionary War might have terminated then and there.[19] Regaining his self-possession, the commander-in-chief permitted the demoralized militia to continue their stampede toward Harlem Heights, although in his report to

Congress he did not fail to denounce their conduct as "disgraceful and dastardly."[19]   He then ordered the immediate retreat of Putnam.

The story of how Mrs. Mary Murray, wife of Robert Murray, whose farm included most of the "commanding height of Inclenberg" (now Murray Hill), entertained the British generals so hospitably that Putnam and most of the remnants of the patriot army still in the city managed to elude the enemy and gain the heights in safety, is too well known to bear repetition.[20]   Suffice it to say that the cake and wine and geniality of this lady, who responded with rare tact and good humor to the bantering of the British officers on her rebel sympathies, as effectually "bowed" her guests "at her feet"—for a while at least—as the hammer and tent-nail of Jael, the wife of Heber the Kenite, had done in detaining Sisera, the captain of the Canaanitish host, when "he asked water and she gave him milk," when "she brought forth butter in a lordly dish."

After having completed their debarkation, the British drew up their lines across the island from the foot of East Eighty-ninth Street to the foot of West Ninety-sixth Street, or Striker's Bay as it was then called, the pickets being stationed between that street and West One Hundred and Fifth Street. Gen. Howe's headquarters were at the Beekman mansion[21] (Fifty-first Street and First

Avenue), while Sir Henry Clinton took up his residence at the Apthorpe house (Ninety-first Street and Columbus Avenue). And in general this was the position of the British for nearly a month. Of the two positions, however, that of the Americans was the stronger. Beginning at Washington's headquarters, One Hundred and Sixty-first Street, the camp extended southward to the "Hollow Way," or the valley now comprised between West One Hundred and Twenty-fifth Street and West One Hundred and Thirtieth Street, through the centre of which runs Manhattan Street. At the eastern end of this depression was a rugged spur called the "Point of Rocks" (One Hundred and Twenty-sixth Street and Columbus Avenue), used by the Americans as a lookout station, whence Harlem Plains could be surveyed as far as McGowan's Pass; while the western portion terminated in a round marshy meadow known as Matje David's Vly, a little to the south of Fort Lee ferry. With the Hudson on the right, the valley in front, the plains on the left, and the rear protected by Fort Washington and the troops at Kingsbridge, the whole well screened by woods and thickets, the Americans could feel that the addition of a few redoubts and entrenchments would make these natural fortifications impregnable. Accordingly three parallel lines of defensive works were constructed between One Hundred and Forty-seventh Street and One Hundred and Sixty-first Street, while a division of soldiers under Greene was posted near the southern edge of the heights overlooking the "Hollow Way," to guard against an assault from that direction.

The unfortunate issue of the encounter at Kip's Bay made precisely the same impression upon the minds of British and Americans as had the battle of Long Island ; the former it confirmed in their belief of absolute superiority, the spirits of the latter it depressed until many had lost practically all confidence in their officers and in themselves. For the moment even nature seemed intent upon rendering their lot still harder to bear. The well housed and equipped soldiers of the king were in forcible contrast to the poorly provided soldiers of the republic, who, says Colonel Humphreys,

"excessively fatigued by the sultry march of the day, their clothes wet by a severe shower of rain that succeeded towards the evening, their blood chilled by the cold wind that produced a sudden change in the temperature of the air, and their hearts sunk within them, . . . lay upon their arms covered only by the clouds of an uncomfortable sky." [22]

But amid all the gloom and depression the leader of the American army never lost his faith in the ultimate courage of the American soldier, however much the timidity of the militia aroused his indignation. His power of keen discernment showed him, further, that, if a fortified camp was a haven of refuge to a soldiery hard pressed by the enemy, so also it might be a tower of strength wherein the very sense of security would inspire the former fugitives with a zeal for action, and, by giving them an opportunity to display their native courage, aid them to regain the confidence which before had failed them. Under such circumstances Washington might well say, "I trust that there are many who will act like men and show themselves worthy of the blessings of freedom." [23] Appreciating the strength of his position, he determined "to habituate his soldiers by a series of successful skirmishes to meet the enemy in the field." [24] This determination was realized in the battle of Harlem Heights.

Sloping upward from the southern line of the "Hollow Way" was another elevation of land, then known as Bloomingdale or Vandewater's Heights, and now called Morningside Heights. In 1776, it was occupied and partly cultivated by its owners, Adrian Hoaglandt and Benjamin Vandewater. The space of land about a mile in extent between the present One Hundred and Fifth Street and One Hundred and Twenty-fifth Street, west of Columbus Avenue, was the "debatable ground," and the scene of the battle of Harlem Heights. It effectually hid the opposing forces from each other. Now, whereas an advance of the British from the direction of Harlem Plains could be easily observed by the American lookouts on the "Point of Rocks," no movement from behind Morningside Heights would be perceptible before the "Hollow Way" had been reached. It was not to be supposed that an enemy flushed with success in the recent campaign would long hesitate to assail the American stronghold. Desirous of guarding against a flank attack, especially from the vicinity of Morningside, early in the morning of Monday, September 16, Washington sent a body of scouts to ascertain what preparations the enemy were making. He himself then rode from headquarters down to the outposts at the "Hollow Way." The men selected were the Rangers, consisting of about one hundred and twenty picked volunteers from New England regiments, and under the command of Colonel Thomas Knowlton, who had done gallant service at the battle of Bunker Hill. Proceeding cautiously under cover of the woods, probably along the line of what is now Riverside Drive, Knowlton and his men had arrived at the farmhouse of Nicholas Jones (One Hundred and Sixth Street, west of the Boulevard) before the British pickets stationed on One Hundred and Fourth Street were startled by the report of shots fired at close range, and spied the forms of the Americans through the trees.[25] The alarm was instantly sounded, whereat a portion of the second and third battalions of light infantry, numbering upwards of three hundred, started to drive back the audacious rebels. In gleeful expectation that this second installment of Kip's Bay militia, as they thought, would fly from before them with the utmost terror and dismay, the British regulars hurried on. But suddenly they were brought to a stop. Upon falling back a short distance, Knowlton had posted his men behind a stone wall and bidden them "not to rise or fire a gun" till the British were ten rods away. Scarcely had the first redcoat crossed the "dead line," when a blaze of fire shot from the stone wall, and the astounded infantry fell back in dire consternation. Then for some time the woods echoed with the sharp crack of musketry in a skirmish. At length Knowlton, perceiving that the superior numbers of the foe menaced his flank, commanded a retreat, which was effected in good order and without the loss of a man.[26]

Meanwhile a rumor spread through the American camp that the enemy were approaching in three columns, whereupon Adjutant-General Reed obtained permission from the commander-in-chief to learn its truth. Riding hastily from the "Point of Rocks" in the direction Knowlton had taken, he reached the scene of skirmish as it was about to begin. "While I was talking with the officer," he writes, "the enemy's advanced guard fired upon us at a small distance; our men behaved well, stood, and returned the fire till, overpowered by numbers, they were obliged to retreat." He further states that the British came on so quickly that he had not left a house (probably Hoaglandt's, One Hundred and Fifteenth Street and Riverside Drive) five minutes before they had seized it. The light infantry continued the pursuit through the fields and woods of Hoaglandt's farm as far as the immediate neighborhood of Grant's tomb. The sight of the scampering rebels restored the gleefulness which they had lost near the stone wall, and, advancing within plain view of the Americans on the heights beyond, they derisively "sounded their bugle-horns, as is usual after a fox-chase." The insult showed the contempt in which their adversaries held the Americans, who three times within three weeks had fled before his Majesty's regulars,—once on Long Island, once at Kip's Bay, and now on the heights just opposite their own camp. "I never felt such a sensation before," says Reed; "it seemed to crown our disgrace." [27]

The appearance of the enemy produced the natural impression that Harlem Heights were to be carried by storm.   Preparations were, therefore, being made for a vigorous defense, when Reed dashed up to the commander-in-chief, "to get some support for the brave fellows who had behaved so well." [28]   With characteristic caution, however, Washington declined at first to hazard his men until exact information of the British strength and position could be obtained.   For the present he felt that a weakened and somewhat despondent army was hardly capable of engaging advantageously in a general conflict.   At this juncture Colonel Knowlton and the Rangers brought the news that the enemy were about three hundred strong, and detached more than a mile from the main body.   Washington now saw his opportunity to cut off this detachment ere it could be reinforced from below, and thereby, as he says, to "recover that military ardor which is of the utmost moment to an army." [29]   If a general engagement could not be risked, a lively and successful skirmish would furnish the very tonic of energy and enthusiasm then so sadly needed.   Still the American commander realized that an attack wholly in front would not only involve the ascent of the steep Morningside Heights, from the top of which the well-posted British could pour a galling fire, but might result in no more than driving them back upon the main body—a contingency he wished most to avoid. Curiously enough, however, this was the very thing that eventually happened, although not with the consequences he had anticipated. The consummate soldier, who had learned the art of stratagem from many an Indian adversary in the tangled forests of Virginia and Pennsylvania, resolved to make a feint in front, while a body of picked men should stealthily creep round to the left and fall upon the enemy's rear. For this purpose he chose about two hundred volunteers, consisting of Knowlton and his Rangers, together with three companies of Virginia riflemen under the command of Major Leitch. Starting from their position near the grounds of the present Convent of the Sacred Heart, One Hundred and Thirtieth Street and Convent Avenue, Knowlton and Leitch, accompanied by Reed, made their way diagonally down the slope, across the now intervening numbered streets and Amsterdam Avenue, near its junction with Manhattan Street, and proceeded toward a rocky ledge, not far from One Hundred and Twenty-fourth Street and the Boulevard. If once they reached this point unobserved they could assail the enemy from the rear, and thus, catching them between two fires, compel their surrender. Stirred by the thought of this brilliant prospect, the intrepid Americans eagerly hurried onward.

In the meantime Washington directed one hundred and fifty volunteers, under Lieutenant-Colonel Crary, to proceed from the vicinity of One Hundred and Thirty-fifth Street and the Boulevard straight down to the "Hollow Way," but not to make any real attack till they saw that the venture of the flanking-party had proved successful.[80]   The bait readily attracted the confident British. Running down the hill across Claremont Avenue to the Boulevard and One Hundred and Twenty-seventh Street, they crouched behind some fences and bushes, whereupon "a smart firing began but at too great a distance to do much execution on either side."[81]   However, if the British could only be kept where they were, or enticed still further toward the American lines, Knowlton and Leitch would reach the desired position, and the light infantry would be prisoners. At this moment Washington judged it expedient to reinforce Crary's courageous volunteers, and for nearly an hour the contest continued. As they dodged behind tree, rock, bush, fence, or other point of vantage, the skirmishers on both sides watched their opportunity to pick off an unwary bluecoat or redcoat. Ere long the British were forced to retreat up the slope of the hill to a field about six hundred feet southwest of their first position, "where they lodged themselves behind a fence covered with bushes "[32] (One Hundred and Twenty-fourth Street and the Boulevard). But this was the objective point which Knowlton's party was straining every nerve to attain. As luck would have it, just as the American rangers and riflemen were clambering over the rocky ledge referred to, they spied the redcoats almost directly in front of them. So far as it was an attempt to hem in the British from the rear the project had failed ; the attack must now be made on the flank. One explanation of the failure is, that through some "misapprehension," as Washington says, the Americans "unluckily began their attack too soon."[33] Another is, that some subordinate officers, in their enthusiasm to meet the enemy, disregarded the commands of their superiors and took the wrong road —commenting on which behavior, in his general orders, issued the following day, Washington declared that "the loss of the enemy . . . undoubtedly would have been much greater if the orders of the commander-in-chief had not in some instance been contradicted by . . . inferior officers, who, however well they may mean, ought not to presume to direct."[34] But perhaps the unexpected retreat of the British and their arrival at the fence in question just as the foremost Americans emerged from the rocks on their right, give the best explanation, and in its light the recklessness of the American soldier and the presumption of the American officer become transfigured into the headlong zeal and self-confident enthusiasm that betoken the militant patriot.

Wherever the mistake might lie, this was no time for conjecture. Their comrades had driven the enemy before them; the gallant example was theirs to emulate. Headed by Leitch and Knowlton, the riflemen and Rangers rushed upon the British and a sharp action ensued. In a few minutes the two leaders fell, mortally wounded, the former lingering a few days, the latter expiring within an hour. To one of his officers who bent tenderly over him as the light of triumph in his eyes darkened and the din of battle in his ears grew fainter, the dying hero of Bunker Hill whispered, "I do not value my life if we do but get the day." [35] To his eldest son, a soldier-boy of only fifteen years, he uttered his last command, "Go, fight for your country!" [36] Thus perished an officer "whose name and spirit ought to be immortalized," says Reed; [37] "the gallant and brave Colonel Knowlton . . . an honor to any country . . . who had fallen gloriously fighting at his post," says Washington. [38]

Meanwhile the struggle was being fiercely maintained. Incited to vengeance by the loss of their leaders, the Americans "continued

The Battle of Harlem Heights

the engagement with the greatest resolution," [39] and soon the British were dislodged
from their position near the fence. The
Americans then "pursued them to a buckwheat field on the top of a high hill, distance
about four hundred paces." [40]   Here the respective antagonists were reinforced and the
British made a determined stand.   The day's
campaign had opened with an attempt to capture the light troops whose "ungovernable
impetuosity," wrote Sir Henry Clinton, drew
them into the "scrape." [41]   The attempt had
failed, and an open conflict had resulted. But,
instead of remaining strictly consistent with
his purpose of avoiding anything like a general engagement, the prudence of Washington
succumbed to surprise and delight at the vim
and courage his soldiers were displaying.
Hence he despatched to their aid about fifteen
hundred men, a number of whom had been
runaways at Kip's Bay hardly twenty-four
hours previous. If the panic-stricken militia
proved to be excellent in a foot-race when the
British were the pursuers, here was another
chance for them to show their vigor at running—but this time with the positions reversed.   Had Washington any misgivings
when he resolved to try the mettle of the
skittish militia under more favorable circumstances, his anxiety vanished when he beheld
the fugitives of yesterday valiantly supporting

their comrades, and charging "the enemy with great intrepidity." [42] Scarcely had the buckwheat field been reached when the remainder of the light infantry, the Forty-second Highlanders, and a company of Hessians came up with two field-pieces. Then occurred the real battle of Harlem Heights— or to speak somewhat more precisely, Morningside Heights—"a smart action," observes a Maryland colonel, "in the true bush-fighting way, in which our troops behaved in a manner that does them the highest honor." [43] During nearly two hours the conflict raged for the possession of the buckwheat field. Terrible as were the British with the bayonet, they proved no match for the accurate marksmanship of the Americans. The field, snowy with the blossoms of coming harvest, an hour before peacefully smiling under the rays of a September sun, was now ruthlessly trampled by the hurrying feet of the combatants, its sunlight obscured by a pall of dust and smoke, its whiteness reddened by the life-blood of many a valiant soldier who furrowed, as he fell, its forest of waving grain. Still, though the harvest of grain might be destroyed, a harvest of hope was to be garnered. Another impetuous charge and the British were driven headlong from the field. Exhilarated by the sight of their fleeing enemies, the Americans enjoyed to the full the novel sensation of a fox-chase, in which they did not personate the fox !

In an orchard near the Boulevard and One Hundred and Twelfth Street the British again stood their ground; but the onward rush of the Americans could not be borne. Once more the enemy fled "across a hollow and up another hill not far distant from their own lines." [44] Here in the vicinity of Jones's house (One Hundred and Sixth Street west of the Boulevard), where the contest had begun in the morning, it ended about three o'clock in the afternoon. For hardly had the redcoats left the orchard, when Washington, surmising that reinforcements would soon arrive, "judged it prudent to order a retreat." [45] But, says Reed, "the pursuit of a flying enemy was so new a scene, that it was with difficulty our men could be brought to retreat." [46] At length "they gave a Hurra! and left the field in good order," [47] just as the foremost columns of the British reinforcements appeared. From Jones's house to the "Hollow Way" the redcoat had pursued the bluecoat; from the "Hollow Way" to Jones's house the bluecoat chased the redcoat, or, in the somewhat picturesque language of Captain Brown of the Rangers, "drove the dogs near three miles." [48] The derisive bugle call of the morning was answered by the exultant hurrah of the afternoon.

" Hail to the shades where Freedom dwelt !
   Where wild flowers deck her martyrs' grave,
Where Britain's minions keenly felt
   The stern resistance of the brave.

" 'T was here in firm array they stood—
   Here met Oppression's giant power ;
Here nobly poured their sacred blood,
   And victory crowned their dying hour." [49]

The effect of this encounter on the drooping spirits of the Americans was simply magical. "A most timely and well delivered return stroke," observes Professor Johnston, "it revived the energies of our army, and had its influence in compelling another delay in the enemy's movements." [50] Its effect is seen in the glow of joyful hope that pervaded the hearts of the patriot soldiers. "I assure you it has given another face of things in our army," writes Reed ; "the men have recovered their spirits, and feel a confidence which before they had quite lost." [51] "The impression it made upon the minds of our people," says Major Morris, "is [that of] a most signal victory." [52] "Our troops," declares Major Shaw, "behaved with as much bravery as men possibly could. . . . Now or never is the time to make a stand, and rather than quit our post [we will] be sacrificed to a man." [53] "An advantage so trivial in itself," remarks Colonel Humphreys, "produced, in event, a surprising and almost incredible effect

upon the whole army. Amongst the troops
. . . every visage was seen to brighten,
and to assume, instead of the gloom of despair, the glow of animation." [54] Colonel Silli-
man and General Knox take about the same
view. Says the former : "They [*i. e.*, the
British] have found now that when we meet
them on equal ground we are not a set of
people that will run from them, but that they
have . . . had a pretty good drubbing." [55]
Says the latter : "They [*i. e.*, the Americans]
find that if they stick to these mighty men
they will run as fast as other people." [56] Indeed, General Greene somewhat extravagantly
asserts that, with good discipline and leadership, the Americans " might bid defiance to
the whole world." [57] And what words of
commendation had the commander-in-chief
to bestow ? In the general orders issued
the next day Washington "most heartily"
thanked the troops for their courageous behavior, and added: "Once more . . . the
general calls upon officers and men to act up
to the noble cause in which they are engaged,
and support the honor and liberties of their
country." [58] The crisis had passed. The
doubts of Washington as to the staying qualities of the American soldier vanished with
the receding forms of the enemy. The mortification of yesterday was replaced by the
gratification of to-day. The success for which

he had so earnestly wished, to retrieve misfortune and infuse new courage, had been attained. Henceforth the devotion of the American soldier to his chief was only equalled by the confidence of that chief in his soldier.

Because the Americans who had enjoyed the rare sport of chasing their enemies for over a mile, and, deeming it unwise to attack the main body, had reluctantly withdrawn, the British construed the "affair of outposts" [59] at Harlem Heights into a victory for themselves. According to General Howe, they "repulsed the enemy with considerable loss, and obliged them to retire within their works" [60]; and in his orders of September 17, he "entertains the highest opinion of the bravery of the few troops that yesterday beat back a very superior body of the rebels," although he disapproves, the "want of attention in the light companies pursuing the rebels without . . . proper discretion." [61] Colonel von Donop, however, who commanded the Hessians, comes nearer the truth when he modestly observes that had it not been for his "Yagers (riflemen), two regiments of Highlanders and the British infantry would have all perhaps been captured." [62] But the utterance of an English officer, as related by an American prisoner on one of his Majesty's ships, affords the best commentary on the events of September 15 and 16, at Kip's Bay and Harlem

Heights. It seems that, on the evening after the unfortunate occurrence at Kip's Bay, this officer went on board denouncing "the Yankees for runaway cowards, and storming that there was no chance to fight and get honor and rise." Quite different the burden, if not the manner, of his complaint when, having fairly encountered the patriot soldiers at Harlem Heights, he again went on board cursing the war, and "saying he had found the Americans would fight, and that it would be impossible to conquer them."[3] Unwittingly the blustering soldier told the truth. From Harlem to Yorktown the story of the Revolution is his witness.

On the buckwheat-field of Morningside Heights, the American soldier studied and learned a lesson of bravery in the school of warfare. The woods and fences, fields and orchards, have long since disappeared, but on their site the genius of education still lives to perpetuate the memory of that lesson, and of that school, in the mind of the American student,—on their site arise to-day the stately buildings of Barnard College and Columbia University. Here, in the centre of what once was the buckwheat-field—the historic landmark of a victory in war—stands Barnard College, a magnificent memorial of a far grander victory in peace, of a victory over the narrowness of Revolutionary days, of a victory for the enlightenment of the nineteenth century, of a victory for the higher education of the American woman.

Present Site of the Encounter

NOTES AND REFERENCES.

1. For a collection of original authorities on the battle of Harlem Heights, see the appendix to JAY, *The Battle of Harlem Plains*, Oration before the New York Historical Society, September 16, 1876 ; JOHNSTON, *The Campaign of 1776 around New York and Brooklyn—Memoirs of the Long Island Historical Society*, iii., part ii. ; *The Magazine of American History*, iv., pp. 369–375 ; viii., part i., pp. 39–49 ; part ii., pp. 627–629 ; JOHNSTON, *The Battle of Harlem Heights*, pp. 125–234. The best account of the battle—particularly for its precision in locating the various sites of the conflict—is *The Battle of Harlem Heights*, by Professor HENRY P. JOHNSTON (Columbia University Press). Indeed, so far as topographical details are concerned, the present sketch is based almost wholly upon Professor Johnston's observations. Besides giving a brief description of the campaign of 1776 around New York City, Professor Johnston also critically reviews earlier versions of the battle, and appends practically all the original authorities.

2. FORCE, *American Archives*, Fifth Series, ii., p. 467.

3. JOHNSTON, *The Battle of Harlem Heights*, pp. 141, 142.

4. *Collections of the New York Historical Society*, *Lee Papers*, i., p. 309.

5. *New York City during the American Revolution*, p. 88.

6. JOHNSTON, *The Campaign of 1776*, etc., part i., pp. 95, 96.

7. JOHNSTON, *The Correspondence and Public Papers of John Jay*, i., p. 47.

8. JOHNSTON, *The Campaign of 1776*, etc., p. 93, note.

9. IRVING, *Life of George Washington* (1857 ed.), ii., pp. 267–270.

10. FORD, *The Writings of George Washington*, iv., pp. 379, 381.

11. GRAYDON, *Memoirs of His Own Time*, p. 174.

12. *Ibid.*, p. 175.

13. *Journals of Congress*, i., p. 465.

14. [MARTIN], *A Narrative of some of the Adventures, Dangers, and Sufferings of a Revolutionary Soldier*, p. 26.

15. For a picture of this mansion, see *The Magazine of American History*, xxi., p. 3 ; LOSSING, *Field Book of the American Revolution*, ii., p. 609.

16. [MARTIN], *A Narrative*, etc., pp. 26–28.

17. Upcott Collection in the library of the New York Historical Society, iv., p. 411.

18. FORD, *The Writings*, etc., iv., pp. 407, 408 ; FORCE, *American Archives*, Fifth Series, ii., p. 370 ; HEATH, *Memoirs*, p. 60 ; GRAYDON, *Memoirs*, p. 174 ; GORDON, *A History of the United States*, ii., p. 327 ; THACHER, *A Military Journal during the American Revolutionary War*, p. 59.

19. FORD, *The Writings*, etc., iv., p. 408.

20. THACHER, *A Military Journal*, etc., pp. 59, 60 ; *Historic New York*, i., pp. 246, 317.

21. LOSSING, *Field Book*, ii., p. 611.

22. HUMPHREYS, *An Essay on the Life of the Honorable Major-General Israel Putnam*, pp. 136, 137.

23. FORD, *The Writings*, etc., iv., p. 409.

24. MARSHALL, *The Life of George Washington*, ii., p. 465.

25. WOODWARD, *Memoir of Colonel Thomas Knowlton*, p. 14.

26. *The Connecticut Gazette and the Universal Intelligencer*, September 27, 1776.

27. REED, *Life and Correspondence of Joseph Reed*, i., p. 237.

28. *Ibid.*

29. FORD, *The Writings*, etc., iv., p. 471.

30. *Memoir of Lieutenant-Colonel Tench Tilghman*, p. 138.
31. FORD, *The Writings*, etc., iv., p. 417.
32. JOHNSTON, *The Battle*, etc., p. 141.
33. FORD, *The Writings*, etc., iv., p. 417.
34. JOHNSTON, *The Battle*, etc., p. 162.
35. *The Connecticut Gazette*, September 27, 1776.
36. WOODWARD, *Memoirs*, etc., p. 15.
37. REED, *Life and Correspondence*, etc., i., p. 237.
38. MARSHALL, *The Life*, etc., ii., p. 468.
39. FORD, *The Writings*, etc., iv., p. 417.
40. JOHNSTON, *The Battle*, etc., p. 141.
41. *Ibid.*, p. 89. Note in the handwriting of Sir Henry Clinton in his copy of STEDMAN, *History of the American War*, now in the James Carter Brown Library, Providence, Rhode Island.
42. FORD, *The Writings*, etc., iv., p. 417.
43. LOSSING, *The American Historical Record*, ii., p. 260.
44. JOHNSTON, *The Battle*, etc., p. 141.
45. FORD, *The Writings*, etc., iv., p. 417.
46. Manuscripts of Joseph Reed in the library of the New York Historical Society, iv. : Joseph Reed to his wife, September 22, 1776.
47. *Memoir of Lieutenant-Colonel Tench Tilghman*, p. 138.
48. *The Connecticut Gazette*, September 27, 1776.
49. These stanzas and four others " appeared originally in the New York *Evening Post*, and were reprinted in the New York *Weekly Museum* of October 5, 1811." They are stated to be " lines occasioned by a ramble over part of Harlem Heights, particularly a spot remarkable for an action said to have taken place there between a party of Americans and a detachment of the British army." See *The Magazine of American History*, viii., part ii., p. 620. The stanzas must have had a special significance in view of the approaching renewal of conflict with Great Britain.

50. JOHNSTON, *The Battle*, etc., p. 90.
51. REED, *Life and Correspondence*, etc., i., p. 257.
52. JOHNSTON, *The Battle*, etc., p. 147.
53. QUINCY, *The Journals of Major Samuel Shaw*, p. 20.
54. HUMPHREYS, *An Essay*, etc., p. 141.
55. JOHNSTON, *The Campaign of 1776*, etc., part ii., p. 56.
56. JOHNSTON, *The Battle*, etc., p. 151.
57. *Ibid.*, p. 163. Extracts from the manuscript literary diary and journal of occurrences kept by Ezra Stiles, D.D., now in the library of Yale University.
58. *Ibid.*, p. 162.
59. *Ibid.*, p. 206.
60. *Ibid.*, p. 204.
61. *Ibid.*, p. 209.
62. *Ibid.*, p. 225.
63. *Ibid.*, p. 164.

BREUCKELEN.

Half Moon Series

Published in the Interest of the New York
City History Club.

VOLUME II. NUMBER XI.

BREUCKELEN.

By HARRINGTON PUTNAM.

THE original settlements which came to be
known as Breuckelen were but a small
part of the present Borough of Brooklyn. The
forested river-front of Long Island, rising over
against New Amsterdam, was still covered
with rich and abundant timber long after a
considerable village was planted on the lower
part of Manhattan Island. The Holland and
Belgium folk, reared in the level and treeless
lowlands, were by no means eager to undertake the severe and unaccustomed labor of
forest-clearing.[1] On Long Island they seem to
have been first drawn to the flats having a
light surface soil, which had received some
rude cultivation in the Indian maize-fields, and
required little preparation for the plow.

What was called Breuckelen was not the
locality of their first settlements. The first
grant of land, in what was afterwards the
city limits of Brooklyn, appears to have been

First
grants

to William Adriaense Bennett and Jacques Bentyn, who in 1636 purchased from the Indian sachem *Ka* a considerable tract at Gowanus, on which a house was erected, only to be destroyed in the Indian wars of 1643.[2] Long afterwards the fame of Gowanus oysters and wild turkeys was carried home to Holland. The Labadist travellers who came there in 1679 said of these oysters that "they are large and full, some of them not less than a foot long."[3] The shells were burned for lime. The supply of oysters remained abundant enough afterwards for great quantities to be pickled and exported to Barbadoes.

Where the East River made an abrupt bend to the north, leaving a wide shallow cove on the Long Island shore, the Dutch soon noticed good land sloping gradually down into the meadows surrounding the water. This was called the *Waal-boght*, and is the present site of the Navy Yard. Two derivations of this name are advanced. It was thought to have been thus styled to mean the Bay of the Walloons, since afterwards many French families settled there, and it was then known as the Walloon quarter.[4] The term *Waal*, however, means a basin or inner harbor, and *boght* a bend. Hence the word may have signified "the bend of the inner harbor," like a similar place called Waal-boght in the city of Amsterdam.[5] This name was sometimes abridged as

Waal, or the Wale. On the faith of old family traditions, it was long and confidently asserted that on the shores of this bay was born the first child of Dutch settlers on Long Island. This claim of priority for the Waal-boght settlement is not established.

Joris Jansen de Rapalje, a Huguenot who had married Catelyna Trico of Paris, and had resided at Fort Orange and later had an inn at New Amsterdam, eventually came to live in a farm on the Waal-boght. The purchase was made on June 16, 1637.[6] It was their eldest daughter Sarah who was erroneously claimed to have been born on Long Island before 1630. After the English conquest, Catelyna's husband died, and she lived on at the Waal-boght —the mother of Brooklyn—affectionately absorbed in her eleven children and their descendants, who in 1679 already numbered one hundred and forty-five. A visitor, who then saw her, described her as devoted with her whole soul to her progeny. "Nevertheless she lived alone by herself, a little apart from the others, having her little garden and other conveniences which she took care of herself."[7] Her house was probably near the present site of the United States Marine Hospital. When Governor Dongan wished to establish, as a fact, that the earliest settlements in the direction of the Delaware were Dutch, he had recourse to the evidence of this venerable dame.

In 1684, she was summoned before his Excellency, and was apparently still vivacious, as she gave her deposition. Describing her arrival here in 1623, she delighted to relate that: "Fouer women came along with her in the same shipp, in which the Governor Arian Jarissen came also over, which fouer women were married at sea,"[8] and afterwards with their husbands were sent to the Delaware.

In 1688, she made another affidavit at her house "in ye Wale." Recalling the bitter struggle with Indians on Long Island and Manhattan, she pleasantly alluded to her previous life with them, for three years at Fort Orange, "all of which time ye s[d] Indians were all quiet as Lambs & came & traded with all ye freedom imaginable."[9]

About 1642, the public ferry was established between Manhattan and Long Island. The landing-places were at Peck's Slip in Manhattan, and at the present foot of Fulton Street on Long Island. A collection of houses soon gathered about the Long Island landing, which little settlement became known as "The Ferry." Southward from the Ferry and along the present Heights and East River shore extended the farms of Claes Cornelissen van Schouw, Jan Manje, Andries Hudde, Jacob Wolphertsen, Frederic Lubbertsen[10]; and ex-Governor Van Twiller had himself taken a grant of Roode-Hoek, so called from its rich

red soil.[11]   It is difficult now to retrace this line
of the water-front, so greatly has the filling-in
of Atlantic Docks changed the contour of the
shore.   Red Hook appears to have contained
about fifty acres, raised up somewhat above
the surrounding meadows.   This small prom-
ontory projected out to the westward, and to
the north of it the shore-line receded inland in
marshes towards Gowanus.   On some of these
farm grants there were slight improvements ;
others were long allowed to remain unculti-
vated.

The Indian wars of 1643, begun on Manhattan, also extended to Long Island.   The white
settlers appear to have been the aggressors.
The retaliation of the red tribes devastated
many of the bouweries.   In the end, the Indians were driven from their maize-fields,
which left attractive sites for habitation, where
the new settlers founded a small compact
hamlet instead of occupying disconnected
farms.

Following the main road (now Fulton Street)
from the Ferry about a mile, the settlers took
up the lands between the Waal-boght and
Gowanus Kill, in the vicinity of what are now
Fulton, Hoyt, and Smith Streets.   The best
parts of this new territory were taken up by
Jan Evertsen Bout, Huyck Aertsen, Jacob Stoffelsen, Pieter Cornelissen, and Joris Dircksen.[12]
In 1645, the West India Company had recom-

mended that the colonists should establish themselves "in towns, villages, and hamlets, as the English are in the habit of doing." These settlers gladly availed themselves of this advice, and notified the Colonial Council that they desired to "found a town at their own expense." This they called Breuckelen, after the ancient village of that name on the Vecht, in the province of Utrecht.

The Governor and Council responded promptly and confirmed their proceedings in June, 1646. No municipal or local liberties were, however, conferred as in New England. The first government grant to this town was merely a ratification of the election of Schepens, and declaration of their authority, as follows:

"We, William Kieft, Director General, and the Council residing in New Netherland, on behalf of the High and Mighty Lords States-General of the United Netherlands, His Highness of Orange, and the Honorable Directors of the General Incorporated West India Company, To all those who shall see these presents or hear them read, Greeting :

"Whereas, Jan Evertsen Bout and Huyck Aertsen from Rossum were on the 21st May last unanimously chosen by those interested of Breuckelen, situate on Long Island, as Schepens, to decide all questions which may arise, as they shall deem proper, according to the Exemptions of New Netherland granted to particular Colonies, which election is subscribed by them, with express stipulation that if any one refuse to submit in the premises aforesaid to the above-mentioned Jan Evertsen and Huyck Aertsen, he shall forfeit the right he claims to land in the allotment of Breuckelen, and in order that everything may be done with more authority,

We, the Director and Council aforesaid, have therefore authorized and appointed, and do hereby authorize the said Jan Evertsen and Huyck Aertsen to be schepens of Breuckelen ; and in case Jan Evertsen and Huyck Aertsen do hereafter find the labor too onerous, they shall be at liberty to select two more from among the inhabitants of Breuckelen to adjoin them to themselves. We charge and command every inhabitant of Breuckelen to acknowledge and respect the above-mentioned Jan Evertsen and Huyck Aertsen as their schepens, and if any one shall be found to exhibit contumaciousness towards them, he shall forfeit his share as above stated. This done in Council in Fort Amsterdam in New Netherland." [18]

Later, on December 1, the authorities gave Breuckelen a schout or constable, and Jan Teunissen was thus appointed, who had been already acting as such for some months before his formal commission.

The origin of these settlers has not been definitely traced to the village of Breuckelen, or to within the jurisdiction of the city of Utrecht. The French wars there, and the Revolutionary war here, have despoiled both Breuckelens of their earliest records. The nomenclature of the little towns on Long Island, however, cannot be regarded as accidental. The association of the names of three hamlets into a triangle, generally similar to the position of the same names in Holland, is a clear proof of the attachment of the colonists to their natal district, between Utrecht and the Zuider Zee. Similar associations appeared at the same time in the new villages to the east of Breuckelen and on the Sound. From the province of Zealand the wish was shown to perpetuate home towns in the names of Vliessingen (Flushing) and Middelburg (Newtown). The identity of village names, and similarity of the relative sites in the neighborhood of Breuckelen to those in the fatherland, are illustrated by two maps from new and old Netherlands.

Amersfoort, Breuckelen, and Utrecht have many historic associations. To the politician and reader of Motley, they are forever linked with the career and tragic end of Barneveld. In 1619, he fell a martyr to the cause of state rights and local self-government. Such an event, comparatively recent in 1646, and still appealing to the sense of individual liberty, may have been recalled by the settlers in America. While the liberties of Utrecht had been the cherished objects of Barneveld's solicitude, he proudly claimed his birth in Amersfoort.[14] In moments of arduous public labor he looked hopefully forward to an honorable and calm retirement from the tumults of party strife to his beautiful estate at Guntersteijn in the village of Breuckelen.[16] Breuckelen, however, was an ancient village three centuries before

the settlement in New Netherlands. Located between Utrecht and Amsterdam, it was early noted for its healthfulness, which soon made it a desirable residence region. The surrounding fields and foliage are strikingly green and luxuriant, even for Holland. Castles grew up about it along the banks of the beautiful Vecht, which all the successive tides of war have not quite destroyed.

Old
Breucke-
len

In the Dutch records, Breuckelen had various spellings, as Broklede, Broicklede, Brackola, Brocklandia, and Broeckland. Hence some say that the name came from its brooks and marshes—*van de drassige en broekactige veen-landen*—meaning a brook or marsh land.[16] It is mentioned as an important place in the year 1317. There were two parishes on opposite sides of the Vecht. These are Breuckelen-Nijenrode, from the castle of Nijenrode, and Breuckelen-St. Pieters. The small river Vecht dividing these towns may be considered an outlet of the Rhine, which parts in two channels at Utrecht. The Vecht turns to the north and emipties into the Zuider Zee. It is navigable for small vessels, and at Breuckelen is a little over two hundred feet wide.

The old country-seats along the Vecht, once set in the prim, geometric gardens of the last century, are now represented by modern villas, half hidden by trees, which to-day form bits of unmatched rural scenery. Eminent landscape painters of the modern Dutch school have loved to make studies amid these gentle windings, and the celebrity of the Vecht in art bids fair to surpass the forgotten fame of the neighboring castles. Old draw-bridges of wood cross the sluggish river. Trees come close to the tow-path, bordered by quaint gardens. Along the garden edges, looking out upon the stream, are *Koepels* or tea-houses, and over all this abundant foliage rises a church spire.

From the fifteenth century the village had a coat of arms. The crown imports a royal grant, but from whom and whence is not known.

SEAL OF BREUCKELEN

The castles of Nijenrode and Oud-aa are admittedly ancient. Indeed, what is now Breuckelen-Nijenrode was once a fief of the lords of Nijenrode.

The settlers on Long Island generally reproduced in wood with thatched roofs the more solid stone cottages of the fatherland. They were mostly of one story, with a garret above. Their fireplaces and chimneys were stone to the height of about six feet, with great ovens alongside. Above the stone they carried up the chimneys with wood plastered thick with mortar inside." But few stone houses were built before the English conquest. Travellers visiting such homes were cheered with good fires, which they noted were of clear oak and hickory, of which there was no scruple to burn with lavish hospitality. The openings of the huge fireplaces were often large enough to seat the family on both sides of the fire, without jambs. A dwelling, sometimes with the barn also, was encircled with strong palisades as a defense against Indians. An institution in the better houses was the *betste*, which was a closed-in bedstead, built into the house like a cupboard, having doors, which shut up the low bunk in the daytime. Other houses had a simple *slaap-banck*, or sleeping-bench, in the room, on which a great feather bed lay in state.

The plantation and farms about Breuckelen, besides their ordinary farm produce, cultivated great fields of tobacco. Some of the best exported from the American colonies grew on the plantations about the Waal-boght. Later, it is recorded that cotton was successfully raised in Breuckelen, although only for home use, to be woven with native wool.[18]

Upon the arrival of Governor Stuyvesant in New Netherlands in 1647, he was obliged to allow an election to be had, so that there should be popular representation in the Council. New Amsterdam, Breuckelen, Amersfoort, Midwout (Flatbush), and other places, elected eighteen of the "most notable, reasonable, honest, and respectable" among them, from whom the Governor chose nine, as an Advisory Council. In this body Breuckelen was represented by its founder and schepen, Jan Evertsen Bout. In the subsequent dissatisfaction with the authority assumed by the Governor in 1653, and the public conventions and remonstrances, Breuckelen took prominent part, being represented by Frederic Lubbertsen, Paulen van der Beeck, and William Beekman, whose maintenance of the rights of the people specially irritated the jealous Governor. Breuckelen, Amersfoort, and Midwout were specially ordered to prohibit their residents from attending any meeting at New Amsterdam.

After peace had been declared between England and Holland in 1654, enlarged local powers were granted, and two new schepens given to Breuckelen. A like increase was conferred on the magistracies of Amersfoort and Midwout, and a superior district court for the three villages was established. This conferred important political privileges. It gave the people rights of local jurisdiction and that right of representation for which they had contended in 1653."

A citizen of Breuckelen could not refuse to continue to hold public office. In 1654, Jan Evertsen Bout declined to act as schepen. He incautiously said he would rather go back to Holland than continue to perform such burdensome duties. No excuses regarding his private business were accepted. Though the schepen-

elect had served for previous terms, and filled
other colonial offices, he was not now allowed
to retire.   The sheriff was formally ordered to
notify him of these summary commands of
Governor Stuyvesant: "If you will not accept
to serve as schepen for the welfare of the Village of Breuckelen with others, your fellow-
residents, then you must prepare yourself to
sail in the ship *King Solomon*, for Holland,
agreeably to your utterance." [20]   This appeal
to the civic conscience of one who had been
prominent as a reformer, coupled with the
grim threat of deportation, was irresistible. No
further declinations in Breuckelen offices seem
to have troubled the Council.

The first church in the present territory
was started at Midwout (Flatbush), the
building of which was begun in 1654. Before
the people of Breuckelen would promise to
contribute to the support of the domine, they
solicited "with reverence" that the Rev.
Mr. Polhemus might be allowed to preach in
Breuckelen and Midwout alternately.   The
Council cautiously assented, declaring they
had no objection that the Reverend Polhemus,
"when the weather permits shall preach alternately at both places." [21]

This met serious objection from the people
of Amersfoort and Gravesend, who pointed
out that "as Breuckelen is quite two hours'
walking from Amersfoort and Gravesend, it

was impossible for them to attend church in the morning, and return home at noon. So they consider it a hardship to choose, to hear the Gospel but once a day, or to be compelled to travel four hours in going and returning *all for one single sermon*—which would be to some very troublesome, and to some utterly impossible."[22] The Council finally settled the difficulty by directing that the morning sermon be at Midwout, and that instead of the customary afternoon service, an evening discourse be preached alternately at Midwout and Breuckelen. It was not till 1660, that Breuckelen had a church and domine of its own, the Rev. Henricus Selyns, who was of a distinguished Amsterdam family. He labored successfully for four years, then returned to Holland ; came out again eighteen years later, was enthusiastically welcomed, and settled in New York. His Latin poem eulogistic of Cotton Mather's great work is printed in later editions of the *Magnalia.*[23]

After the settled pastor, came the schoolmaster. He, too, was a learned and distinguished man—Carel de Beauvois, an educated French Protestant from Leyden, who was appointed in Breuckelen in 1661, and was also required to perform the offices of court messenger, precentor (*voorsanger*), "ring the bell, and do whatever else is required."

In 1660, Breuckelen numbered thirty-one

families amounting to one hundred and thirty-four persons. It may be doubted if any hamlet of its size in the entire American colonies was favored with better spiritual guides, or more learned and helpful teachers—a preeminence in school and in pulpit that Brooklynites may well endeavor to keep. Thereafter the growth of the village was steady and uneventful. English settlers came into the neighboring towns of Gravesend, Jamaica, and Flushing, but not without friction with their Dutch neighbors.

On a morning of August, 1664, a British fleet, unannounced, anchored in Gravesend Bay. Staten Island was first seized. A body of New England volunteers came through the Sound, landed on Long Island, and encamped near the Ferry. Governor Stuyvesant indignantly declined to yield. A part of the fleet came up the East River and landed more troops below Breuckelen. Governor Stuyvesant's historic "I would rather be carried out dead" than surrender, was at last overborne by the entreaties of the women and children. On September 8, 1664, Governor Nicolls raised the flag of England on the Fort, and named New Amsterdam, New York. Long Island and Staten Island, and probably Westchester, were made an English "shire." After passing through various phases of Dutch spelling, Breuckelen became Brockland, Brocklin, Brookline, and at last Brooklyn, in the West Riding of Yorkshire.

In 1683, when the counties of Kings and Queens were established, the settlement of Newtown was detached from the West Riding and made part of Queens County, leaving Kings County with its present territory. In 1816, Brooklyn became an incorporated village, which grew to the dignity of a city in 1834. Williamsburg was united with Brooklyn in 1855, followed by the absorption of the towns of Kings County in 1886 and 1894. In the consolidation with New York in 1897 this enlarged municipality, embracing all the county of Kings, has now become the Borough of Brooklyn.

From Village to Borough.

REFERENCES.

1. Stiles, *Hist. Brooklyn*, i., p. 23 ; also see lease of land in Breuckelen, August 1, 1647, for four years, rent free, tenant to cut, burn, and remove the timber, but at liberty to leave the stumps.—*Doc. Col. Hist. of N. Y.*, vol. xiv., p. 75.
2. Stiles, *Hist. Brooklyn*, i., p. 49.
3. *Journal of Voyage to New Netherland—Collections*, L. I. Hist. Soc., vol. i., p. 123.
4. O'Callaghan, *Hist. New Netherland*, i., p. 101.
5. *Literary World* (N. Y.), May 20, 1848, p. 309.
6. *Doc. Col. Hist. N. Y.*, vol. xiv., p. 4.
7. *Journal of Voyage to New Netherland*, p. 342.
8. Stiles, *Hist.*, i., appendix, p. 413.
9. Stiles, *Hist.*, i., appendix, p. 414.
10. Stiles, *Hist.*, i., chap. ii.
11. *Doc. Col. Hist. N. Y.*, vol. xiv., p. 48.
12. *Doc. Col. Hist. N. Y.*, vol. xiv., pp. 60, 64, 65, etc.
13. Stiles, *Hist.*, i., pp. 45, 46.
14. Motley, *John of Barneveld*, ii., p. 229 (ed. London, 1875).
15. *Ibid.*, ii., p. 185.
16. *Kabinet van Nederlandsche en Kleefsche Oudheden*, by Mattheus B. van Nidek, Isaac le Long, J. H. Reisig, and others, p. 262, Amsterdam, 1793.
17. Stiles, *Hist. Brooklyn*, i., p. 222.
18. Stiles, *Hist.*, i., p. 232.
19. Stiles, *Hist.*, i., p. 110.
20. *Doc. Col. Hist. N. Y.*, vol. xiv., p. 255.
21. Stiles, *Hist.*, i., p. 129.
22. Stiles, *Hist.*, i., p. 130.
23. *Magnalia*, vol. i., pp. 20, 21 (Hartford, 1820). The poem ends as follows :
   "Tu dilecte Deo, cujus Bostonia gaudet
    Nostra Ministerio, seu cui tot scribere libros,

Non opus, aut labor est qui Magnalia Christi
Americana refers scriptura plurima.   Nonne
Dignus es agnoscare inter Magnalia Christi ?
Vive Liber totique Orbi Miracula Monstres
Quae sunt extra Orbem.   *Cottone,* in saecula vive;
Et dum Mundus erit vivat tua Fama per Orbem."

References

THE "NEUTRAL GROUND"

Half Moon Series

Published in the Interest of the New York
City History Club.

VOLUME II.   NUMBER XII.

THE " NEUTRAL GROUND."

By CHARLES PRYER.

Location
of the
" Neutral
Ground "

URING the War of the Revolution the
County of Westchester, and particularly the lower towns (now forming the
Borough of Bronx or Bronck's '), was the prey
of the foraging parties of both armies, as it
lay directly between them and was permanently occupied by neither. Being common
property to both parties, it was, therefore,
called the "Neutral Ground." The views of
the inhabitants themselves at the outset of the
struggle were much divided, and if popular
sentiment was not absolutely loyal to the
crown of Great Britain, it was much more
conservative than in New England or in the
southern colonies.

Many of the leading families were staunch
loyalists and afterwards prominent leaders of
the Royalist Refugees. Amongst these were
the Van Courtlandts, DeLanceys, Philipses, and

Wilkinses, and these were the names which the people of that period were accustomed to follow. On the other side, however, were the Morrises, Livingstons, and Tomkynses, families who belonged in the same region, so that parties may be said to have been pretty evenly divided. The first meetings called to consider the question of electing delegates to Congress were broken up by the violent efforts of Philipse, Wilkins, and other Royalists, and when the matter was finally decided in the affirmative, the delegates chosen were instructed to do nothing disloyal to "the government of his Majesty the King," and it is an historic fact that New York was the last colony to authorize its delegates in the Continental Congress to sign the Declaration of Independence.

This conservatism, however, was not altogether induced by loyalty to the British government, but by a selfish interest. It was perfectly self-evident to such men as "Squire" Van Cortlandt, Oliver de Lancey, and others, that one of the main objects of the home government, in case of war, would be to separate the more southern from the New England colonies, and New York was the keystone of this position. With her deep harbor, and the broad Hudson stretching far to the northward, it would be easy for England to bring in her invincible fleet, and with it materially aid any army that might invade the State from loyal Canada ; so what they feared, and what actually came to pass, was that the locality would be made the theatre of war and devastation.

But let us follow events more in detail. Boston had been evacuated, and the brothers Howe had sailed from Halifax ; already rumors were current that the General had been largely re-enforced, and that My Lord the Admiral had taken his entire command on board his magnificent and irresistible fleet, and was on his way to capture New York. Washington was even now in the city to defend it with the Continental army. On June 28, 1776, the British fleet appeared, and General Howe's troops were landed upon Staten Island without opposition. Washington had entirely too much ground to cover with his meagre force of eighteen thousand men, a large proportion being raw troops, and he found it impossible to defend that comparatively distant point.

It will be necessary here, to understand the campaign in the Neutral Ground, to give a short sketch of the capture of New York and Brooklyn Heights. It is now conceded that Washington made a mistake in attempting to defend New York with the very limited resources then at his command, but he was urged to do so both by the inhabitants and by Congress, and his own good judgment was entirely outweighed. Howe lost much

time in vain attempts to negotiate a peace
with the exasperated colonies. It may be
here said to his credit, that he always carried
the olive-branch with the sword, and fought
with the greatest reluctance, so it was not
until August 22, that he landed at Graves End,
with twenty thousand men, his army in the in-
terim having been augmented by the arrival
of Sir Henry Clinton from the South. To
oppose this force the Americans had nine
thousand men under General Putnam. Most
of these were behind earthworks on Brooklyn
Heights, and on a wooded ridge commanding
some of the roads from Graves End.

Howe spent several days in reconnoitring,
and it was not until August 27, that any
serious advance was made ; then he sent his
brother, the Admiral, to threaten the city with
the fleet and to keep Washington occupied,
while he attacked the forces under Putnam.
Four roads led from his Graves End camp towards the Continental lines, one of which ran
along the shore, which was defended by General Lord Sterling with his division. Against
this renegade Scotch peer, Howe sent General
Grant with his Highlanders. Two of the remaining three roads joined near the village of
Flatbush, and crossed the ridge which was defended by General Sullivan ; and here advanced
General Heister with his Hessians. The fourth
was the Jamaica Road, along which the main

body of the army marched with Howe himself, Clinton, Percy, and Cornwallis at their
head. Their object was to march by the
ridge where Sullivan was stationed, and then
to wheel near the village of Bedford in order
to attack him on the flank and rear. In this
movement Howe undoubtedly out-generaled
Putnam ; Sullivan was completely routed,
with the loss (including those of Sterling's
division) of about four hundred killed and
wounded, and one thousand taken prisoners ;
among the latter was the General himself.

The troops of Sterling did much better
fighting, and it was not until Sullivan was
defeated, and the main army of Howe joined
Grant, that the Maryland brigades gave ground.
Even then they succeeded in gaining Putnam's main line without disorder. Howe's
troops were now tired, and he did not advance at once against the works on Brooklyn
Heights. Washington at first re-enforced Putnam, supposing an immediate assault would
be made, but finding Howe was in no hurry
to fight, and seemed rather inclined to lay
seige to the position, he took advantage of a
very dense fog on the night of August 29,
evacuated the forts, and took his entire army
over to the New York shore. This is one of
the most masterly retreats in the face of a
superior force on record, and if Howe had
shown his ability in his flanking march on

the night of the twenty-seventh, Washington
more than equalled him by his brilliant retreat
on the night of the twenty-ninth, or two days
later. Washington, with the main body of
the army, retired to Harlem Heights, where he
established himself in a very strong position,
leaving Putnam with four thousand men in
the city proper.

In 1776, the city of New York did not extend beyond Chatham Street, and the Island
was much narrower at that period, as several
blocks have been filled in on both rivers since
those days; thus the command in the town
did not have so much territory to cover as
might appear at first sight, but it was perfectly
self-evident that, from the moment that Long
Island was lost, the city could not be held, and
that Putnam's stay would be short ; his position was, indeed, extremely perilous, for could
Howe get some troops up either river in his
ships, to a point between the city and the
Continental army, he could land them, cut off
the four thousand under Putnam, and capture
his entire command.

Howe, seeing all this, sent two ships up the
Hudson to Bloomingdale, disembarked his
army on the other side of the Island at Kip's
Bay (near the foot of the present East 34th
Street), and attempted to cut off Putnam's
division ; but the genial gentleman was too
strong for the soldier. Mrs. Robert Murray,

understanding the condition of things thoroughly, and seeing Howe and his staff passing, invited the General and officers to lunch with her. A halt was immediately called, and the lunchparty commenced which saved the American cause one general officer and four thousand men; for while this entertainment was in progress Putnam marched his entire division northward and joined Washington.

Howe now had New York, but it was of very little use to him so long as Washington's army occupied a strong position extending from the mouth of "Harlem Creek" right across the Island to the Hudson. The British commander, however, had two alternatives besides a direct assault ; he could pass between Forts Lee and Washington with his fleet, ascend the Hudson, and make the position of the Americans untenable by landing in their rear. But to do this he would have to stand the fire from the forts, which might do considerable damage to his men-of-war and transports. The East River, or Sound, was, however, entirely free from forts, and afforded him almost as good an opportunity of getting into the rear of the Americans as the Hudson; this alternative was therefore selected, and on October 12, 1776, Howe embarked the greater part of his army and sailed up the Sound or East River as far as Throg's Neck[2] (now a portion of Greater New York), where he landed,

leaving Lord Percy to keep Washington occupied at Harlem.   He hoped by this movement
to get directly in the rear of the Continental
army, and so force it either to surrender, or
entirely to rout and scatter it; but the rebels
had not been sleeping.

General Heath, with a force of several
thousand men, had been sent to defend the
causeway and tear down the bridges across
Westchester Creek, so it would be impossible
for Howe to gain the rear of the Americans
without a fight.   Howe did not care to advance through a marsh in the face of so strong
a force, and delayed on the Neck six days, in
which little but ineffective skirmishing was
accomplished.   At the end of this period he
took to his boats again, proceeded northeast
about three miles, landed his forces on Pell's
Neck [3] or Pelham Neck, (now Pelham Park),
and advanced towards the Albany and Boston
roads.   Heath threw a couple of brigades in
his way, and attempted to check his progress.
For a time quite a spirited fight was the result; but the Americans were out-numbered
and compelled to retire with a loss of about ten
killed and forty wounded.   Howe had at last
succeeded in reaching the place he wanted, but
it was too late for his purpose of capturing
the Continental army; for the Americans had
evacuated Manhattan Island, except Fort
Washington, and were now comparatively

safe on Chatterton Heights, near the village of White Plains. For a few days Howe's army covered a wide field, and we hear of some of his troopers almost as far north as the Connecticut line. This, however, was probably done merely in search of forage, for he soon concentrated them on the Albany Road near the scene of the recent engagement.

It was a beautiful autumnal morning, October 23, 1776, that the greatest military pageant took place that the fair county of Westchester ever saw, at all events in the eighteenth century. Howe, preparatory to following Washington, drew up his entire army for review, along the road and on the meadows (very near the present boundary-line between the city, and the now much curtailed County of Westchester), then known as Pelham and Eastchester flats. Some ten thousand men took part in the ceremonies, and the effect must, indeed, have been inspiring and beautiful. The bright scarlet of the British regulars, contrasted well with the more sombre green of Knyphausen's Hessians, and with the background of the yellow sedge grass covered with sparkling frost. This was a fine picture by which, on that chill October morning, to impress the inhabitants with the invincible power of England's chivalry, and the politic commander had thought it wise to invite a few of the more distinguished proprietors of loyal tendencies to witness the affair. There was the fiery Philipse, and the philanthropic colonist who is said to have sprung from the grand old House of "Kourlandt" (Cortlandt), to witness the glorious return of their sovereign's banner, and, while the bands played and the sun glistened upon the bright arms of the troops, this little band of officers and gentlemen rode along the lines and inspected the army. As the sun rose higher in the heavens the day became warm and genial with that Indian summer balminess, so common to our American autumn. By noon the party before alluded to, were glad to halt for refreshments under the golden shade of what, even then, must have been a group of grand old chestnuts. That lunch just before the march to White Plains has become historic, and the old resident can still point out the trees with pride to any visitor who may be passing that way. Let us hope, however, that the meal of these fine gentlemen was not spoiled by the presence of that rough old German, the Count von Knyphausen, who, though a dashing soldier and a brave man, was no courtier, and anything but a pleasant dining companion. All that is left of this gallant assembly, are the old trees that have defied all change in this change-loving land, and as recently as the beginning of the winter (1897–98) still stood, the only landmarks of those long-departed days.   But, old trees, you are not to stand here always.   Though you may have seen the Indians of the seventeenth century; Washington, Howe, and Clinton, of the eighteenth; and all the celebrities of the nineteenth; yet those trunks of yours, sixteen feet in circumference though they be, are but hollow shells; the gales of two hundred winters have lopped many a fair limb, and ere the twentieth century shall grow old the squirrel will no longer play on your boughs, nor the frosts of autumn turn your leaves to gold !

In the fall of 1876, just a hundred years after the day of the "Great Review," two gentlemen were lunching under the same old trees. "The days of old" were discussed, and the historic spot examined in all its bearings; but after a time the conversation flagged, and they sat gazing up into the shady trees, whose leaves were fast turning into those brilliant hues with which the American forest-trees bid good-bye to summer, when the elder man turned to his companion and said: "Here is the pistol which my grandfather carried when with General Howe on the day of the 'Grand Review,' when they lunched under these trees just before the Battle of White Plains; now, as I want you to remember this occasion, I present you with the derringer as a memento of the anniversary of that parade." As they gazed upon this weapon of a former age, the nineteenth century seemed to fade into the Indian summer mist, and they could only see the scarlet of the British regulars and the green of their Hessian allies; the figures of the chivalric Cornwallis; the gallant but peace-loving Howe, and the rough old soldier, Knyphausen.

But to return to our narrative. The day after the "Grand Review" Howe went in pursuit of the Continental army and on October 28, stormed Chatterton Heights near White Plains, and forced Washington to retire to North Castle. He himself, however, did not go farther, but soon withdrew to the city proper, to rest and refresh his troops, evidently thinking he had done enough for one campaign.

We have now finished with the great armies of either party in the Neutral Ground, and must hereafter content ourselves with resting in their shadow, and try to keep the war spirit alive by cavalry raids, the robberies of the Skinners and Cowboys, and such expeditions as were sent out for foraging purposes. DeLancey's and Tarleton's cavalry scoured this part of the country in all directions, and Heath and others were scarcely less active. The Cowboys (ostensibly Royalists), and the Skinners on the American side, vied with each other in the atrocity of their acts; they respected neither friend nor foe, only caring whether their victims had anything of value.

After Howe had established himself securely in the city, and Washington was at distant North Castle, the British had to take Fort Washington, on the northern part of New York or Manhattan Island, to make their conquest complete. It would have been far wiser for the Continentals to have evacuated the stronghold, as it was evidently impossible to hold it in the face of such an army as was now in the city ; but General Greene, instead of doing this, reinforced the post against the advice of Washington. The result was as might have been foreseen, that the fort had to be, after a desperate struggle, surrendered, and the Americans lost just so many more of their best troops.

Now, at last, the island was free from armed rebels, and there was no regular force of the enemy for many miles north of it ; but a number of foraging bands or cavalry of both parties, were wandering through the country in all directions, and when these parties met there was apt to be more or less trouble.

The first, and probably most tragic of these affairs occurred very soon after the events just related, or in the early winter of 1776. A party of Americans belonging to the army of General Charles Lee, which was still posted in the northern part of the county, came south as far as Ward's house (which is within the district we have attempted to describe), bent upon forage. In this time-honored mansion they found much that was to their taste, and after a few bottles of their absent host's very good wine had circulated among them, the discipline of Captain Delavan relaxed, and the guards were allowed to join in the general merry-making. As night came on they became as reckless of their safety as though the country was in a state of profound peace, and they were enjoying themselves in the village inn.

But the American foragers were not left long to enjoy their carousal. As the night advanced one or two of the more sober ones heard the distant sound of horses' hoofs, and at once tried to arouse their stupefied and sleepy companions, but without much success, while the tramp of many hoofs grew nearer and nearer, as the troopers galloped over the frozen ground. The jingling of the sabres and the word of command proved that they were soldiers, and before even those who were able had time to attempt either to defend themselves or to escape, the house was surrounded, and Captain Campbell, who was in charge of the Royal Cavalry, (for such the horsemen proved to be), demanded the immediate surrender of the Americans. Delavan, seeing that resistance was hopeless in the existing condition of his men, immediately complied, and stepped forward to hand his sword to Campbell, when a shot was fired⁴ by one of the half-inebriated soldiers, and Campbell fell dead at the feet of the man whom only a second before he had considered his prisoner.

This irresponsible act was nothing less, of course, than murder, as the terms of surrender had actually been agreed to, and the captured party would in all probability have been treated by Campbell as simple prisoners of war. This breach of faith, however, changed the entire aspect of things. The vilest passions of the British soldiers were aroused, and the only man with sufficient authority to control them was dead before their eyes. The fact that his life-blood was treacherously shed, served to justify almost any crime that might be committed. It was hardly to be expected that they would take into consideration the intoxicated condition of the man, nor did they, but sprang forward, sabre in hand, and cut down the innocent and unfortunate Delavan first; then they rushed into the house and took the lives of all whom they met, or, as the old farmers used to say, "stuck them like so many pigs." Some of the victims jumped from the windows, and were killed by those who remained outside to watch for them; some tried to secrete themselves among barrels and rubbish in the cellar, but were found and hacked to pieces. Not more than a half-dozen in all escaped to tell the story of this fearful night of the first year of the Republic. About twenty-five are known to have perished, and it would seem that Campbell was pretty well avenged.

There are other incidents of the time handed down which are not so tragic ; we must now turn to an event less bloody but somewhat more amusing. An old homestead, situated not far from the scene just narrated, had not been deserted as were most of the houses in the vicinity. During the long, cold winter the occupants lived in constant fear of those marauders who subsisted by plundering the inhabitants, under cover of the pretended espousal of one cause or the other, the Skinners being the Continental robbers, while the Cowboys claimed to be loyal to the King. They were both absolutely indifferent to the politics of the unfortunates whom they robbed.

It was in January, 1777 ; the night had set in cold and forbidding ; a keen northwest wind had been blowing all day, and as the sun sank into heavy banks of clouds, the thermometer [5] almost touched the zero point. The snow creaked under the feet of the farmer as he returned to the house after attending to such cattle as the marauding parties had left him. Throwing his hat on a chair he remarked:

"I hope those Skinners will leave us alone to-night !"

The darkness increased, and as the night wore on, all that could be heard was the roar

Tbe
Skinners
Raid upon
an Old
Home=
stead

of the wind, as it drove the still drifting snow against the window-panes ; but a crackling fire burned in the ample fireplace, and all within was genial and comfortable, when—hark ! between the gusts of the winter wind could be heard the distant tramp of many feet. The farmer jumps up and rushes to the door to listen,—*no* there is no mistake, nearer and nearer come those ominous sounds, and soon a party of some fifteen men or more, can be seen advancing like spectres of the night. In a few moments they reach the house and enter without invitation. With small cere- mony, they make their business known, by demanding all the money and valuables to be handed over to them at once on pain of death.

All are armed with the military muskets of the period, and the majority carry pistols and knives in addition. but, they have no other insignia of regular soldiers about them ex- cept cartridge boxes, belts, etc. They are, for the most part, dressed in the ordinary clothing of the common people of the country, with here and there a stolen military garment, made conspicuous by its incongruity. To their demand the owner of the house replies that he has no money, and is therefore unable to give it to them. The intruders reiterate their threats of instant death unless they get what they desire; but finding it useless to parley longer with the farmer, they leave a couple of their number to guard him and his family, and proceed to search the house for themselves. After an absence of about half an hour, during which time all the upper rooms are thoroughly ransacked, the party return with very little booty and again threaten the unfortunate proprietor, who can only tell them just what he did before, that he has nothing to satisfy them; which answer is in all probability perfectly true, as previous visitors of the same kind had helped themselves to everything worth carrying away on the premises.

The Skinners, therefore—this particular band happened to be of that persuasion—thought, or at all events acted, as though all that was left for them to do was to carry out their threat of hanging the farmer. After warming themselves well before the great log fire, they obtaincd a rope and compelled him to leave his comfortable hearth and walk before them into the cold winter night, with the pleasant prospect of being hanged from the first convenient tree. Silently they walked for a few moments, when the Skinners were much surprised by hearing their victim burst out laughing. They were curious as to the cause of his merriment, when he informed them that he was laughing because he thought it such a funny idea to suppose that hanging him would fill their pockets. This remark

set the robbers to thinking that there might
be a little absurdity in what they were doing.
After assuring themselves that he was not
shamming in regard to having nothing, they
let him return to his fireside, much to the sat-
istaction of himself and family.   In the morning, he was not much astonished that his few
remaining cattle were gone, but was, on the
whole, glad to get off so easily.

A similar visit occurred at the same mansion
a few years later, but before the close of the
war.   A friend of the family spent the night
at the house on his way north, and upon part-
ing the next day left thirty pounds in coin in
charge of the daughter of the farmer, thinking perhaps that it would be less unsafe in
her possession than on the highway.   Be this
as it may, everything was reasonably quiet
around the place during the remainder of the
day, but shortly after nightfall, a small party
of Cowboys (for they were Cowboys this
time) was observed approaching.   The young
woman immediately concealed the money
about her person, and putting on a bold front
prepared to receive them.   Soon they entered,
but instead of demanding valuables in a general way, they went immediately up to the
girl and asked for the money that had been
given her that morning.   She, of course, de-
nied that she had any, whereupon one of the
marauders seized her and shook her so vio-

lently that the bag of money fell upon the floor; the man instantly let go of her, picked up the gold and departed, followed by his companions. It was never known how they became acquainted with the fact that the money was in the house, but it was always suspected that one or more of the band must have been looking in the window when the young woman received it.

It becomes unavoidable, in writing of the Revolutionary occurrences of this locality, to change the scenes constantly, as there was no connected campaign or regular army in the vicinity after Howe drove the Federalists from Chatterton Heights. There was only a series of events entirely independent of each other. Somewhat nearer Kingsbridge than the homestead visited by the Skinners and the Cowboys, stood the Lefferts' mansion, which, unlike the other, was deserted by its proprietor, who, probably being a loyalist, had fled to the city. At all events he wrote a very queerly worded petition to Congress from New York City, which ran somewhat as follows:

" *To the Continental Congress &c.*

    " MOST RESPECTED SIRS :

" Will your Honorable Body grant a pass for my two children to leave my mansion in Westchester County, and proceed to meet me in New York City. The house above referred to is, or of late was, occupied by thirty men in the Colonial service, who have eaten all the horned cattle, sheep and pigs, and driven nigh unto death all the horses;

and I now fear for my children confined in the house; and I would therefore humbly beseech your Honorable Body to grant a pass for the said children and such servants as may be deemed necessary to their safety in the present unsettled condition of the country. With the Greatest Respect Your Most Obedient and Humble Servant,

"DIRCK LEFFERTS."

Now, in reading this, the question that one naturally asks is, did he fear the children were to be eaten, or driven to death?

Again we change the scene. It was the dead of winter, and the snow lay thick upon the ground, when General Parsons collected a force of American troopers for a foraging expedition into Morrisania. The party of a hundred or more, desiring to be as silent as possible, to avoid a conflict with the Royal Refugees under Colonel De Lancey, were all put into sleighs and driven rapidly through Morrisania Manor towards Kingsbridge. No merry jingle of bells in this sleighing party; no laugh, no sound save the grim click of a musket's lock, or the rattle of the officers' side arms. On and on they sped over the silent, yielding snow, until their goal was almost reached, when suddenly an order rang out loud and clear upon the frosty air of midnight, and on all sides, like spectres from their graves, appeared armed and mounted men. Undismayed for a time, the Americans defended their sleighs with courage, almost with desperation, but the Light Horse were too numerous for them, and ere long they were cut to pieces or captured.

Before the retreat of the Americans northward the Westchester Church was used by General Heath as a hospital, and he quartered a number of his cavalry in the rectory, while the unfortunate rector, being a Royalist, was compelled to hide in a neighbor's stable.

The Wilkins family did much to protect the English clergy during the war. Being strong Tories they threw open their house, and even had a secret closet in the chimney, where several were hidden safely when searched for by the Colonial troops. The Graham house was burned by accident during a magnificent banquet, given by Colonel Fowler, of the British army, who was using it as his temporary headquarters. The table had been covered with flowers and beautifully decorated with cut-glass and silver, and the guests, many of whom were ladies, were strolling about the grounds in the balmy summer evening, when a servant suddenly rushed from the house and informed the Colonel that the building was burning. That officer, not in the least discomposed, calmly ordered the tables brought out on the lawn, and seated the company, who watched the conflagration while enjoying their repast. The cool and gallant Colonel was unfortunately killed in a skirmish, very soon after this event.

The skirmishes between the Light Horse of the two armies were entirely too numerous and too barren of permanent result to chronicle in their entirety. One or two more, however, to show the general character of these expeditions may not be out of place.

Colonel Burr, afterwards so famous, or, rather, infamous, as the slayer of Hamilton, destroyed Colonel De Lancey's blockhouse, after a slight skirmish. The Colonel secretly approached the building in the night with quite a large number of men, threw a hand-grenade into the building, setting it on fire and killing a number of men. Most of the rest were captured while attempting to escape.

At the time of Washington's retreat before White Plains, a series of forts and earthworks were erected from the East River to the Hudson across Morrisania and the lower part of the present city of Yonkers. After their desertion by the Continentals, these works were often utilized by both parties in their expeditions against each other, and held for longer or shorter periods of time as might be advisable. General Heath, of the American forces, often occupied them, as did Lincoln and many another Continental commander, and on the British side, Simcoe, Tarleton, and Colonel James De Lancey made favorite resorts of them.

At one time the American forces, in considerable strength, advanced to Kingsbridge and took up their position for some time behind newly made earthworks. The sentries annoyed each other by continual firing, though it was against the orders of both armies by an agreement between their officers. As time passed, however, the men were better controlled on both sides, and became more accustomed to each other's presence, until finally the British put a raw Scotch recruit on guard, who immediately discharged his gun at the American sentry across the stream, who as quickly replied, and wounded an officer who happened to be standing near. This brought out the guard and its commander, who called across the river, "I thought we had agreed not to have any more of that business." The Continental replied, "Your man began it." "What! this Scotchman? he shall be punished": and in future there was no more firing. In fact the sentries became so amicable after a while that they would talk together, and even exchange pipes, tobacco, etc., by tying them to stones and throwing them across the creek.

Out of the British works at Kingsbridge often rode Colonel Simcoe and Colonel Tarleton on expeditions against the "Rebels." Sometimes success attended their efforts, and at others they were fruitless. On at least one of these occasions they were accompanied by Prince William Henry (Duke of Clarence), afterwards William IV. of England (1782). He was then a junior officer in the navy. Just above Manhattan Island, on the Albany Pike, stood the "Old French Inn," kept by Gainos, who served many distinguished people in his day, as they travelled northward in the old mail coach. When the war broke out and the American army was in that vicinity, many of the officers frequented the tavern, and even the commander (who was very fond of French cooking) often dined there, and is said to have become quite fond of the dishes of Gainos. At all events, when the Continentals retired northward, the poor Frenchman thought the British would maltreat him for having fed the rebels, and he, therefore, left his inn in charge of some neighbors, and fled with Washington's army.

The first night after the landlord's departure the house was attacked by a party of Cowboys, who evidently thought the place practically deserted. In this supposition it happened that they were mistaken, for a number of the country people had collected in the tavern as was their wont, in spite of the absence of the proprietor, to gossip over the exciting condition of affairs. When they saw the band of robbers they determined to defend the place, and as few people went out at night in those troublous times unarmed, they were all in possession of weapons of some kind. Therefore when the marauders demanded admittance to the house, they were much surprised to be received by a shower of bullets, and soon came to the conclusion that the wisest thing for them to do was to leave the vicinity as rapidly as possible.

So the Cowboys picked up one of their number who had been hit, and proceeded through the meadows, woods, and orchards, for they seldom followed the roads, towards Kingsbridge. They had not gone far when they discovered that their wounded companion was dying from the effects of his injuries. This discovery made a halt necessary; they laid the poor fellow down on a grassy bank in an old orchard, and seated themselves, waiting for him to breathe his last. They were not delayed long, for after a few gasps his blood-stained soul departed. Small ceremony sufficed for the poor fellow's funeral ; the man who happened to be nearest simply said : "It 's all over with him ; let 's be moving, or more of us may get the same pill." Then they picked up the body again, as it might serve to track them to their fastness should they leave it where it lay, and carried it to a well that happened to be under one of the trees ; there they let the poor wretch fall into the water, and he was soon lost to sight, after which they proceeded on their way.

The next day some of the residents came for water and were horrified to find the liquid stained with blood, and to this day the spot is called the bloody well. Many are the tales that are told of supernatural sights and sounds that emanate from the locality. As to the truth of the ghostly part of the occurrences, we are unable to say, but certain it is that even as recently as our own times, the mouldering remains of a man were taken from the well. Let us hope that the removal and decent interment of the body also quieted the restless soul.

Once more the scene changes, not much as to locality, but radically as to events. The brave but unfortunate Stockbridge Indians had espoused the cause of the Colonies, and came down through Yonkers nearly to Kingsbridge on an expedition against Simcoe's forces. That officer having got wind of the enemy's approach, at once prepared to give them a warm reception. Selecting a well-wooded portion of the road he concealed most of his troops on both sides of it ; then he sent a small party of cavalry northward to attract the attention of the Indians. They had not far to go ; for soon they descried them silently advancing in single file as is the wont of these sons of the forest ; but long before the troopers had discovered their swarthy foes the sharp eyes of the Indians had seen the horsemen and prepared for action. As was planned, the British horse only skirmished lightly and then fell back, the Indians following them in hot pursuit, until they were within the ambush, where over forty, out of a total of sixty, were killed or captured. When the old chief saw the situation he shouted: "Save yourselves, my children ; my time has come and I am ready," and he fell dead with a bullet in his heart. This leader was quite a well-known man for one of his race, having visited England and been presented at court. He could read and write fluently and had a very good idea of history.

To show what a crude idea the British ministry had of the topography of this country, it may not be out of way here to insert an order received by Lord Admiral Howe :

"As the County of Westchester is in a very unsettled condition, and our troops are much harrassed by the 'Rebels,' whenever in that vicinity, you will send a couple of frigates up the Bronx River, to protect our forces and fire into the enemy whenever seen."

Now as this stream has an average breadth of about seventy-five feet and a depth in some places of not more than eighteen inches, it might have troubled his lordship to obey this command. Did they confuse this river with the Hudson ?

In 1778, Colonel Gist of the Continental army occupied quarters near the Babcock mansion, where then resided Mrs. Babcock, the handsome widow of the Rev. Luke Babcock, and it was whispered that the gallant Colonel had selected this locality for his command, which was much nearer the enemy's line than was at all safe or advisable for so small a force, that he might pay his addresses to this fair widow. Be that as it may, Lieutenant Colonel Simcoe got wind of his whereabouts in some way, and resolved upon the capture of the entire command. He therefore sent out his forces at night to surround the encampment of Gist. His plan apparently succeeded perfectly ; the Americans were not in any way disturbed until the enemy supposed they had entirely surrounded their intended victims. The Colonel himself was oblivious of all outside events, for never had the beautiful widow been more engaging, and never had he remained at her house so late. But all evenings however enchanting, must come to an end, and this one was no exception ; so finally he bade his fair friend adieu and started for his camp. Just as he was departing reluctantly, looking back as he went to see her waving a final farewell with her handkerchief, he heard a shot quickly followed by a scattering volley. Forgetting instantly his romance, he rushed rapidly to where his men were quartered ; there he found every-thing in the direst confusion. Barring his weakness for the widow, the Colonel was a good soldier and soon restored a semblance of order even in the face of the enemy. He took in the situation at a glance and resolved to fight his way to the main army northward. It is very doubtful if he would have been able to do this, however, had it not been for the fact that one of the enemy's commands had lost its way and thereby left a passage open for him, which he was not slow to use. He therefore reached his friends, not indeed without fighting, but with the loss of only about one third of his command. How his affairs prospered with the widow after this interruption we know not ; but let us hope that if he again ventured in that quarter, he did not involve his entire command in this sort of a conquest.

When the Skinners and the Cowboys were struggling for the sovereignty of the "Neutral Ground," and shortly after one of the scions of one of our old county families had been shot down while standing under a walnut tree[6] near the door of his mansion by one of these gentry[7] for refusing to blacken his boots, the people found it necessary to bury all valuables which they chanced to possess to escape these marauders from both sides.

One day it was whispered abroad that a

rather stronger party of Skinners than usual was about to visit the district of lower East-chester. Several of the people came together, unhung the bell of the "Old East Chester Church," filled it with money and other valu-ables and buried it. Among these individuals were two brothers named Wilson. One of these young men, Harry, was a drunken, worthless chap, who had caused the death of his beautiful and devoted wife by his brutality, while the other seems to have been a very respectable member of society. Some time after the visit of the before-mentioned party of Skinners, both brothers (who were not on good terms) by a strange coincidence resolved to dig up the bell and procure the treasure on the same night. Harry, whose wife had re-cently died, came to the spot first, with the necessary tools, and also a bottle of his never-failing companion, brandy. The night was dark and cold, and the winter wind sighed in the old apple-tree over his head as he struck the first blow upon the frozen ground with his pick. The work was severe as the ground was hard from frost, but with the aid of many a pull upon the black bottle, he soon had the satisfaction of hearing the pick ring upon the metal of the bell. After cleaning out the dirt a little and taking a look at the precious things within, he sat down to rest and finish the last of the contents of his beloved bottle.

He had hardly done this and sent the empty vessel crashing amongst the stones and *débris* of the excavation, when he thought he saw a light approaching. He took an instant to assure himself he was not mistaken, then put out his own lantern and stepped behind a tree to await his visitor. In a few moments he saw his brother, pick in hand, advance to the spot, and heard him exclaim: "What! somebody has been here before me, but they must have left hurriedly, for nothing is taken." Harry waited no longer, but stepping from behind the tree, informed his brother that his time had come, and suiting his action to his words, seized his unfortunate victim by the throat. For a time they struggled, but the first comer, made strong by drink and frenzy, soon conquered, and left his opponent dead upon the ground. The next morning a neighbor discovered the remains, but the murderer was never seen again. Strange to say, however, he only took from the bell just what belonged to him, leaving the rest as he had found it.

The remains of the murdered man were buried in the old churchyard from which the bell was taken, and a few days later his *fiancée*, who had died from the shock of the news, was laid by his side. The bell was soon replaced in the church tower, and rings out each Sunday morning, as it has done since the time of good Queen Anne. It is said that upon every anniversary of this horrible event the bell tolls, and suppressed groans are heard in the time-honored tower.'

One evening an old Indian, the last of his race, sat at the door of his wigwam watching the fading rays of the chill October sun disappear from the western sky, when two rough-looking men and a dog crossed the farther end of the clearing. The chief, whose head the ashes of time had long since whitened, recognized the newcomers at once to be members of a band of Skinners, supposed some mischief might be brewing, and resolved to follow the miscreants. They led him across a brook and through the woods, until they came to a small hut where a third member of the band was making a fire. The Indian secreted himself in some bushes within hearing and awaited events. One of the men whom he had followed hailed the man by the fire and said:

"Did you get the girl, Paul?"

"Yes, she is in the hut."

"Did she tell where the old man's money was buried?"

"No."

"Then she must die. Bring her out."

The man called Paul disappeared within the hut, and soon returned leading a terrified but still beautiful young girl, whom the ruffians tied to a tree and then prepared to shoot.

"I will give you one more chance," said the man who appeared to be the leader. "Tell us where the money lies buried."

"I know of no money," was the faint, gentle answer.

"Then prepare to die. *One—two—*"

He raised his gun to fire at the word three, but before he could utter it the unerring aim of the Indian had sent a bullet through his heart, and before his companions could recover from their surprise the old chief rushed in with knife and tomahawk and despatched them both. He picked up the poor girl, who had fainted, and carried her to his wigwam, where she was soon revived. The poor old man, however, perished at the battle of White Plains while fighting gallantly in the Colonial army.[6]

But our tales are finished, and the "Neutral Ground" is neutral no longer. The great city has stretched out its long arms and encircled it in its grasp. The days of the Cowboy and the Skinner are over. The British soldier and his Hessian ally are seen no more. Clinton, Howe, Washington, and Lee, all sleep with their fathers, and the drum and the bugle of the Revolution are silent.

> " Soldier rest, thy warfare o'er,
>   Sleep the sleep that knows no breaking;
> Dream of battle-fields no more,
>   Days of danger, nights of waking."

NOTES AND REFERENCES.

1. The name is taken from Jonas Broncks, one of the early proprietors of the district.
2. The original owner of the property was Throgmorton. Throg's Neck is a corruption of Throgmorton's Neck.
3. Thomas Pell was the first proprietor.
4. The shot was fired by Lieutenant Paddock.
5. We do not mean to assert that there was a thermometer as we understand it.
6. Some thirty years ago this tree was cut down by the proprietor. Some of the wood has come into the possession of the writer, through a relative to whom it was given. It now forms a couple of book-cases.
7. Some writers state that a Hessian officer committed this deed, but we think the Cowboy version is correct.
8. The last two anecdotes were told to the writer by Mr. William L. Stone, the historian.

R. A. BOLTON's *History of the County of Westchester.* New York, 1848.

GENERAL HEATH's *Memoirs.* Boston, 1798.

Itinerary of General Washington, from June 15, 1775, to December 23, 1783. Philadelphia, 1892.

COLONEL JOHN THOMAS SCHARF's *History of Westchester County, New York.* Philadelphia, 1886.

Works and Documents of William L. Stone.

JOHN FISKE's *American Revolution.* Boston, 1891.

WILLIAM WATSON WALDRON's *Huguenots of Westchester.* New York, 1864.

Guide to New Rochelle (1842).

Papers on Yonkers, by HENRY B. DAWSON (26 copies printed for private circulation only.) Yonkers, 1866.

www.ingramcontent.com/pod-product-compliance
Lightning Source LLC
LaVergne TN
LVHW051349190726
843642LV00007B/2579